ALSO BY JESSICA B. HARRIS

Hot Stuff

Iron Pots and Wooden Spoons

Sky Juice and Flying Fish

Tasting Brazil

The Welcome Table

A Kwanzaa Keepsake

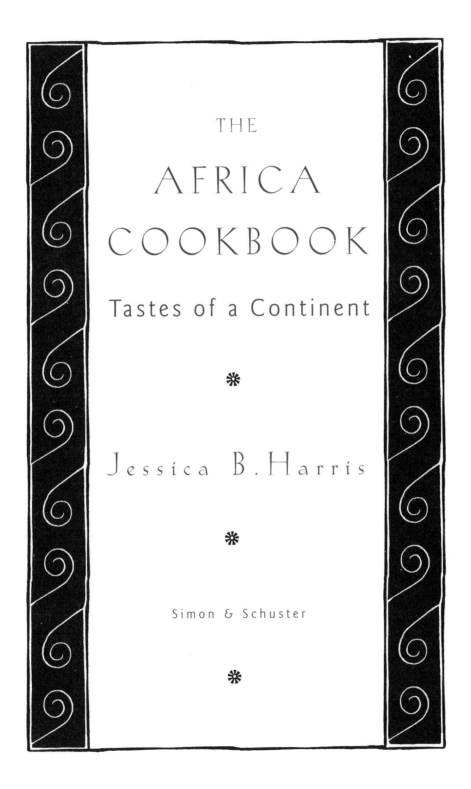

THE
AFRICA
COOKBOOK

Tastes of a Continent

✳

Jessica B. Harris

✳

Simon & Schuster

✳

SIMON & SCHUSTER
Rockefeller Center
1230 Avenue of the Americas
New York, NY 10020

SIMON & SCHUSTER and colophon are registered trademarks
of Simon & Schuster Inc.

Designed by Katy Riegel
Map © 1998 by Anita Karl and James Kemp

Manufactured in the United States of America

1 3 5 7 9 10 8 6 4 2

Library of Congress Cataloging-in-Publication Data

Harris, Jessica B.
The Africa cookbook : tastes of a continent / Jessica B. Harris.
p.   cm.
Includes bibliographical references and index.
1. Cookery, African.   I. Title.
TX725.A1H284   1998
641.596 — dc21   98-38882
CIP

ISBN 0-684-80275-9

ACKNOWLEDGMENTS

Cookbooks are inevitably the sum total of the knowledge of all who go before. Therefore, I must begin by acknowledging the millions of unknown women and men from all parts of the African continent who, over the millennia, created these recipes, tested them on their families, and perfected them with loving hands. The recipes are theirs; I have simply gathered them here.

This African journey has been one that has been over twenty-five years in the making. and so a complete listing of all of those who should be thanked would take up enough pages to create an encyclopedia of African hospitality. A blanket thank-you will have to do for those who spoke with me, ate with me, put up with my questions, and encouraged me during the decades that this project was perking.

My West African family has become a part of my lifeline to the continent. I could not have written this without their help with everything from recipes to overweight luggage. Théodora Houémavo-Komaclo, Aimée Houémavo-Grimaud, Suzanne Houémavo-Adotévi, and Léonie Houémavo-Koumah and their families have become quite simply a part of my life. Michéle Rakotosan, my Malgache sister; Mammadou Sy of Mali; and Nicole Ndongo, widow of my Senegalese big brother, Moctar, must also be mentioned here, as well as Anna Kamara, Marie-Pierre Djigo, Thierno Ndongo, and the late Ababacar Samb Makharam. Souad Segroughni in New York, Fatéma Hal in Paris, Shareen Parker in South Africa, and Danny and Karen Matovu, Harry and Emma Matovu, and Rovianne Matovu in London have also joined the African friendship train.

In the more immediate realm, thanks and praises are due to fellow authors, food scholars, and librarians who jumped on the idea with interest and helped with everything from botanical identifications to ancient sources. Particular thanks must go to William Woys Weaver, Fritz Blank, Nancy Harmon Jenkins, Paula Wolfert, Hoppin' John Taylor, Karen Hess, Betty Fussell, John T. Edge, Patricia Ogendengbe, and my newest African sister, Dorinda Hafner.

Then I must thank those who enabled me to keep heading to the continent that so fascinates me. Théophile Komaclo at Air Afrique, and before him Charles Librader, Gail Moaney at Ruder-Finn/ South African Airways, Peggy Bendel and the South African Tourist Board, Marcella Martinez for ongoing help and research with all of my projects. The members of the Moroccan Tourist Office under more than three directors, as well as the tourist offices of Senegal, Kenya, Zambia, and South Africa, must also be acknowledged for their continuing support. Editors who have enabled me to write about the continent and therefore continue my research must also be included in the list of those to whom I am indebted: Robert Arndt, the staff at *Travel Weekly,* Fred Dodsworth, Barry Estabrook, and Rux Martin. Dunn Gifford and the folk at Oldways Preservation and Trust, with their educational sojourns, have enabled me not only to meet the experts in Tunisia and Morocco but also to get to know my culinary colleagues on the road.

Then there are others in North, South, East, and West Africa as well as Africans who no longer live on the continent, including Dinia; Hayat; Mina El Glaoui; Marida Awada; Farakacha Nawal; Hachoume Sossey Alouai; Assmaa Ben Maimoun, in Morocco; Magda Abdou, in Egypt; Mohammed Driss, in Tunisia; Ramola Parbhoo; Fadela Wiliams; Achmat Marcus; John Giese; Portia de Smit; Nomzamo Gertrude Cuba; Liz McGrath, owner of Cellars; Margot Janse; Ebrahim Rahim; Garth Strobel; Elmerie de Bruyn; Janette Sheilpe; Margi Biggs and Janet Malherbe, in South Africa; Rose Odera and family, in Kenya; Xen Vlahakis, in Zambia; Biram and Ndioro Ndiaye, in Senegal; Maurice and Nadège Yaba in Côte d'Ivoire; Carrie Dailey, in Guinea; Tamaro Touré, in Mali; the Francisco Paraiso family; the Desiré Vieyra family; and the Gbokede family in Benin; and many, many others.

On this side of the Atlantic pond, I must thank Ayo Fenner for information about Yoruba ritual, Priscilla Martel for thoughts of North African sweets and the recipe for *makroud,* Debbie Mack for goodwill and illegible Sudanese recipes, Sheila Walker for encouragement, Dara René for help with typing, Abena Busia for understanding it all, Martha Taylor for allowing me to keep her Egyptian book for way too long, Bob Christgau of the *Village Voice* for making me a more thoughtful writer, and Gray Boone for always being there to give a hand, raise a fork, and lend an ear.

Thanks also to Mae Tata and the *filhas de santo* at Ile FunFun in Bahia, Brazil, my spiritual lifeline; the staff and faculty of the SEEK program at Queens College; and the QC lunch bunch: Cecily Rodway, June Bobb, Frank Franklin, Charles Lloyd, and Phyllis Cannon Pitts, who keep me going;

Ron Cottman who continues to keep the rain off; Ralph Taylor and the folk at Almond Beach Resorts for believing; Patrick Dunne, Kerry Moody, and the gang at Lucullus for welcoming me and my madness to New Orleans; Eugenie Vasser, for helping me to find a way. Thanks as always are due to my spiritual daughter Patricia Hopkins and her kids Jan'ie and Charles Anthony, who are always there.

Then, there are the usual suspects: Daphne Derven; Chester Higgins and Betsy Kissam; Asantwaa Harris; Yvettte Burgess-Polcyn; Martha Mae, from Chesapeake Bay; Angie Johnson; Richard Alleman; C.H.L., Willy Baba and Liv Blumer, friend extraordinaire; and the one that I forgot—who all show up, eat, and encourage me.

Thanks must also go to Carole Abel, my agent, who has ably been there for over a decade, and to Sydny Miner, my all-suffering editor, who has become my friend. This project has seen her through three assistants who must also be thanked—Diana, Monica, and Andrea.

Finally, to my mother, my culinary secret weapon, who provides the stability and love that allow me to soar and who has armed me with the education and the courage to make my dreams realities.

To all of these and to the Supreme Creator, without Whom nothing would ever be written by me.

THANK YOU

TO

my mother, Rhoda A. Harris,

my father, Jesse B. Harris (ibae),

my grandparents, Ida Irene Harris and Miles Harris (ibae), and

Bertha Philpot Jones and Arthur Dempsey Jones (ibae),

my great-grandparents, Harriet Hornbeak (ibae), and

Rhoda Cobbs Philpot and Samuel Philpot (ibae),

AND

my newly rediscovered great-great-grandparents,

Merendy and Thomas Anderson (ibae) and

Amy and David Cobbs (ibae)

AND

All of the unknown African Americans and Africans whose lives lead my

blood back to the continent from which we all spring.

May the tastes of this continent of cuisines—palm wine and plantains,

cowpeas and couscous, millet, meloukhia, *and so much more—honor their*

memory and the memory of millions of others like them.

ASE.

CONTENTS

✳ Contents

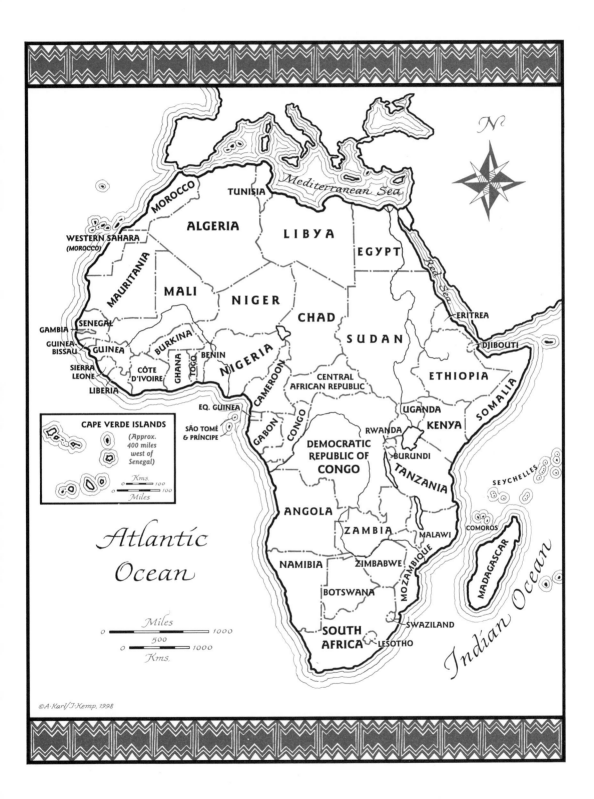

N

Mediterranean Sea

MOROCCO
TUNISIA
WESTERN SAHARA
(MOROCCO)
ALGERIA
LIBYA
EGYPT
MAURITANIA
MALI
NIGER
CHAD
SUDAN
Red Sea
ERITREA
GAMBIA
SENEGAL
GUINEA-BISSAU
GUINEA
BURKINA
BENIN
NIGERIA
DJIBOUTI
SIERRA LEONE
CÔTE D'IVOIRE
GHANA
TOGO
CAMEROON
CENTRAL AFRICAN REPUBLIC
ETHIOPIA
SOMALIA
LIBERIA
EQ. GUINEA
UGANDA
KENYA
SÃO TOMÉ & PRÍNCIPE
GABON
CONGO
RWANDA
DEMOCRATIC REPUBLIC OF CONGO
BURUNDI
TANZANIA
SEYCHELLES

CAPE VERDE ISLANDS
(Approx. 400 miles west of Senegal)
Kms.
0   100
0   100
Miles

Atlantic Ocean

ANGOLA
ZAMBIA
MALAWI
COMOROS
NAMIBIA
ZIMBABWE
MOZAMBIQUE
MADAGASCAR
BOTSWANA
Indian Ocean

Miles
0   1000
500
0   1000
Kms.

SOUTH AFRICA
SWAZILAND
LESOTHO

©A·Karl/J·Kemp, 1998

✳

Niam N'Goura
(Eat so that you may live.)
—Toucouleur proverb

AFRICAN ATTITUDES

An Introduction

Africa! The mother country, *that* was my destination. I had traveled before—Europe had seen my black face several times, in fact—but this trip was something quite different: I was going home. I cannot claim to have thought of Africa that way all my life. In fact, I was a recent convert to nationalism and pan-Africanism. My new identification was something of which I was doubly proud. I wore it like a flag. This trip was a confirmation of all that I looked for.

The excitement of the trip was by far overshadowed by the knowledge that I was going to a home that I had never seen and to relatives who had never seen me. We didn't even know of each other's existence. Nigeria, Ghana, Côte d'Ivoire, Senegal—all were places that were as familiar to me as dreams, yet far and forbidding in reality. The towns on the itinerary that I had chosen unfurled like a banner that held all my history: Accra, Abidjan, Ouagadougou, Cotonou, Bamako. I was going home, home, home, *home.*

So I wrote in the summer of 1972 with all the enthusiasm of the twenty-four-year-old that I was. I have been returning to Africa with the same wonder and excitement for almost three decades. It is a place like no other. While I can look back now at the musings of my youth and smile at the naïveté that I displayed about the continent and myself, I also marvel at the accuracy of my observations. Africa *is, was, and will always be* home to me.

My African home is a continent made up of hundreds of ethnic groups. It is a continent of such vast geographical diversity that no one can claim to truly understand the whole. Despite all that, we all labor under a burden of misconceptions, trite inaccuracies, fanciful inventions, and just plain lies about the continent where man was born. Africa is dark indeed, not from any malevolence of its own but rather from our own ignorance. No continent has a longer record of continual unflattering images in the history of the modern world. So let's begin our culinary journey by ridding our minds of the negative elements that today's headlines and yesterday's news broadcasts have imprinted on our collective memory banks.

Banish the photographic images of babies with begging bowls and Bokassas crowning themselves. Delete the pictures of warring nations and despots with their diamonds. Eliminate the dissension and contention left in the wake of colonialism. Forget about *National Geographic*'s bare-breasted maidens, Ubangis, and cannibal cooking pots. While we're at it, eradicate the concept of the "noble savage" and the idea of the slave trade being an issue that can be defined in black and white. Remove all notion of the legendary kingdom of Punt, where the Egyptians traded for spices, and while we're at it, let's also leave out King Solomon's Mines, *The African Queen*, the Marx Brothers' Dr. Spaulding, The African Explorer, Tarzan, Sheena, and yes . . . George of the Jungle.

Too many of us still tend to regard Africa as a country. It may come as a brutal shock to realize that the African landmass is three times the size of Europe and four times that of the United States. Madagascar, which is a part of Africa, is the fourth-largest island in the world. Too many folk still talk about people speaking African, ignoring the fact that over 1,000 different languages are spoken on this continent that comprises many worlds.

Much like the story of the blind man and the elephant, those who visit different areas of Africa return home with different tales of the "part" that they have touched. It is a continent with many doors, many different points of entry into a world that is wondrous and strange.

Travelers who visit capital cities like Nairobi, Capetown, Abidjan, and Dar es Salaam return home with tales of an Africa where the sophisticated badinage of the drawing rooms of the *mondaine* is larded with discussions of art shows in London's Chelsea, Paris's Rive Gauche, or New York's SoHo and interspersed with references to stock markets in London and Tokyo. If they head to Lagos, Nigeria, or Cotonou, Benin, they return with tales of traffic jams and go-slows, of people wearing designer *agbadas* that match the car being driven that day, of weddings where the bride makes three or four complete changes, from dress to jewels—white with diamonds, pink with rubies, and blue with sapphires—where the best dancers at the reception are rewarded with Niara or CFA or Cedis plastered to their sweating brows.

Others travel to game parks and return with tales of an Africa that looks as though it might have appeared the day after God rested. They tell of a vast and unspoiled land whose beauty is so staggering as to be truly indescribable. Some will talk of the ancient marvel of pyramids, the haunting silence of the stone ruins at Greater Zimbabwe, the thatched great palace gate at Ketou in Benin, or the Roman ruins at Volubilis in Morocco. Still others describe vast dunes and profound lagoons, dense rain forests and sun-dappled vineyards. Some will not be able to see beyond the poverty and the problems, while others will discover a continent of myriad opportunities for growth and betterment.

Africa is a continent that can leave no one indifferent and where everyone will find at least one thing to his or her taste. It is where the exotic meets the ordinary, a place that is at the same time strange and familiar. Africa, with all its conflicting images, is a continent of diversity, and nowhere is this diversity better expressed than in the Africa that is a continent of cuisines.

Over the years, I've explored these cuisines, unconsciously (as a traveler who loves to eat) and consciously (as a food historian and cookbook writer). My sojourns on the continent have taken me from north to south, east to west. I've ridden on the back of a motorbike from the Hilton hotel deep into the souks of the Chellah in Rabat in search of spices and eaten blood sausage in the open market in Kenya on a dare. I've sipped champagne served by white-gloved servants in the homes of high government officials in Côte d'Ivoire, been served cool water in a chipped enamel basin by tattooed co-wives in Benin. I've danced to high-life music under the stars in Accra and sipped innumerable Flag, and Stork, Star, and Tusker beers. In Kenya, I saw the Indian Ocean for the first time with an old man who had never been there and ate biryanis and curries and marveled at the cultural mix that is Mombasa. I've had dinner with the Virgin Mary, as you will see later, eaten in a tent, and placed my hand in the communal bowl in too many countries to note. I've slept in fancy hotels and dined under the stars in the bush.

I cannot claim to know Africa, but I can claim to have eaten in all of its cardinal points. I cannot claim expertise, but I admit, indeed crow, about my extended African circle of friends who have become the matrix of my overseas family. Berber and Bantu, Fon and Falasha, Afrikaner and Akan all sit down at my African table, along with the descendants of Europeans, Indians, Malaysians, Lebanese, and those who share ancestral blood with the enslaved sons and daughters of the continent who have returned home from Brazil, the Caribbean, and the United States. In short, in the more than a quarter of a century that I have been visiting Africa since I first wrote of going home in 1972, I have become a part of this continent that fascinates and attracts me as much now as it did then. My Africa is a continent of ancient history and profound spirituality: a continent of madness and marvels, where the past walks side by side with the present and both show the way to the future. It is a continent of history and culture, of music and science, of art and imagination, and yes, of cuisine.

BEYOND BARE-BREASTED MAIDENS AND CANNIBAL COOKS

◎◎◎

2,001,998 Years of Food, from the Paleolithic to the Present

Archaeologists now feel certain that eastern and southern Africa provide the world's earliest and most continuous record of human evolution. If so, then this history includes what is arguably some of humankind's earliest food production. In *Africans: The History of a Continent*, John Iliffe reminds us that "there is evidence as early as 20,000 to 19,000 years ago of intensive exploitation of tubers and fish at waterside settlements in southern Egypt near the First Cataract, soon followed by the collecting of wild grain."

The early grains included five races of sorghum, pearl millet, finger millet, African rice, and teff. The grains were developed in different areas of the continent. Sorghum (*Sorghum bicolor*) developed in the northeastern quadrant of the continent, near Chad and Sudan. Pearl millet (*Pennisetum glaucum*) originated in the edge of the Sahara. Finger millet (*Eleusine curacana*) can be traced to the highlands of eastern

Africa, while African rice (*Oryza glabberima*) is native to the savanna. Teff (*Eragrostis tef*) was first domesticated in Ethiopia. The Sahel and the Sudan developed plants later than other areas of the continent, but were responsible for two agricultural systems that are still important today, one based on sorghums and a second based on African rice.

It must also be noted, though, that while much emphasis had been placed on cereal cultivation, there is increasing evidence that tubers also played an important role in African diets as well and seem to date back to 18,000 to 17,000 years ago. Yams became so important within the western section of the continent that they took on mythical proportions. Festivities mark their planting and harvesting in countries like Ghana and Nigeria even today. In the medieval empire of Mali, murderers were beheaded in a yam field so that their blood could fertilize the crop. It is generally agreed upon by botanists that certain species of yams were first protected and later domesticated in the tropical rainforest zone of western Africa. It is thought that the oil palm (*Elaeis guineensis*) was also domesticated in the same region at around the same time.

Archaeological sites in today's Ghana reveal that the race of hunter-gatherers who moved around the forests and savannas of the zone in the period from 1750 to 1350 B.C. ate a wide variety of foods, including tortoises, monitor lizards, freshwater turtles, and a type of giant land snail. Rock paintings in Tassili n'Ajjer in the Ahaggar Mountains in the Sahara show buffalo chases, hunting, and cattle herding. In South Africa, researchers have determined that domestic crops grown in Africa by Iron Age farmers also included sorghum and different species of millet. They have found that the people living at different archaeological sites hunted and consumed animals such as antelope, bush pig, buf-

falo, and ostrich eggs. Those who lived in zones near lakes or lagoons consumed fish, mussels, crabs, and tortoises. Remains of members of the yam family have also been found.

✳

Food of the Pharaohs

> Think of it! In Egypt we
> Had fish for the asking,
> Cucumbers and watermelons,
> Leeks and onions and garlic.
> —Numbers 11:5

Certainly one of the most complete records of early foodways on the African continent is that of Ancient Egypt. There it is possible to see food featured prominently in Egyptian wall paintings and reliefs of all periods. Much of our knowledge of Ancient Egypt comes to us through the funerary art of the country. We can surmise from the number of paintings, models, and other art that food was important to Ancient Egyptians. They wished to ensure that their dead would enjoy in eternity the foods that they so prized in life. There have even been finds of foods that have been preserved through the ages, including funerary offerings of duck, loaves of bread, figs, and dried fish.

The Ancient Egyptians were gourmets, and the hieroglyph for taste is an abbreviated profile. The same hieroglyph also means smell and, more important, enjoy. Ancient Egyptian society was one that placed importance on grains. Barley *(Hordeum vulgare)* and emmer wheat *(Triticum doiccum)* were both used to prepare a flat loaf of bread similar to today's pita, and to make porridges similar to the mashes that are served with soupy stews throughout the continent. Wheat bread was considered to be finer bread than that made from barley. The Egyptians were the first to make leavened bread as we know it. Loaves were available in a variety of shapes: ovals, triangles, animal and human forms, and more. Some loaves were flavored with various spices and seasoned with honey. There were also some forms of pastry; pastry cooks were called "workers in dates," a term that refers to the use of the date as a sweetener. One of the uses of grains that most appeal to many modern diners is brewing. Egyptians were one of the first peoples to brew a beverage that is close in style to beer. The alcoholic drink was sometimes flavored with fruit or vegetable products and widely consumed.

A passage from a Nineteenth Dynasty schoolboy quoted by Hilary Wilson in his monograph

Egyptian Food and Drink, admonishes against overindulging in one grain product while emphasizing the importance of another. "Beer will turn men away from you and send your soul to perdition. You are like a broken rudder on a ship . . . like a shrine without its god, like a house without bread."

It was not all bread and beer in Egyptian households. Onions and garlic were consumed in vast quantities, and the air of the construction site of Khufu's pyramid must have been fragrant indeed, as the workers were paid in onions and radishes! Onions and radishes may have been the mainstays of the diets of the poor, but the aristocrats savored lettuce, cucumbers, watermelons, figs, dates, grapes, and pomegranates. Vegetables may have also included *meloukhia,* a leafy green that is today prized in much of North Africa. A variety of broad bean *(Vicia faba)* and the smaller beans that find their way into dishes like *ful medames* were both available, as were lentils. Other available legumes included yellow peas, *luba* beans, and black-eyed peas.

While fruits and vegetables were available in fair abundance, the Ancient Egyptians were far from vegetarians. The wealthy ate beef; those of more modest means consumed fish and wildfowl. Meat was usually roasted or grilled, while the fish was smoked and dried, as it is today in much of the continent. Fish were also pickled in oil. Ducks were eaten, and a relief on the walls of a Sixth Dynasty tomb seems to show a scene of ducks being force-fed in much the same manner as they are in southwestern France today. Could it be that the Egyptians had a taste for foie gras? Those who wished to savor the wilder side of Egyptian culinary life could sniff mandrake fruit. It was reputed to be an aphrodisiac, and its hallucinatory properties would have given revelers a buzz.

Salt was the major condiment and was used to cure meat into a form of jerky as well as to preserve fish. It seems also to have been served in an herb-and-spice mixture of some form in much the same manner as today's *dukkah.* There were many different types of salt; Herodotus mentions a purple salt from Libya. Milk products were probably readily available, with goat's and sheep's milk being most common. There was even a form of cheese. A wide variety of cooking fats was used, from olive oil to lard. Nouvelle cuisine chefs would perhaps be surprised to learn that there is nothing new under the sun: Ancient Egyptians also sweetened and thickened their sauces with fruit purées and syrups. Honey was much prized and came from Lower Egypt. Flat-leaf parsley, rosemary, coriander, celery, cumin, and fenugreek have all turned up at ancient burial sites and would have made the cuisine of the pharaohs very rich indeed.

Cooks went about their tasks wielding knives of copper and bronze and wooden spoons and spatulas. Grinding stones and a pierced metal skimmer, as well as fanner baskets for winnowing and woven sieves, were all part of the cook's arsenal of tools. Serving pieces included wooden bowls, pottery plates and cups, and further up the social scale, tableware in silver and gold. The society reveled in its love of food and fine banquets and established continent-wide precedents for a lavishness of hospital-ity that are still in effect today.

Life after death, though, was always foremost in the minds of Egyptian hosts and guests, and the Greek writer Herodotus reported in *The Histories* that:

> In social meetings among the rich, when the banquet is ended, a servant carries round to the several guests a coffin, in which there is a wooden image of a corpse, carved and painted to resemble nature as nearly as possible, about a cubit or two in length. As he shows it to each guest in turn, the servant says, "Gaze here, and drink and be merry; for when you die, such will you be."

It was a chilling memento mori to be sure, but one that accurately symbolized the preoccupation of Egyptian life and hospitality.

❋

Delenda Carthago — "Carthage Must Be Destroyed"

North Africa was one of the hubs of the Mediterranean world, and by the sixth century B.C., Carthage was the greatest city in the western Mediterranean. Hanno, a Carthaginian, is thought to have sailed as far as the Guinea Coast of West Africa. Others traded British tin, as well as North African and Sardinian grain, to the rest of the Mediterranean region. Following the first Punic War Carthage was forced to abandon its holdings in Sicily and Sardinia and became subject to the rule of Rome, though the state continued to prosper and remained the ruler of the North African hinterland. Roman jealousy of Carthage's prosperity escalated to the point that Cato the Elder is reported to have held up a fresh fig in the Roman Senate one day and remarked that only a few days prior it had been growing on a tree in Carthage. This, to him, and indeed to all Romans, meant that Carthage was too close and that it must be destroyed *(Delenda Carthago)*. It was, in 146 B.C., and was colonized by the Romans as a part of their growing North African empire. The North African colonies of Rome were noted for their production of grain, olive oil, and wine; in fact they produced as much as two-thirds of Rome's supply of grain, as well as melons, olives, grapes, peaches, pomegranates, and, of course, figs.

The Romans who colonized brought their own lifestyles with them, and the region became an outpost of the wealthy and the ambitious. Roman ruins in Tunisia and Morocco testify to the lavish entertaining that went on during this period. In the houses of the well-to-do, the dining room floors were paved with intricate mosaics depicting what would have ended up there after the banquet: Shrimp shells, fish heads, broken eggshells, vegetable parings, and cherry pits all turn up in mosaic detail. Others depicted wine-filled nights complete with servers, hosts, and more than one inebriated guest.

✳

Dar el Sudan

It is difficult to reconstruct the foodstuffs that were cultivated and eaten in western Africa prior to European contact, but from archaeological evidence and early Arab chronicles, it is possible to make some deductions. From them we learn that while the African larder was significantly smaller prior to the Columbian Exchange, there were certainly grains, which were prepared as fritters, porridges, mashes, and couscous-like dishes much as they are throughout the continent today. Pumpkins (*Cucurbita* spp.), calabashes, and gourds (*Lagenaria vulgaris*) are reported by the chroniclers as being eaten in Timbuktu, in Gao on the Niger, and in other areas within the Niger Basin. By the fourteenth century, there were turnips (*Brassica rapa*), which were probably imported from Morocco to the north; cabbage (*Brassica oleracea*), which most likely arrived earlier from Morocco and Muslim Spain; eggplant (*Solanum melongena*), including a variety that is grown for its greens which are cooked in stews; and cucumbers (*Cucumis sativus*), which some scholars feel may have originally come from central Africa. In addition, there were onions and garlic.

There was also okra (*Hibiscus esculentus*), which is indigenous to the continent. It was used both fresh and dried, appeared in soups and stews, and was used to thicken sauces. A number of legumes were available, including the black-eyed peas (*Vigna sinensis*) that have found their ways into many dishes emblematic of the African-American experience, and Congo or gunga peas (*Cajanus cajan*), which have been found in Egyptian tombs. They were native to the continent, and their names in English and French—Congo peas and *pois d'Angole*—may hint at a central African connection. There were also broad or fava beans (*Vicia faba*), and more than likely chickpeas, kidney beans, and lentils. All were eaten in Ancient Egypt and had made their way to the western part of the continent through trade. The beans were used in soups and stews, and Ibn Battuta, during his 1352 journey through Iwalatan and Mali, observed, "They dig from the ground a crop like beans and they fry and eat it. Its taste is something like fried peas." He also commented on women selling a type of bean flour from which porridges were prepared. It seems that he was discussing the Bambara groundnut, a legume that has virtually disappeared from tables, although it was popular and used by American cooks well into the last century.

There were a variety of fruits. There was tamarind, which was and still is consumed as a cooling beverage called *dakhar* in today's Senegal and which is also used medicinally for its laxative qualities. Wild lemons and oranges were available in parts of the Sahel; the Portuguese traveler Diego Gomes found lemon trees growing in Senegambia in 1456. There were also melons, including watermelon *(Citrulus lantanus)*, which has been cultivated in Africa for millennia and which seems to be indigenous to tropical Africa. Certainly, there were dates *(Phoenix dactylifera)* and figs *(Ficus carica)*. Mangoes arrived more recently and were immediately taken to heart.

More unusual foods included ackee *(Bligha sapida)*, the bland-tasting red tropical fruit that turns up in one of Jamaica's most popular dishes. While ackee originated in West Africa, it can be found from Senegambia to Gabon, and is eaten by the Yoruba of southwestern Nigeria, it would seem that its uses there are more medicinal than culinary. It is considered a sacred plant in parts of Côte d'Ivoire, where it is used medically, and is employed by the Krobos of Ghana to wash clothing and to fix dyes.

The baobab tree *(Adansonia digitata)*, which grows from Senegambia to Zimbabwe, offers virtually all of its parts for matters culinary. The leaves are dried and pulverized for soup, and the pulp of the white gourdlike fruit is eaten. The seeds are roasted and taste like almonds; they are occasionally ground into a powder and used to thicken soups and stews. Leo Africanus records that there were truffles—some so large that a rabbit could make his burrow in them—which were peeled and roasted on coals or cooked in a fat broth. These, though, were most probably some other form of vegetable fungus than the black or white truffles that we know today.

Sesame oil was also used for cooking, as were vegetable butters like shea butter (or *karité*, as it is known in French). It is mentioned by Ibn Battuta and called *gharti*, a variant on the Soninke *kharite*. Farther south there was also the oil of the palm tree *(Elaeis guineensis)*. This oil crosses the Atlantic to become Brazil's *dende*. The same tree also provided palm wine, which could be cooling and refreshing, or if allowed to sit and ferment, could pack the kick of a country mule (an early variety of white lightning).

Aside from palm wine, there were Ethiopia's meads, all manner of beers, and drinks prepared from tree barks. There was also the drink prepared from the deep red flowers of a bush of the hibiscus family known in the Caribbean as roselle *(Hibiscus sabdariffa)*. It is consumed today as *carcade* or *karkadeeh* in Egypt and as *bissap rouge* in Senegal.

Meat was used sparingly and primarily for seasoning. At times of feasting, though, meat was important. In coastal and river areas there was fish, which was usually sun-dried and smoked. Dishes tended to be soupy stews served over or alongside a starch.

Leo Africanus, writing of Tunis in his *A Geographical Historie of Africa*, published in London in 1600, writes about the bread of Tunisia in the fifth book:

> Bread they make very excellent, albeit they leave the bran still among the flower, & they bake their loaves in certain mortars, such as the Egyptians use to beat flaxe in. The merchants and most part of the citizens use for a food a kind of homely pulse or pappe called by them besis, being made of marley meale in forme of a dujpling, whereupon they pour oil or the broth of pome citrons.

To spice things up there were members of the pepper family, some native, others acquired through trade, most notably grains of paradise *(Amomum* or *Aframonum melegueta)*, as well as other variants like long pepper *(Piper longum)*; West African, Guinea, or Ashanti pepper *(Piper guineense)*; Monk's pepper *(Agnus castus)*; and cubebs *(Piper cubeba)*. In the Middle Ages, these were much prized in Europe and traded in limited competition with pepper from the East *(Piper nigrum)*. In the past, they were used in conjunction with ginger to season dishes calling for a more spicy outlook. Today, these are mainly used in the cooking of Ghana and Nigeria. However, they all turn up in the more elegant variations of ras al-hanout, Morocco's legendary spice mixture. Salt was highly prized and used mainly as a preservative. It was mined in great blocks from salt mines in northern Mali, where the salt caravans still run. In addition, there was kola *(Cola acuminata)*. The nuts of this plant are chewed as a stimulant and contain kolatine and small quantities of theobromine, which allow people to function for extended periods of time without rest or nourishment. The plant's importance is also religious, as it is used in divination by the Yoruba and several other groups. In many parts of western Africa, kola has social and ceremonial importance, notably in the payment of bride prices and dowries, and in other exchanges of gifts and demonstrations of wealth. The sharing of kola is still considered a sign of friendship in many West African countries today.

Cooking and eating utensils were made from earthenware, wood, or metal, and many of the dishes and food-storage vessels were prepared from calabashes and other gourds. Indeed, many of these everyday utensils have found their way into the art museums of the world for their beauty of design and their arresting appearances.

The major culinary techniques were those that could be used on the traditional three-rock stove.

1. Boiling in water. (This may not have been used throughout the continent, as it remains unknown to some of the traditional people even today.)
2. Steaming in leaves.
3. Frying in deep oil.
4. Toasting beside the fire. (This can also be described as grilling.)
5. Roasting in the fire.
6. Baking in ashes.

❋

The Columbian Exchange

With the arrival of Europeans and the extension of the culinary cornucopia that was the result of the Columbian Exchange, the African larder expanded to include such American foods as tomatoes, corn, chiles, and manioc or cassava, brought by the Portuguese in the early part of the sixteenth century. These were rapidly embraced (given the slowness of transport in the era), and became a major part of the dietary norm. In fact, many contemporary Africans would be hard-pressed to acknowledge that such staples as cassava and corn, tomatoes and hot chiles are not indigenous. Indeed, it is impossible to think of Senegal's *thiebou dienn* without tomatoes or the food of southwestern Nigeria and Benin without the cassava meal called *gari.*

❋

The Explorers Arrive

The cuisine of western Africa, both with and without the American additions to the diet, drew praise from missionaries and explorers in their travel logs for over 700 years. René Caillé, who traveled overland from Morocco through Mali into Guinea in the early nineteenth century, repeatedly speaks of the foods he ate in his 1830 travel account. He mentions a "copious luncheon of rice with chicken and milk" that he ate with delight and that filled the travelers for their journey. He also speaks of a meal offered to him by the poor of a village he was visiting, which consisted of a type of couscous served with a sauce of greens. A similar millet couscous is still traditional in many parts of Mali and northern Senegal. He is astonished by the lavish hospitality, as the hosts ate only boiled yam with a sauce prepared without salt. The prodigious hospitality to which visitors were treated was worthy of commentary by virtually all writers and is certainly a pan-African hallmark. Those who think of the foods of Africa as lacking sophistication, however, should also note that Caillé and others were as astonished by the preparations and the tastes of the food as they were by the prodigious hospitality they were offered.

Theophilus Conneau, another Frenchman, records that on December 8, 1827, he partook of an excellent supper:

> of a rich stew which a French cook would call a *sauce blanche*. I desired a taste which engendered a wish for more. The delicious mess was made of mutton minced with roasted ground nuts [or peanuts] and rolled up into a shape of forced meat balls, which when stewed up with milk butter and a little malaguetta [sic] pepper, is a rich dish if eaten with rice *en pilau*. Monsieur Fortoni of Paris might not be ashamed to present a dish of it to his aristocratic gastronomes of the Boulevard des Italiens.

✳

Colonial Rush

After the explorers had traversed the continent, the rush to colonization began. By the middle of the nineteenth century, each European nation had set up outposts that were soon small enclaves of their mother country. While India was noted for its colonial life, Africa was more daunting for the housewife, be she British, French, Belgian, or Portuguese. Nevertheless, households had to be manned and the aura of European normalcy maintained, even when the last shipment of products from home had arrived in the local canteen weeks, if not months, prior. Manuals for departing wives dispensed the accumulated wisdom of those who had gone before and admonished women to wash all vegetables in a purple solution of potassium permanganate and boil all water. One housewife bemoaned the culinary tedium of the colonial existence. "There was no refrigeration, no means of electricity, no means of keeping your food. Whatever you had was killed that morning and eaten either for lunch or dinner." This lack of European ingredients led the colonial wives and their African cooks to astonishing feats of culinary inventiveness, with mashed yams substituting for mashed potatoes, plantain chips instead of game chips, and at times, dark-roasted peanuts as a coffee substitute. Newcomers depended on the wisdom of those who had been there longer, and soon a few cookbooks even appeared, to help them out. Works like *Chop and Small Chop: Practical Cookery for Nigeria,* by Nora Liang, and *The Kenya Settler's Book* gave advice to those who cared. *Living off the Country,* a Nigerian cookbook published in that period, advised replacing unavailable or scarce European ingredients with African substitutes and suggests that the colonial ladies had learned a few things from their resourceful African cooks after all. This work suggests using papaya leaves as meat tenderizers and substitutes *yakua,* or roselle pods, for lemon juice in some recipes. It also features some adaptations of traditional dishes of the country.

Maintaining the household was most emphatically *not* done alone. And while European wives may have complained of the lack of European products, there were ample numbers of African workers who stood at the ready to explain and help them if they were willing to learn. African houseboys and cooks usually did the marketing, the cooking, and the serving in all but the smallest households. They worked diligently and adapted their traditional dishes to European tastes while at the same time taking some of the tastes of the European tables home with them. The continent's cuisines were enriched once again by contact with other worlds.

From the time of Napoleon's conquest of Egypt, travel to the continent had increased and so had the colonial hotels. In Cairo, the New Hotel and Shepheard's beckoned with large rooms decorated in traditional style and restaurants that offered menus to tempt the Europeans. The Mount Nelson, in Capetown, South Africa; the Mamounia, in Marrakesh, Morocco; the Grand Hotel, in Tripoli, Libya; the Croix du Sud, in Dakar, Senegal; and more sprang up like a chain of diamonds greeting travelers and later tourists. In the English-speaking areas of the continent, they served as havens of European lifestyle, complete with dressing for dinner and afternoon teas.

MOUNT NELSON HOTEL, CAPE TOWN

The French took a bit more readily to the food of the continent, but even they craved the foods of their homeland. They solved the problem by opening a series of restaurants where the atmosphere was such that to cross the threshold was to take a trip back to a bistro in any provincial French town. Holiday *réveillons* and drinking and dining fraternities continued, as they would have in Nantes and in Nancy, France. As the colonial worlds expanded and as bureaucrats moved from one sphere of influence to another, they brought their increasingly international tastes with them. The British were soon enjoying the spices of the Arabian Peninsula and the savory tastes of the Indian subcontinent in Uganda and Nigeria, while the French nibbled on Indochinese *nem* in Dahomey and Dakar. The Lebanese and Syrians arrived from the Levant to become shopkeepers in French-speaking areas, while Indians had a monopoly on minor trade in those that spoke English. As African labor worked as waiters, cooks, countermen, and sales help, new ingredients and new techniques again joined the mix.

✳

Nation Time

Day after day, I began to wonder if I could plan a meal
that would satisfy the tastes of all of our people.
—Rhoda Omosunlola Johnston,
Never a Dull Moment

The independence celebrations for the Gold Coast in 1957, which featured the lowering of the Union Jack and the raising of the Ghanaian flag, and photographs of kente-clad Prime Minister Kwame Nkrumah dancing with a seemingly nonplused Duchess of Kent, were the signal of the transfer of power on the African continent that occupied much of the decade of the 1960s and the first half of the 1970s. As went Ghana, so went the rest of the continent, as the map slowly turned from the wash of British colonial pink and French colonial turquoise to the patchwork of independent nations that it is today. Nation time called forth a new wave of national pride and resulted in a new pride in traditional cooking. But in many cases, the African elite who would become the continent's new rulers, while knowing the tastes, were as unfamiliar with the preparations of their own food as the European colonizers.

Pioneering home economist Rhoda Omosunlola Johnston tells of the duality in her autobiography, *Never a Dull Moment*. On one hand she had to teach students from all parts of Nigeria how to use

European utensils and etiquette; on the other, she forged ahead and instructed her charges on the preparation of traditional dishes such as *fufu*. She wryly notes that she had to learn how to prepare the latter before teaching the methodology, as she did not know it herself; her family had always purchased already prepared *fufu* from market women. The complexity of her task and that of others like her was that they had to research and understand the ethnic diversities that were rampant in the new countries that had been divided along colonial and not ethnic lines.

The emerging African elite took pride in its culture and restaurants, like the legendary Jimmy Moxton's Black Pot in Accra, Ghana, which presented traditional dishes in baskets and wooden bowls atop the brightly hued batiked cloths.

For the literate, there were new types of cookbooks, ones that stressed local dishes. The first generation of African home economists wrote works in traditional languages and crisscrossed the fledgling countries, speaking with women and advising them on how to cook nutritious meals in a manner that still leaned heavily on European models. "Kitchens are not what they should be in Nigeria," begins *Miss Williams' Cookery Book*, before going on to explain and explore the riches of local cuisine. The book, written by Rhoda Omosunlola Johnston, gave housewives hints on such things as how to use a Players cigarette tin for consistent measurement and how to prepare many of the national dishes. For those who wish to get a feeling for the times, one of the most interesting sections is on how to select ingredients in the market for freshness and economy. It advises housewives to make sure that the tomatoes have not been eaten by maggots and not to select cereals that have been eaten by weevils, that okra should be fresh and not wilted, and that fresh shrimp should not be smelly and fly-covered. Pride in the local diet joined with European considerations of hygiene and proportion was the hallmark of this and other early works that are still the standards throughout much of the continent. The continent's cooking was beginning to come out of the closet and come of age.

✳

Tourism and Tastes

With independence came tourism. The new nations rapidly became the focus of world curiosity and more important of the African diaspora. Nations whose independence had been spawned in no small measure by the civil rights struggle of American blacks now hosted their cousins as visitors. These visitors, unlike many of those who had preceded them, were interested in the food of the continent, and many of them found similarities with their own. Senegal became an independent nation in 1960; it hosted the African-Atlantic world at the Festival des Arts Nègres in 1966 and dazzled visitors with its *teranga*, or welcome.

By 1972, when I made my first trip to the continent, the Hôtel Ivoire had been constructed in Abidjan, Côte d'Ivoire. This pleasure palace on the lagoon boasted five dining rooms including a coffee shop, a casino restaurant, a circulating restaurant with a view of the lagoon and Abidjan, a poolside venue, and a snack bar overlooking the continent's first, much-debated ice-skating rink! In each, while the food was basically European, African dishes slowly crept onto the menus. *Pili pili* turned up in the mayonnaise in the coffee shop that bore its name. Plantains filled the starch portion of the plates, and a traditional dish of the day appeared on many of the menus. Cuisine began to be exploited as a means of satisfying an international tourist clientele who wanted not only to see Africa but to taste it as well. What happened in Abidjan happened around the continent, as increasingly sophisticated tourists, Peace Corps volunteers, missionaries, and businesspeople began to search out the true tastes of Africa and demand that they find their way to the center of the plate.

The story doesn't end here. New cuisines are coming out of the homes and finding their way to restaurants. With the collapse of apartheid's regime in South Africa, more and more people are discovering the country at the continent's tip and it is discovering itself. From Dakar to Dar es Salaam, African restaurants are taking the food of the continent out of home kitchens and bringing it to restaurants. In Capetown, the Africa Café spotlights the food of the continent and offers tourists a taste, while the major hotels are adding restaurants that showcase the culinary diversity of the country.

✳

Famines and Food for the Future

African cooking has gone home to Europe and North America in the taste buds of immigrants and in the mouths of those who have visited the continent. It's possible to get *thiebou dienn* or *poulet moambé* in Paris and *kitfo* and *doro wat* in Washington, D.C. African cooking is out of the closet and here to stay. The all-too-widely held vision of the continent as an enormous begging bowl filled with bloated bellies and incapable of feeding itself is being revised. The naysayers are having to change their opinions and regroup, as the tastes of a continent, a continent of cuisines, is revealing itself, from the creolized cooking of Saint Louis's *signares* who carefully skin and bone a fish and then reconstitute it, complete with minced garlic and bread forcemeat, to make *dem farci à la Sainte Louisienne*, to the *dada* of Morocco, who are known for their confection of bastilla and its gossamer-fine *ouarka* pastry. There are the delicately flavored curries of the so-called Cape Malay of South Africa and the complexities of Ethiopia's various and varying berbere spice mixtures. You can enjoy the taste of bread baked in a Dutch oven over a wood fire on the savanna in Zambia after a day trekking through the grass on foot watching lions sun themselves and hippopotami frolic in the mud of the Zambezi, or luxuriate at a formal dinner in one of Marrakesh's palace restaurants. New ingredients like *waterblommetjie* and *rooibos* tea offer surprising tastes and new direction, while familiar ingredients flavor dishes like Cape Verde's *catchupa*, the biryanis of the Indians from Africa's east, and the *cocidos* of the Brazilians who have returned to the country of their ancestry.

The dishes of Africa are part of the legacy of this continent of many civilizations and of many cuisines, where all of life's events from the coming in to the going out are celebrated with food. All you need to join in is an open mind and a willing spoon.

A CORNUCOPIA
OF CUISINES

◎◎◎

North Africa: The Maghreb and Beyond

Fatéma Hal and I were destined to meet. The first words that I heard her utter publicly were an answer to an unspoken prayer. It all happened in Morocco during a food conference run by Oldways Preservation and Trust, a group devoted to preserving the old foodways.

The following day cemented our friendship. I was to make a brief presentation on a panel on varying views of Moroccan food. I selected the *dada* of Morocco, descendants of former slaves who had become first nurses and then master cooks. They fascinated and still fascinate me, and I used them as an indication of the unresearched culinary links between the Maghreb and the lands to the south. I ended my discourse with a wish to learn more about the *dada* of Morocco.

Fatéma gave the next presentation, which fit mine like the missing piece of a puzzle. She began with an invocation to the *dadas* she'd known growing up in Oujda, on the Moroccan/Algerian border. By the time she'd finished, we were both in tears; I'd received many of the answers to my unasked questions, and found another culinary sister.

Fatéma is impassioned by the history of the food of her people. She has a restaurant in Paris, La Mansouria, that is one of the top spots for Moroccan food in that city. One day we set off to the me-

dina in Marrakesh; Fatéma was in search of service items for her restaurant, and I was just happy to tag along. We began in the Djema el Fna, the Square of the Dead, perhaps the liveliest place in all of Marrakesh. Soon we were in the midst of the sun-dappled souk, where the sounds of the busy square were only a muted hum. We stopped at a tiny stand, heady with the scent of spices and incense. Fatéma spoke to the wizened owner. She'd purchased ras al-hanout in Fez, but she thought she'd need some more. She watched with the skeptical eyes of the seasoned shopper and sniffed as the owner brought out the ingredients: long pepper and cubebs, rosebuds and cassia, ginger and turmeric, cloves and caraway. The ingredients vary from merchant to merchant, each one jealously guarding the secret of his own personal mix. Some versions of ras al-hanout have as many as twenty-seven different spices. The one that Fatéma purchased in Fez, from the legendary spice merchant ben Choukroun, contained such esoteric ingredients as dung beetle eggs and Spanish fly! Here, in Marrakesh, we hoped to do as well. After making sure of the quality of the individual spices and the complexity of the mixture, we purchased several kilos for her and a small bag for me and continued on our way.

As we walked, we talked about the foods we knew and the similarities of traditions in the sub-Saharan and northern parts of the African world. I spoke of the black American and Senegalese love of buttermilk, and she told me about Morocco's *rayeb*, a milk curdled with the "whiskers" of arti-chokes. She spoke lovingly of the *tangia* of Marrakesh and Taroudant, where the meal is cooked in one pot, and I countered with tales of the *kedjenou* of Côte d'Ivoire. We compared notes on what was con-sidered good manners and proper guest behavior and she let out peals of laughter when I described how in many black American households you eat before going to dinner because you don't want anyone to think that you're hungry. "That's exactly how folk behave in Tlemcen," she replied.

As the afternoon continued, we found that there were more similarities than differences in the matrix of the cooking that we both loved. Fatéma was a real confirmation of what my mouth had been telling me all along—that the Sahara was a very permeable veil indeed and that the cooking of northern Africa shares many similarities with that of the sub-Saharan region and with that of the African-Atlantic world as well. We both had a fondness for the food lovingly prepared by "Mama cooks," as I call the women cooks around the world who nightly prepare dinner for families and whose handiwork truly defines the culinary richness of their home regions.

By the end of our voyage, we'd exchanged manuscript notes, ideas, pieces of jewelry, and friendship. *Les Saveurs et les Gestes,* the cookbook on which she was working when we were together in Morocco, has been published in France and is a masterwork of culinary history, detailing the food and foodways of Morocco with affection and insight.

Our first meeting will always be cemented in my memory by images of my trotting dutifully along behind her through the souks of Marrakesh and Fez. It will also be sealed by my knowledge of our shared appreciation of the *dada* of Morocco—black and brown women who have transcended their ancestry as slaves and whose hands keep many of the country's culinary secrets.

✳

The Sahara — A Permeable Veil

A Maghrebi proverb has it that Algeria is a man, Tunisia is a woman, and Morocco is a lion. Whether the first two parts are true or not can be debated, but Morocco is definitely a lion, and a lion king at that. I've traveled to Morocco too many times to count, but I will always remember my first trip, with my parents over two and a half decades ago. On a bus tour rest stop in a small café near Tangiers, we were ceremoniously ushered behind the bar by our tour guide. He pointed reverently up to the picture of King Hassan II and said, "This is our king; this is your country. Welcome to Morocco and welcome to Africa."

Over the years since that first visit, I've thought many times about my initial welcome as I have been welcomed as long-lost kin in houses throughout North Africa from Casablanca to Cairo. It has only been recently, though, that I thought much about the links between the northern part of the continent and its neighbors to the south.

Too many geography lessons separate out North Africa as though it were a different place from the rest of the continent. Morocco, and all the countries of the northern part of the continent, are the same continent we visit when we journey to Kenya or Senegal, Benin or Tanzania. These links are evident when the mud-brick kasbahs of the south are compared with the mosques of Djenné and Timbuktu in Mali or when keening music of the Gnaouia musicians is compared with the sounds of the griots of Niger or Mauritania. Pieces of the puzzle came together as I thought of why I tasted hints of home in many of the dishes that I sampled. Nowhere is it more obvious than in the food of the region. Senegal's *tiere* or millet couscous is just another cousin of its Moroccan relative to the north. The Gnaouia food of Tunisia, with its accent on the slippery tastes of okra and *meloukhia,* is a reminder of the masters and slaves from the former empire of Ghana who journeyed northward, including the scholars of Timbuktu who studied and taught at the university near the Kairaouin Mosque. The Egyptian love of okra and its appearance in dishes like *bamia maloukah* and other synchronicities and similarities are all reminders of the fact that the divisions between northern and sub-Saharan parts of the continent are recent ones. Trade in salt, spices, and yes, slaves; wars and jihads; and dynastic intermarriage have made those to the north familiar with their cousins to the south. It's all there on the plate.

✳

In Seach of the Dada of Morocco

On an early trip to Morocco, a friend's daughter had referred to me as *dada.* How nice, I thought, mistaking the term for a variation of *tata,* the honorific "auntie" sometimes given to family friends in Senegal. "Oh no," replied her mother, "the *dada* in Morocco are black women cooks who prepare specialty dishes at feasts known as *diffa.*" At first offended by the seemingly racist quip, I was then intrigued. Who were these *dada* and where did they come from? There was scant information to be found. When I asked Moroccan friends, even the term seemed fraught with controversy. Some argued that the *dada* were not truly cooks, but rather nursemaids who took over the role of cook after their charges grew up. Others were unwilling to discuss them at all. Still others rolled their heads back, smiled, and said "Ah!!!"—recalling the delights that they had tasted prepared by the ebony hands of one of the *dada.* Clearly the *dada* had a culinary magic all their own.

The next time the *dada* turned up in my consciousness, I was reading the introduction to *Come with Me to the Kasbah: A Cook's Tour of Morocco,* by Kitty Morse. In his foreword to the book, Abderrahim

Youssi, a professor of Linguistics and Anthropology at Mohammed V University in Rabat, compared Morocco's *dada* with the black cooks of the American South. Many visits to the country had revealed that there were indeed a number of black and brown women who were entrusted with particular culinary tasks. They were known for their adeptness at preparing the transparently thin *ouarka* pastry that is used in preparing bastilla, the pigeon pie that defines the elegance of Moroccan cooking, and for their mastery of various different tajines. At the Ecole Royale in Rabat, I would watch as the descendants of the *dada* prepared other of the country's specialties, and I began to learn a bit about their history. It seems that the women are the descendants of slave women who arrived from the region that the French call the Soudan (today's Mali) and Senegal. They were prized for their looks and many were indeed hired as wet nurses. Over the years, though, as their charges grew up, they often turned to cooking for the family, learning the Moroccan specialties and investing them with their own talents for spicing and seasoning. The older generation of the *dada* are dying out today as family life has changed and the younger generation is no longer subject to the career choices of their parents. Some remain, however, and I met two of them—one short and energetic, the other tall and majestic. Both were the color of burnished ebony. Both were Moroccan to the core. They and others like them throughout the kingdom of Morocco hold a part of the country's culinary heritage in their hands and in their heads.

✳

Islamic Cooking from East to West

The majority of people who live in the belt of countries from Egypt to Morocco in North Africa are Muslim and follow the dietary rules set down by the Koran and its interpreters. Islamic traditions forbid the eating of pork and the meat and blood of any animal that has not been sacrificed to God. This form of preparation is called Halal butchery, and it is similar to the kosher butchery of Judaism. Followers of Islam must also not consume alcoholic beverages of any kind. The result is that there are numerous drinks available using fruit syrups, most notable Egypt's *karkadeh* and Tunisia's *orgeat*. Most of us know about Morocco's mint tea, but Egypt's love of coffee is also a result of the interdiction against alcohol.

Breakfast, *fatour al-sabah,* may consist of tea or coffee with either a porridge prepared from millet or chickpea flour, or small cakes of many different types. Occasionally, there will be one of the flat breads that characterize the region.

Lunch, *al-ghada*, is usually three courses. The appetizer may be a selection of small plates of vegetable salads, which may also appear later in the day as hors d'oeuvres. A main dish such as couscous, a tajine, or any of the numerous fish dishes follows these appetite teasers. Sometimes there is pasta, which is served with a variety of sauces.

Dinner, *al-acha*, is usually a single fish or meat dish, which is accompanied by bread or pasta. Sometimes there is one of the seemingly infinite varieties of soups. When there is a festive gathering, there's feasting indeed. A Moroccan *diffa* can conjure up visions of the *Arabian Nights* with its lavish presentation of food.

The celebration may begin at the doorway with rose petals scattered on the ground to perfume the path that the diners will take. Guests are seated at banquettes or on poufs around low round tables covered with tablecloths embroidered in the tiny cross-stitch work that is typical of Fez, and frequently strewn with more rose petals. The dinner begins with a ewer of water passed by the daughter of the family so that guests can wash their hands in perfumed water. This is only natural, as forks and spoons will not appear. Hands and pieces of bread will be the "cutlery." (Right hand *only*, please! Don't ask why.)

Good table manners mean that you eat what is in the section of the bowl in front of you. The host or hostess will make sure that your section is filled with the most appetizing morsels. It's considered poor form to reach over the bowl to select the piece that you want. Don't fill up on the salads; they're just the opening salvo. Next come the tajines, and there will probably be more than one, so pace yourself accordingly. Finally, just when European diners are ready to cross their hands over full stomachs, the couscous arrives. The ewer is passed again and hands are rewashed, then it's time for the tea that closes the meal, along with a series of pastries and perhaps fresh fruit of some kind. The meal is bracketed by prayer—*Bismillah* signals the beginning, and it ends with the guest repeating the word *Hamdullah* (Thanks be to God), to which the host will reply *B'sahatkoum* (To your health).

The holiday cycle brings families together around the table throughout the year, beginning with New Year's Day, *ras al-sanah al hijri*, which is a changeable date celebrated on the first day of the Muslim month *mouharran*. That day many families will savor a dish of chicken and pasta or crepelike pancakes with honey and sugar. The birth of the prophet Mohammed, *al-mawlid al-nabaoui al-charif,* is celebrated by some with a soup called *assida*. Ramadan is a month of fasting during the daylight hours. From the time that it is light enough to distinguish between a black thread and a white one until the time that they again become indistinguishable, no food or drink passes the lips of devout Muslims. The daytime fasting is countered by nighttime feasting, as families gather to break their fast with dates and milk or honeyed fritters. Then comes one of the many varieties of the soup that is known as *harira* in

Morocco, followed by a copious meal. The pilgrimage to Mecca, or hajj, is signaled by a festive meal for departing pilgrims on the eve of their departure and a celebratory feast on their return.

Whatever the time of day or the season of the year, food in North Africa is the occasion for communion, for the celebration of family and friends. Hospitality is considered a prime virtue, and rare is the individual who is not invited to a home or at least to a café to partake of a meal or a snack with a new friend. Families pride themselves on their welcome of *marhaba* and value the ability to receive well.

✳

The Southern Rim of the Mediterranean Diet

Over the past few years, the Mediterranean diet has become for many the paradigm of a healthy diet. It's low in animal protein, places the emphasis on consumption of whole grains and fiber, includes lots of fruit and fresh vegetables, and uses vegetable oils for cooking. Mediterranean influences can be seen in the new-style Italian restaurants that have proliferated like rabbits, each with its own version of grilled vegetables and its obligatory olive oil bottle on the table for bread. They can be spotted in the culinary vogue for sun-dried tomatoes and in the seemingly endless varieties of olive oil that we find on our supermarket shelves.

Most of us, though, have not really looked at the food of the region's southern rim. Aside from the occasional couscous salad or a piece or two of flat bread, the food of the southern half of the Mediterranean rim is relatively unknown. This is a shame, because the rich tastes of a slow-cooked tajine or a simmering pot of *meloukhia*, the unctuous savor of a plate of ful, the delightful crunch of deep-fried fava beans are all Mediterranean as well. The case is being made that these tastes are perhaps even older than the more familiar ones. After all, many of the tastes of today's Mediterranean region were strongly influenced by the tastes of the North African Moors who ruled the region for over seven hundred years. Certainly, they are as tasty and as healthy as the foods of their relatives to the north.

Recipes from this region highlight the tastes of cumin and caraway, clove and cinnamon. They play with harmonies of sweet and savory and tantalize with mixtures like oranges and radishes, or lamb and pears. The sophistication of the court cooking and the food of the descendants of the pharaohs are all a part of the food of this region, one that offers a different look at the familiar Mediterranean diet.

✳

SOUTH AFRICA

The southern end of the hemisphere has long been an area of contradictions. For years, I refused to visit a country where my brethren were not able to enjoy full rights as human beings. I relented and journeyed to South Africa only a few years ago, after Nelson Mandela had become president, and I was amazed with the country I found. While many in South Africa are busy rewriting history and forgiving recent inequities, I was fortunate to meet Shareen Parker, a woman who looks forward to a new future, while at the same time revering and preserving the memory of the past. She is the most recent inductee into my group of African culinary sisters, but one who by her intensity and fervor is in the front ranks.

We met when she was assigned to be my guide for my short stay in Capetown. In the bad old days, Shareen carried a passbook that labeled her as colored, and she would have been called Cape Malay, although this is a term with which she disagrees violently. The Cape Malay, she contends, were not a uniform or homogeneous group, as the name would imply. They were rather a mixing of many peoples from places as diverse as Malaysia, Madagascar, and more northern and western sections of Africa, as well as the indigenous Khoi and San peoples who were the original inhabitants of South

BREAKFAST AT A SOUTH AFRICAN MISSION

Africa. The creolized folk were then given the name Cape Malay, although that's only one of the peoples in the mix.

As we drove along the streets of Capetown, Shareen acquainted me with tales of Capetown before, during, and after apartheid. We visited Bo-Kap, the traditional Cape Malay neighborhood, and the District Six neighborhood, where she'd grown up. In the small museum, I saw the streets where people of all races had lived in harmony in a tiny enclave of peace. As a travel writer, I've learned not to make assumptions about the politics of other countries based on that of the United States, but Shareen's intensity was genuine and moving, and I agreed with her politics.

We drove partway up the side of Table Mountain and stopped to look at the breathtaking view of the town and the water beyond. There were antelope in the fenced-off area fronting the highway, and a covey of tiny quail crossed our path as we left the car for a brief stroll. They reminded me of the diversity of this land that offers not only the familiar fruits and vegetables, like cabbage and pumpkins, but also strange new ones like *waterblommetjie heuning*, an edible seedpod from a water plant that tastes like a cross between asparagus, artichokes, and fiddlehead ferns—this land where the bounty includes *heuning bos* and *rooibos* teas, native plants that grow without tannin and caffeine.

I was pleasantly surprised when Shareen asked me to her home for dinner with her family on my last night in South Africa. She made the two-hour drive from Capetown to Paarl to make sure that I'd get there. When I arrived, she'd invited her sister and a few friends with whom she was working on a special project for UNESCO. That one of them turned out to be the sister of a woman I know in Barbados is a testimonial to the smallness of *my* world.

The table in Shareen's large kitchen was set Western-style, but Shareen, her husband, Feisal, and her sister Yasmeen ate the traditional way, with the tips of their fingers, though Yasmeen's son ate with a fork. Whatever the utensils, the food was delicious, redolent of all the flavors of home and hearth and love of a well-cooked home-cooked meal. There was a sugarbean *bredie*, a sort of cousin of cassoulet in which the beans are slow-cooked to deliciousness. A tomato *bredie* had the taste of slightly caramelized tomatoes and the surprise of meat. Shareen complained about the dal, deriding it as watery and not worth serving, but I suspected it was modesty, as it was the dish she'd prepared and it was quite fine as far as I was concerned. The snoek biryani, richly seasoned pieces of the fish nestling among the grains of rice and pieces of vegetable, was the centerpiece of the meal. White rice also accompanied the meal for those who wanted a bit with their food. We washed the whole down with an apricot nectar that was, for once, aptly named.

The meal was one of my favorite kinds, just friends and family sitting down at a table having good conversation, good fun, and good food. It somehow seemed to be a fitting ending for my brief South African sojourn. We ended reluctantly, but the airport and my luggage piled high with a case of wine, bags of maize and mealie, cookbooks, and more waited the following day. As we drove the two hours back to my hotel, we vowed that this would not be the last time that we shared food. I just don't know whether it will be my place or hers.

✳

The Butcher of Guguletu

"Guguletu Butchery/Superette, Best Meaty Place in Gug's," reads Nomzamo Gertrude Cuba's business card. She's a competent, capable, and energetic black woman of the type that I've seen behind market stands in Jamaica and Brazil, at work in the fields in Senegal and Haiti, and in front of stoves at church suppers in the United States. I'm speaking with her in her small office cubicle in the convenience store and meat market that she owns in the township of Guguletu, near Capetown.

Guguletu is my first look at what life in South Africa for black South Africans must have been like before Mandela. Shareen would later tell me that the location of Guguletu was chosen with diabolical exactness. It's situated where it is strafed by winds that are alternately blisteringly hot in summer and frigid in winter. The views are bleak and the folk are dressed in heavy sweaters and woolen caps, but there are pockets of brightness, like the small yellow flowers growing on the side of the road and in front gardens, and the smiles of playing children. Although it is late summer in the Northern Hemisphere, in Capetown winter is yielding its grip to the softer weather of spring. We pass a *shabeen,* or beer bar, where people congregate for scattered moments of joy amidst what is still a harsh environment. They were outlawed under the old regime and are now the main gathering spots in the townships, rocking with beer and music until all hours.

Other gathering spots include spaces like Nomzamo's butcher shop, which offers special *braais,* or South African barbecues, on weekends and for special occasions. "You should come back then. There's music and dancing and laughter and lots of food," she tells me while showing me the enormous barbecue grills that she's had constructed, stacked with firewood awaiting the next bash. I think of rearranging my schedule but know only too well that time is already too short.

Back in her office, we turn to the realities of life for women around the world and feeding a family. Nomzamo is very aware of the price of maize. At 2 Rand 29c a kilo, it's expensive (about 50 cents U.S.), but ten people can eat off one kilo of maize. I confess to her my confusion about the use of the terms *maize* and *mealie,* and she explains patiently that maize is dried corn. She brings out a small package of the precious commodity that she generously gives me as a gift. It is similar to what my family has always called samp, or broken bits of dry white corn that has been processed. Mealie, on the other hand, is cornmeal. Both forms are in abundant use in South Africa. Corn is not only expensive to buy, it is expensive to prepare, as it uses about three hours' worth of fuel for cooking, but it is still a major staple.

Nomzamo explains some of the most common dishes to me and some of their regional and ethnic distinctions. Mealie pap is cornmeal porridge prepared from white or yellow cornmeal. It is accompanied by a number of sauces and fits into the continent-wide paradigm of a mash over which a soupy stew is served. Then there is Xhosa *kramel* pap, which is crumbled porridge. A similar dish goes by the name of *umphokoqo* in the Transkai and is called *puto pap* in Lesotho. It is served with fresh or sour milk and is considered a delicacy. When vegetables are used, cabbage and spinach, turnips and turnip tops are favorites. Meat is something that men eat more than women, although there is an increasing number of lady butchers in the townships, because it is a field that is open to them; Nomzamo prided herself on her innovations, like her introduction of smoked pork to her community.

She was particularly interested in my questions about gender-specific foods. Certainly, in her South African experience there were things that women could cook and eat, and things that they could cook, but not eat, and things that they didn't cook, but did eat. Traditionally, she informed me, men are meant to hunt, so they're meant to eat a lot of meat. Women have taken a taste for meat as well, as I would find out in later days when a visit to a bookstore revealed a book of traditional tales with the title *Women Like Meat.*

By the end of our conversation, night was falling, the lights in the houses were giving off a pale yellow glow, and a chill wind was beginning to whistle through the now abandoned streets of Guguletu. We drove off with Nomzamo standing in the door of her shop. The butcher of Guguletu was waving, her blue fleece jacket the lone spot of cheer in the deserted streets.

✳

The Cape of Good Cooks

Capetown was a startling experience for me. The sheer beauty of the region constantly surprised me: it is at the top of my list along with Rio de Janeiro and Hong Kong for scenic magnificence. The warmth of the greeting of the people that I met always delighted me. I was also thrilled by the food. Wherever I turned, there seemed to be someone talking about food, or eating, or planning to eat, or cooking, or selling something delicious.

It all began for me on the plane ride from New York to Capetown. On any other fourteen-hour plane ride, I'd have been a squirming wreck, but the food on South African Airways told me that the South African palate shared a North African/Southeast Asian love for the combination of the tart and the sweet. The salad was served with currants and walnuts and a sesame seed dressing, and a curry selection was offered. About an hour later, I was almost humming along with the township music playing on my earphones and finishing up my dinner with a piece of Stilton cheese and a sizable glass of port before retreating to chocolate and Champagne. East meets West and Europe meets Africa on the plates of this land, and when doing research my motto has always been Trust your mouth and—eat!

Later in the flight, just before touching down to change planes in Johannesburg, I was greeted with a breakfast that included yogurt, shredded wheat, croissants, fresh fruit, eggs, and bacon sausage (and more). It was clear that no weight would be lost on my trip. In the airport, I was fascinated to hear my first Afrikaans. It sounded a bit like Dutch with a southern lilt. On the two-hour flight to Capetown the snack was an egg salad sandwich, a green salad topped with peanuts and raisins, and a pastry for dessert.

I managed to arrive at my hotel, The Cellars–Hohenort in Constantia, just in time for dinner. The classically elegant dining room was decorated in sunshine yellow with accents of polished brass, dark woods, and blue-and-white china hanging on the wall. As I was ushered to my seat, I reflected that this was not the South Africa that many see and this was not one that I'd have enjoyed even a few years ago. The food is amazingly inexpensive and staggeringly good. My rack of lamb came to the table napped in a hazelnut and oyster mushroom sauce and was served with a daisy-shape wafer-thin potato galette. The lamb was achingly tender and the string beans and *mange tout* that accompanied it were steamed to verdant perfection. I bade a final farewell to the diet and accompanied the meal with a bottle of Groot Constantia Governers Reserve 1987 that went down like ruby velvet, then I followed up with some locally made red Leicester, green sage cheese, and a bit of Stilton. In the interest of research, I finished with a small glass of the *vin de Constance* that was so loved by Napoleon I and Tsar Nicholas II, hoping that my fate would be better than theirs. I staggered off to bed, but not before musing that my meal total, including wine, came to about $40 U.S., startling when I realized what a similar one would have cost me in the States.

By the time morning dawned and I breakfasted on wonderful apricot preserves and crusty croissants, I knew that Capetown was a city I could learn to love, an undiscovered culinary capital of my African-Atlantic world.

During the following days, I would meet some of the chefs who create the culinary diversity that is Capetown. Over lunch, I would speak with Ramola Parbhoo about the Indian cooking of South

Africa and learn that Natal province and its capital, Durban, are where to go for the best Indian food. The main influences are Hindu, and the earliest wave of immigrants came in the late nineteenth century from southern India to work the sugarcane, much as they had in the Caribbean. The 1920s through 1940s brought a second wave of folk from the Gujarat region, so there are a variety of cuisines. Indian families live authentically and traditionally within their own communities, Ramola told me. One of the first books that a new bride receives is *Indian Delights,* an Indian cookbook for South African housewives that offers variations on all the special dishes as well as advice for the novice written in motherly tones. Ramola has written several cookbooks, including tomes on vegetarianism and ayurvedic food habits.

Cass Abrahams appealed to me right away, because she'd begun her career as a teacher. After a baptism of "hellfire and brimstone" because she couldn't cook, Cass discovered that she had to learn to justify her existence in the Cape Malay community of which she is now a part. She defined Cape Malay food as a harmonious mixture of Dutch food and slave spicing. Since the slaves came from various points, the spicing was diverse and distinct. The Cape Malay food has so gained in popularity today that all the major hotel restaurants serve it. This food was basically the food that was served in homes on the Cape flats until 1992 by the folk that Shareen had told me about. With the rebirth of the tourist industry, this food came out of the closet.

Cape Malay cuisine is hot right now in South Africa. It's a cuisine that everyone is trying to define, but it's so vast that as Achmat Marcus, the chef/owner of the Cape Manna restaurant, put it, "Everyone's granny has a different recipe for every dish."

Unfortunately, Fadela Williams and I just did not have enough time to talk. We met on my last day in Capetown as she joined me for a lunch at my hotel that was interrupted when I had to rush off to jump on my hopelessly overstuffed suitcases. Our conversation revealed another aspect of the cooking of the Cape Malay—the round of Muslim holidays that mark the traditional life of many in Capetown and the dishes that accompanied the holidays, from the fast-breaking soups of Ramadan to the celebratory pastries that accompany a pilgrim's return from the hajj. It was only a glance at my watch that told me that I'd have to cut short our conversation or miss my plane. With the improvisational skill that I'm sure that she uses in her cooking, she decided to ride to the airport with me so that we could continue to talk. She even organized a brief detour to a spice shop on the way that further jeopardized my on-time departure, but convinced me that no matter what, I must make it my business to return to the city that I now think of as the Cape of Good Cooks.

✳

The Wines of Nederborg

"Hurry up," said Janet, my guide. "These folk are major Afrikaners and they don't appreciate lateness."

I knew of the wines of South Africa, but I was going to be treated to a wine tasting and luncheon at the site of the world-famous wine auction. The building itself is impressive, set atop a knoll where iris and daffodils were showing their first blooms and signaling the coming of spring.

The grand salon, where I was met by the charming woman who was to be my guide and hostess, was imposing, with massive bouquets of flowers and a baronial fireplace. The luncheon was delicious, a mutton pie with fresh vegetables: parsnips, string beans, carrots, new potatoes, and the South African version of candied sweet potatoes prepared with boniato and brown sugar seasoned with cinnamon sticks, allspice, and nutmeg. Following lunch we adjourned to the wood-paneled tasting room where the wines were set up. Now, I can fake my way through most wine tastings, but the burgeoning friendship of the morning compelled me to confess that I really am a wine drinker and not a connoisseur. I like my wine red, liquid, and alcoholic. That seemed to endear me to her all the more. "You know," she said, "I see a lot of 'experts.' It's very nice to see someone who wants to know about the wine." Confession made, I proceeded to hunker down to learn about the wines of the region and to exercise my taste buds. Nederborg, my guide explained, is better known for its red wines than for its whites (that was fine with me, as I am a confirmed red wine drinker). and has 25 percent of the South African wine market. Then she began by pouring a young sauvignon blanc which we swirled and sipped. For the first time, it was not so much blah-blah—I could actually taste the slight *pétillance* and the faint spice of green peppercorns. We moved on through a 1996 chardonnay to the reds that I had been anticipating. While California is known for its varietals and France is known for its regional styles, the wines of South Africa are named many different ways. At Nederborg, I was taken by the 1993 Baronne, a cabernet sauvigon/shiraz blend where the cabernet provided tastes of black currant and the shiraz gave a slightly smoky tone.

My favorite of all was a 1994 pinotage. This wine, which takes its name from the pinot noir and hermitage grapes that are blended together, is uniquely South African. I came to know it well during my stay. A young pinotage is eminently drinkable, and with a little age it can become as soft and enveloping as liquid garnets. I tasted wines in several other parts of the wine-growing region around Capetown, but somehow, the pinotage always came out my favorite. I even hauled a case home with me, which I save for special occasions.

✽

EAST AFRICA

Michèle Rakotosan came into my life like a whirlwind at a conference on writers of the Francophone world at Brown University a decade ago. We'd seen each other during the conference, but as she read from her work *Le Bain des Reliques,* I was struck with her intensity and with her connection to her home, Madagascar, where she is one of the leading playwrights. We spoke after her reading and I invited her to visit New York City, which she'd seen only on a group tour.

A week later found me at Pennsylvania Station hoping that I would recall what she looked like so that we'd be able to hook up. I shouldn't have worried. She emerged from the crowd of train riders, bristling with energy, with her aureole of curly black hair, and we headed off to explore my city as sisters of color. She felt right at home in my Brooklyn house and evidenced her comfort by heading off on her own to explore the neighborhood. She displayed superb urban street savvy by returning home at nightfall, before my disquiet had reached panic levels.

She returned with her impressions of the city. "New York has its own apartheid. On my first visit, I'd only seen the area around the big hotels and I didn't know where the people of color lived. I can see now that they're all here near you. I had the greatest time," she continued in her breathless enthusiastic manner, "and I found the most amazing greens. You've got everything that I need to make a real Malgache meal, you've even got some things I can't find in Paris. I've been dying for my food. Why don't I make dinner for us tomorrow night?"

The following day, we headed off to the markets of Fulton Street. We talked about everything, from the kinds of food that are eaten in Madagascar to the differences in tastes between the more Indian peoples of the population and the more African ones. All the while, Michèle was peering at the greens. "What are these?" she wanted to know. "These are collards, the ones that are classically black American. These are mustards, these are turnip tops, and these are kale. Over here, these are more commonly eaten by people from the Caribbean and are called callaloo or malanga." "Great, I'll take some of each." She also stocked up on vegetables: carrots, tomatoes, a small turnip or two, and some other items. Then it was off to the butcher's for a chicken. By this time I was curious. "What are you going to make?" "I'm not sure. I'll figure it out when I'm in the kitchen. Right now, I'm just enjoying the abundance and the wonderful choices."

"What kinds of seasonings do you have at home?" Michèle asked. I replied that I had salt, pepper, hot chiles in varying forms, nutmeg, cinnamon, cloves, lots of garlic, and more, much more. "Do you

have fresh ginger? Fresh young ginger?" she inquired. I replied in the affirmative, and we set off to get to work in my kitchen.

We discussed family celebrations as we worked. Michèle reminded me that the piece that she had read at Brown dealt with the walking of the ancestors in her native land, the annual perambulation of certain parts of the island with the corpses of those who had gone before. She informed me that food was also a part of the ritual and that the ancestors had to be fed before they were returned to their graves. We never discussed just what the ancestors ate, but somehow I knew that they ate what they had liked in their lifetimes.

As we talked, Michèle and I had stripped the greens and worked our way through preparing the vegetables, and the pot with the chicken was now bubbling away on the stove. The rice was next. She spread a bit out in her hand, determined that she didn't have to pick through it to remove impurities, and proceeded to measure it into the pot, add water, and put it on to boil. By the time we sat down to eat we'd established that there really wasn't that much difference in our methods of cooking. We had even ventured far enough to suggest that there really wasn't that much difference in our lives. Michèle confessed that she'd always been teased in her family for being the one with the most African hair, and I admitted that I'd always been the most involved with the continent in my family. Our moment of truth came when we sat down to eat and both sensed that we had been trained to say grace. "What religion are you?" she questioned. "I do many things now, but I was raised a Presbyterian," was my reply. Gales of laughter accompanied my admission. "I'm a lapsed Presbyterian too!" she confessed. Friendship cemented, we said a good lapsed-Presbyterian grace and proceeded to eat a meal that crossed continents and oceans and yet held the tastes of home for both of us.

Since our initial meeting, I've seen Michèle several times in her adopted city, Paris. We've shopped the market stalls of the rue Mouffetard and of the suburban area in which she lives. On each visit, we're more and more aware of the fact that the differences that separate us in many ways are not as great as our similarities. She's promised to take me to her island home one day, and I look forward to tasting the food that she reproduced so well in my Brooklyn kitchen. She's even promised to take me to the walking of the ancestors, an event that celebrates her forefathers and who knows, perhaps my own.

✳

Looking to the East: The Food of the Indian Ocean

When most of us think of Africa, we think of the continental landmass. Cartographers differ and remind us that the islands of the Indian Ocean are indeed part of Africa. The Seychelles, the Comoros, Mauritius, and Madagascar, the fourth-largest island in the world, can all claim to be a part of the history and culture that is Africa. These islands, though, look to the east as much as they look west to their African origins, and their food is a magnificent mixture of Africa and Middle East, India, and Southeast Asia.

These islands are magical. Mauritius was the home of the dodo bird until its extinction. The infamous *coco de mer*, a coconut shaped exactly like a woman's nether half, also comes from this area.

Mauritius, which lies on important trade routes, was not permanently settled until 1721, when the French arrived. The Portuguese and the Dutch had already passed through, leaving culinary traces in the names of dishes like *brèdes touffé*, a spicy dish of sautéed greens, and *camarons* with rice, a prawn and rice pilaf. But they didn't stay. The French established cane plantations and set up societies similar to those in the sugar islands of the Western Hemisphere. Eastern Africans were enslaved, and they brought with them their own culinary traditions. The British arrived in 1810 and in turn brought workers from the Indian subcontinent. Later the Chinese would arrive to complete the cultural mix.

The Portuguese also first charted the Seychelles, though they may have been visited earlier by Arab traders. The pendulum swing of invaders and colonizers saw the islands in French and then British hands prior to attaining independence in 1976. Europe, Africa, and Asia come together in the population of the islands that produce such wonders as cinnamon and cloves, tea and vanilla for export.

The Comoros have a similar history. This time the cast of conquerors comes from Africa, Indonesia, and the nations of the Persian Gulf. The Comoros, though, cannot boast the agricultural diversity of Mauritius. Instead, they produce coffee, cacao, coconuts, and vanilla as well as exotic essential oils for many perfumes. Today, tourism lures many travelers to these worlds of *dolce far niente*, bringing the diversity of international chefs to the culinary mix and adding new influences to the cooking pots.

✳

Wild Game

The game parks of eastern Africa are one of the region's major lures for visitors from other continents. Anyone who has driven down into the Rift Escarpment and into the valley floor can well imagine what the world must have looked like on the day after God created it. The annual migrations in the Rift Valley are a visual encyclopedia of African wildlife, with thundering herds of everything from antelope to zebra. I had the good fortune to visit Zambia more than twenty years ago to participate in a walking safari in South Luangwa National Park.

There, we slept in tented camps under the stars by night and ventured through the tall grass during the day on foot as we walked and watched and lived with the animals on their own terms. Each morning we'd awaken with the sun to track herds of majestic kudu and lechewe. We giggled nervously as we watched an elephant drunk on marula nuts prance about on massive legs the size of tree trunks, rubbing against a tree in ecstasy. We eavesdropped on the honking, snuffling sounds of hippos as they frolicked in the muddy waters of the Zambesi and played peeping Tomasina with lion families as they fed their young. At dusk, we returned to our movable camp to savor some of the most delicious meals ever: hearty stews prepared from the ingredients that we'd brought with us and from the game that the wardens had culled. I remember a Cape Buffalo stew that I was persuaded to eat. Surprisingly toothsome with the rich dense flavors of game, it made me understand the beauties of the natural life. It was accompanied by wonderful bread baked in a Dutch oven in the ashes of the fire.

The meal remains in my mind even twenty years later—the fresh taste of the simple but delicious food, the smoky hint of the flame in the stew, and the crusty sweetness of the bread. This meal has remained in my memory as a totem, for it reminds me of the meals that must have been eaten throughout the continent for centuries by adventurers who traversed the continent in search of adventure and in search of themselves. I think of Livingston and Stanley, of Caillé, Clapperton Burton, and of Mary Hall, the first European woman who journeyed from the Cape to Cairo. The mind travels further back in time and I see Ibn Battuta and Leo Africanus and all those who packed their belongings on their backs and ventured off into unknown worlds. East Africa, more than any other part of the continent, recalls these intrepid travelers, with its open spaces and communication with nature in its pure form. It reminds us that for most of the world, Africa in its culture and cuisine remains unknown to us and offers itself to us for discovery.

✳

Sheba's Children

The lands of the Horn of Africa feature some of the oldest continuous civilizations on the continent. The nation that was known once as Abyssinia has a history that reaches far back into the Biblical past. This is the nation of the Queen of Sheba, the legendary woman about whom Solomon wrote some of the most sensuous love poetry in the Bible. To the lover of food, the poetry is alive with the richness of culinary metaphor and the sensuality of food, for Sheba was "black, but comely," with lips that dripped as the honeycomb and milk and honey under her tongue. The roof of her mouth was as the best wine for her beloved. It is somehow fitting that Solomon's love should be detailed in terms so lush with the appreciation of food, for Ethiopia, where the rulers claim descent from the union of Solomon and Sheba, is a country with some of the most original food on the continent.

This diverse area has long been a crucible for many of the world's religions: The Falasha, or Ethiopian Jews, are considered by some to be descendants of one of the original twelve tribes of Israel. The Coptic Christian stone churches at Lalibela are some of the oldest in the world, and the Muslim and animist traditions are also well represented.

Ethiopians have a long tradition of feasting. Their country can boast of being the watershed for a number of unusual crops that are only now beginning to make their way into specialty markets. With its combination of grassy northern and eastern highlands and heavily forested southwestern uplands, Ethiopia was one of the African sites of early plant domestication. Tef or teff (*Eragrostis abyssinica* and *Eragrostis tef*), a grain that is a staple food for much of the community, and *nug* or *noog* (*Guizotia abyssinica*), an oilseed, are two little-known ones. Teff is now being cultivated in the United States and is billed as "a super grain." It boasts an iron content that is three times that of wheat barley or grain sorghum and levels of minerals and other nutrients that are significantly higher than those of other grains. Also grown here early on were mustard, finger millet, and false banana. Then there is coffee, without which many of us would not be able to begin our daily culinary life.

As in much of Africa, hospitality is important in Ethiopia. Sometimes guests are even fed huge chunks of food as a mark of respect and honor, an honor that must be repeated again and again. To not do so marks the host as stingy. Hospitality depends on both host and guest, so accepting too much marks the guest as ill bred.

Food is so important in the Ethiopian scheme of things that a young girl of marriageable age is as prized for her cooking, and particularly for the subtle complexity of her berbere, or spicing mixture, as she is for her looks. Any visitor to an Ethiopian home or restaurant can testify to the fact that berbere indeed makes the cook in many parts of Ethiopia. The complex spice mixture is made in such vast quantities for home use that recipes call for as many as 15 pounds of chiles and 5 pounds of garlic. Berbere is so important to life that an Amharic expression has it that a man who is a coward is a man who has no pepper. Indeed, the heat of some berberes requires a brave heart for consumption.

Those who have had the pleasure of eating in an Ethiopian restaurant know that large wooden baskets with conical tops form the tables called *mesob*, which are covered with overlapping layers of the tart crepelike injera, upon which the meal will be served. Protocol dictates tearing pieces of injera off with the right hand, wrapping them around the meat or stew, and then popping them into your mouth. One nineteenth-century traveler to Abyssinia mistook the large folds of injera for napkins and placed it in his lap, earning immortality in the annals of faux pas. Others took quite a liking to it. C. F. Rey and his wife, early travelers to the region, pronounced it "very good when eaten with jam and butter." As a result of years of political unrest in the Horn of Africa, there are numerous Ethiopian and Eritrean restaurants in many cities in the United States, so that tasting the foods of this area of the continent may be as easy as a trip across town.

✳

WEST AFRICA

Theodora came into my life with a telephone call over twenty years ago. I was sitting in her husband's office in Dakar when he spontaneously asked my friend and me to join him and his wife for dinner. We accepted with alacrity. We met at the pre-arranged hour and drove to their home in Pointe E, *the* suburb at the time. As we drove up to the imposing structure, I found myself wondering what we'd have for dinner.

We entered the spacious living room and were met by a short energetic woman whose ample hips gave her a rolling gait. Her twinkling eyes smiled and she invited us to sit down for a pre-dinner drink. My nose twitching, I said yes, but there were no smells of food cooking. What would dinner be? I was soon answered as we finished our drinks and headed back into the car and off to a restaurant.

MARKET IN SENEGAL

Chez M'Baye M'Barrik was an outdoor spot located in the Almadies area. It was a popular place and known to locals for its *méchoui*, or whole roasted baby lamb. Theodora and I talked about everything from birthdays (we are both Pisces) to the food, beginning with the succulent tender pieces of lamb that we were pulling off the carcass with our fingers. By the end of the evening, we had so bonded one with the other that I pulled out a Pisces charm that I had just purchased and presented it to Theodora, telling her that we were now twins and she must come to visit me in New York, where she'd never been. She accepted both the charm and the invitation and came to visit me two weeks later.

We've been talking about food and eating together ever since. I've cooked in her huge kitchen in Dakar, once planning a sit-down dinner for ten at which I served fried chicken, Hoppin' John, and other black American favorites to a few of my Senegalese friends. When she moved to Abidjan, Côte d'Ivoire, I followed and we cooked some more. She now actually lives in New York, and so we've cooked together on this side of the Atlantic as well. It would take a separate book to note all of our culinary adventures. We've headed to markets in Abidjan, Dakar, and Cotonou, where she's from, in search of different ingredients and unusual dishes.

Several years back, while I was researching a story on the food of Benin for *Eating Well* magazine, Theodora arranged for me to watch as one of her country's leading cooks prepared *kpete*, a rich goat stew.

As we arrived at the cook's home, a small boy was herding several goats into the open courtyard. We entered and were offered breakfast while the goats gamboled nearby. After breakfast, a man arrived who I was informed was the butcher. He started to sharpen his knives, and preparation for the meal began.

If I were to write it as a recipe, it would begin, "First select your goat. . . ." The unfortunate goat was chosen and quickly dispatched. The butcher scraped the fur from the goat's hide, as the skin is considered a delicacy and is a part of the dish. He eviscerated the animal and cut the meat into bite-sized pieces. Meanwhile, the cook and her assistant were preparing the spices for the sauce. The most noticeable ingredients were black pepper and a funny little pepperlike item that I later learned are cubebs. The assistant then took over and patiently and carefully washed the goat chitterlings several times, cut them into small pieces, and rolled each piece into a ball. (These, I was informed, were special treats and savored only by those who paid extra.) As she worked I was reminded of my reading about hog-killing time in the American South.

Theodora, who was with me through the entire process, told me that when someone is working and you want to encourage her, you say *couchay* in Fon, her language, so I would periodically urge the assistant on with a shout of *couchay.* As the sun got hotter and the day grew longer, much encouragement was called for. The *yovo* (which means "peeled orange" and by extension, in some circles, a foreigner) enjoyed herself and didn't flinch when the goat was dispatched. Family members seemed to come from throughout the compound to watch the strange proceedings. Finally, the *kpete* was ready to be cooked—the wood fire had been burned to the right point and all the pieces of goat and the highly aromatic mixture of pepper, cubebs, and a bit of the goat's blood had gone into the pot. It was time for a break. We wandered off for photographs and fun as the *kpete* bubbled away on the fire. We returned later in the day to savor the final product, which was a rich, thick stew heady with the bite of peppery cubeb, which is called *piment pays* in Benin. We packed a bowl of it to take home, and the rest of the goat meal went to the cook.

Theodora has been my guide to the food of the western part of the African continent. Over the years, I've come to know not only her immediate family but also most of her sisters and her mothers as well. (Yes that's an *s*—her father had two wives!) I cannot see the twinkling lights of the night markets of Cotonou, or wander through the crowded stalls of the Marché de Treicheville in Abidjan, or drink chilled Laurent Perrier Grand Siècle champagne in the continent's grand receptions without thinking of our adventures together. She has been the perfect guide to the cooking of what is to me the most fascinatingly familiar region of the continent, because she, like it, is warm, welcoming, and brimming with excitement.

✳

The Salt Mines of Taoudenni

I don't use salt when I cook. I'd rather season with mixtures of spices and herbs that I enjoy concocting, one to suit each dish. There are a variety of reasons for my aversion to the white stuff—the staggering toll of high blood pressure in the African-American community, the tendency many of my friends have to salt food before tasting it, and I suspect, an evening that I spent with a man named Alioune in Dakar over twenty years ago.

For several summers, I was a virtual regular at the Hôtel Nina, a small place off the Place de l'Indépendance in Dakar, Senegal. The tiny hotel offered a convenient location and great rates, and best of all it was run by close friends of mine. I'd developed the habit of dropping into the tiny bar for a nightcap with them before heading off to my room. One night, I noticed that there was a newcomer to the crowd of regulars who usually ended their evenings in a similar manner. His name was Alioune. Tall and spare, he chain-smoked pungent French cigarettes with an intensity that was riveting. He had, I was told, been a political prisoner in the northern reaches of Mali in a place called Taoudenni. Alioune didn't have much to say, aside from furtive asides whispered to my friend Moctar.

One night, though, Alioune broke his silence. Peering through a cloud of smoke, he told us in haunted tones of his incarceration in a Saharan salt mine. The brutal extremes of temperatures, the backbreaking labor, the salt that was ever-present all came into vivid existence as he recounted his years at Taoudenni. Salt is mined, he informed us, and comes out as large tombstone-like slabs that are piled up and kept until the caravan arrives. Twice a year, the caravan arrives in Taoudenni; it was the only break in the spirit-deadening, monotonous work. No Paris–Dakar cortège of Land Rovers or heavy-gauge trucks, this caravan is a camel caravan, for the salt is still carried from Taoudenni on the backs of camels, several of the heavy slabs per camel.

As Alioune told his story, we sat transfixed. His voice took on animation as he painted a vivid word picture of the place and time. We could feel the oppressive heat of the mines, taste the grit of the Saharan sand on our tongues, and feel the sting of salt as it burned every cut and made eyes water. Finishing his story and returning to his drink, Alioune sighed, a man with too many ghosts, and I headed upstairs with the name Taoudenni burned into my brain with the sandstorm of words that Alioune had unleashed.

Later, I looked the spot up in my atlas. Due north of Timbuktu, just below the Tropic of Cancer, it is surrounded by a wide expanse of nothingness that my atlas has marked as SAHARA. The daily temperature, it informed me, can reach as high as 140 degrees. Recently, a friend who travels frequently to Niger said that on her next trip she was going to purchase a slab of salt to hang in her living room. I asked her to get me one as well. I'll keep the salt out of my food, but perhaps I'll hang some on the wall to remind me of Alioune and Taoudenni.

✳

Yoruba Cooking: A Cuisine That Crossed the Sea

Obatala, Shango, Yemoya, Oshun, Ochoosi, Oya, and others are the names of some of the venerated ancestors and forces of nature that are celebrated by the Yoruba people of southwestern Nigeria. These forces are called *orisa,* a word that derives from the term "selected heads." Celebrated with ceremony and music, dancing, and feasting, the *orisa* are like humans in that they are picky and have preferences as to colors they wear, rhythms they dance to, and foods they eat. These preferences mean that they have a veritable menu of foods that are offered to them. Derived from the everyday foods of the Gulf of Benin, these dishes are touchstones for the votaries of the religion.

Worshipers of Obatala, the *orisa* of purity, know that he does not like spicy foods and will not accept offerings including the red palm oil that is virtually a necessity in offerings for Shango, the justice-rendering *orisa* of lightning and thunder. Yemoya and Oshun, riverine goddesses in their native Nigeria, feast on the bounty of the rivers and the seas and are placated with offerings of fish and sea plants. Oya, the woman warrior, eats virtually the same foods as Shango, whose lover she is, but with variations in form and size. Ellegba, the messenger of the *orisa,* loves slippery, staining red palm oil. The culinary web surrounding the *orisa* is dense and vast, and dishes like the *akara,* a white bean fritter fried in palm oil; *amala,* a yam flour porridge; and pounded boiled white yam are only the tip of the market basket.

These demanding gourmet gods, like so much that is West African, crossed the Atlantic Ocean in the fetid holds of slave ships during the more than three centuries of the transatlantic slave trade. Yemoya is celebrated in Bahia, Brazil, and Brooklyn, New York. Oshun is venerated in Matanzas, Cuba, and Miami, Florida. Shango dances with his double axe in houses of worship from Haiti to Harlem. The *orisa* of the Gulf of Benin have maintained their culinary tastes from home, and so wherever they have traveled, worshipers attempt to replicate with what they have at hand the African dishes favored by the *orisa.* Thus *akara* can be found in *terreiros* in Brazil on altars dedicated to Shango. In Cuba, his *amala* is still prepared, although in the New World it is made with cornmeal instead of the traditional yam flour. Yemoya becomes Yemaya or Iemanja. From a river goddess, she becomes the mother of the waters and the ocean. She still dotes on the finny bounty of her depths. Obatala's love of white yam crossed the ocean as well, and in the houses of Candomble, in Brazil, an annual yam festival is held that is a shadow of those that are a traditional part of life in western Africa.

Invention and innovation mark the food of the African continent. When natives of that continent were transported to other parts of the world, they took that love of improvisation with them. The ritual foods of the Yoruba religions on both sides of the Atlantic have a specificity that is a part of their continuity. New World *orisa* are celebrated with meals that replicate their Old World favorite foods as closely as possible. The spirit of innovation and continuity that is both African and African American lives on in these dishes and in the *orisa* that have survived and thrived in another Africa, across the seas.

✳

The Ubiquitous Yam

Yams immediately conjure up visions of an orange-hued candied Thanksgiving dish that appears on countless sideboards only for residents of the United States, who have been laboring for centuries under what I call yam confusion. True yams, not the sweet potatoes that we confuse with them, are large, sometimes hairy tubers that can grow to great length and weight. They can weigh up to 45 pounds, but Jane Grigson in her book on exotic fruits and vegetables records a yam that weighed in at a quarter of a ton.

True yams were one of the earliest foods cultivated in the world. Botanists are not sure of the yam's place of origin, but they do know that the tubers were cultivated as early as 17,000 to 18,000 years ago on the African continent. The flesh of the yam can vary in color from pristine white to light purple. Closer in taste to white potatoes than to sweet potatoes, yams have only recently become widely available in American markets. This is because they are used a great deal in the cooking of the West Indies and in that of the Hispanic New World and new immigrants have brought this old food to the United States.

The mythology of yams is extensive in western Africa. In the ancient empire of Mali, it is said, criminals were ritually beheaded in the yam fields so that their blood could fertilize the crop and ensure its fertility. Much of the yam's mythological potency comes from the fact that new yams are planted from sprouted old yams. For this reason, the yam has come to be the symbol of renewal and rebirth in many West African societies and yam festivals are a part of the annual calendar of events in many places. These festivals are joyous occasions.

Among the Aburi of Akuapem in the eastern region of Ghana, a large yam festival is celebrated for two days during the month of September or October. Forty days before the festival, a ban is placed on bringing new yams into the town. This is done because Ntoa, the god of the harvest, is being celebrated at the festival and he should be the first to enjoy the bounty of the new harvest. All merrymaking is forbidden, to encourage farmers to return to their villages and to their yam fields to oversee the harvesting of the yams. The choicest specimens are selected for offering to Ntoa in gratitude for his blessings over the past year.

On the days preceding the festival, the religious shrine to Ntoa is cleaned and the footpaths and fences leading up to it are repaired in preparation. A senior priest remains in confinement during the forty days to make sure that all is done correctly. On the day of the festival, water is sprinkled on the streets to purify them. Around noon, the priest appears, dressed completely in white and wearing the insignia of his rank. He is handed a knife and a tuber of new yam and is carried through the streets on the shoulders of the worshipers. At every important stop, he stops and slices off three chips of yam. The three yam chips are an oracle. If two or more fall with the brown side to the ground and their white side facing upward, prosperity is ensured for the incoming year.

Similar ceremonies take place in other areas throughout the country, with regional variations. All involve the outing of the new yams. At some, a communal meal of yam *fufu* and chicken, at others, a mashed yam and a soup prepared from smoked river fish, at still others, goat's meat. Whatever the meal, the celebration is one where the farmers and their communities bring vividly to life the dictum, First thank the food.

OUT OF THE DARK

◎◉◎

Traditional African Diets
and Modern Health

The African continent has long been dubbed the Dark Continent. Needless to say, this appellation is incorrect. More appropriately, the landmass where man originated should be baptized the "Continent About Which We Are in the Dark." Nowhere is this more evident than in the realm of food. I recently taught a master's-level course on international cuisine at a major university. On the first day of class, I asked my students what they knew about the food of the African continent. They dithered at first, arguing that they didn't know anything about the continent's food. I gently challenged them, and finally they came up with "Very hot," "Really spicy," "Soupy stuff." That was it. No more from these food and nutrition scholars. Finally, one bright student added, "Couscous." There was no more, not even from the student whose parents were Egyptian. She thought I meant only sub-Saharan Africa and didn't realize that her Sephardic Jewish cuisine was also a part of the diverse culinary heritage of the continent.

Nothing could have brought Africa's place in the culinary world more startlingly home. It's easy to see that African food has gotten a bad rap. With the awareness of the food of the continent at such a low level, it's only natural that there is no thought at all to the healthful aspects of the diet. When African food is brought up, people's minds turn more to palm oil and hot chiles, mucilaginous soupy stews, and mystery meats than to appetizing healthful dishes. Certainly, all those things can be found in the diet of the continent, but along with them, there's more, so very, very much more. There's spit-roasted lamb and an infinite number of couscous dishes prepared from hard wheat and millet. The bounty of the vast coastline is served baked, stewed, and fried and can range from grilled sardines to fish curries. The continent's touch with spicing and the spices that inspired this talent were legendary before Columbus sailed westward. If that's not enough, the hands in hues ranging from saffron through cinnamon to deep, dark chocolate that have stirred the continent's pots for millennia are acknowledged virtually worldwide as gifted in the art of food preparation. Think of the enslaved cooks of the so-called New World. From the south of France to South Brooklyn, much of what we eat daily has been inspired by the food of Africa.

The diet of the continent is arguably at the origin of the much-vaunted Mediterranean diet; after all, the Mediterranean, after it was the *mare nostrum* of the Romans, was a Moorish sea for several centuries. Think of the paradigms. As in the Mediterranean diet, meat is not the centerpiece of the plate but rather a taste-enhancing addition to the vegetable-rich main courses. Think of the couscous of Morocco or the *thiebou dienn* of Senegal. Grains are consumed in abundance. Think of the millet couscous of Mali or the rice that goes under the main dish in much of Sierra Leone. Think of all the starchy mashes prepared from corn and millet in many parts of the continent. Corn from the Americas has pre-eminence in South Africa as mealie, but it also turns up in the fermented starches of West Africa. The continent can even boast grains of its own, like Ethiopia's teff. In other areas of the continent, mashes prepared from tubers replace grains and provide a starch base for the meal. And the paradigm of a soupy stew over a mash applies to dishes north, central, and south, ranging from the tajines of Morocco to the groundnut stews of Ghana to the curries of the east and south.

The ingredients of the continent's cooking themselves are not only rich in taste but also rich in nutrition. Garlic, which flavors many pots and was used extensively by the ancient Egyptians, may lower blood cholesterol. The leafy greens that go into pots from Ethiopia to Côte d'Ivoire are rich in beta-carotene and vitamin C. They are also a good source of fiber and of minerals like iron and calcium. Legumes like black-eyed peas and the fava beans that are the basis of Egypt's ful are some of the best plant sources of protein and some of the oldest agricultural crops in the world. When they are mixed with rice or other grains, as they are in many dishes, the result is almost perfect in terms of nutrition. Millet, one of the world's oldest grains, has been used on the continent for millennia. The rice that turns up on many American tables actually arrived in South Carolina from Madagascar and was cultivated with African know-how.

The okra that flavors much of the cooking of the continent is rich in vitamin C as well as in folic acid and other B vitamins and is a good source of dietary fiber. Chiles have been found to aid digestion and act as a natural thermostat in the torrid zones by making individuals sweat, thereby lowering their body temperatures. They are also rich in vitamin C and some are good sources of beta-carotene. Beyond the temperate zones of the northern and southern ends of the continent, sugar is used sparingly, and the taste for things sweet is satisfied with fresh fruits. Watermelon not only provides a good source of potassium and vitamin C but offers liquid as well. Salt is not the villain that it is in many other parts of the world, because it is traditionally used sparingly as the precious substance it once was.

The sidebars of the Mediterranean diet pyramid are two notations indicating that exercise and wine in moderation may also form part of this much-vaunted diet. For those who live traditional lives on the continent, exercise of the pumping-iron, aerobic type is laughable. Exercise is gained simply in the daily going about the business of living—pounding grain in mortars and carrying water, and more.

But with increasing Westernization, the traditional diet is being changed, as it is throughout the world. Animal protein is becoming a large part of the meal, along with the empty calories of foods that are packaged and prepared when compared with those that are caringly cultivated. Nutritionists, though, are looking at ways to adapt traditional tastes and ingredients to modern lifestyles. One thing that needs no adaptation is the incalculable role played by the commensality of food. The sharing of meals and the communing with friends and family across bloodlines and generations that takes place at the tables of the continent every day is perhaps the healthiest aspect of the African diet and indeed the easiest to duplicate on this side of the Atlantic in our own homes.

CALABASHES AND CASSAVA MEAL

◎◎◎

A Glossary of African Ingredients and Utensils

ALMONDS *(Prunus amygdalus* or *Prunus dulcis)*   These fruit seeds of the sweet almond tree seem to have originated in Iran or Arabia, but they spread to the Mediterranean Basin in ancient times and are mentioned in the Bible as one of the gifts sent by Israel to Joseph in Egypt. They contain more calcium than any other nut. They are used extensively in the cooking of North Africa, where they turn up in courses from appetizer snacks through desserts. Almond paste, or marzipan, is a filling in many North African desserts.

When purchasing almonds, look for shells that are not cracked and that don't have wormholes or any other sort of visible damage. If purchasing shelled almonds, look for uniformity of size and crisp, fresh nuts. Unshelled nuts will keep for about six months if stored in a cool, dry place. Shelled nuts will last about half the time in similar conditions. For fresher taste, blanch and prepare your own almonds. Simply dip them into boiling water to loosen their skins and then slip the skins off with your fingers. Almonds are readily available and can be purchased at supermarkets and health-food stores.

ANISE PEPPER *(Zanthoxylum piperitum)*   This berry, which is not a member of the pepper family, is sometimes referred to as Szechuan or Sichuan peppercorns, or *fagara.* It is the small dried reddish-brown berry of the prickly ash tree and has a spicy, woody aroma. The spice turns up in some West African spice mixtures as well as occasionally in some mixtures of Morocco's ras al-hanout.

Anise pepper can be found in markets selling Chinese products, as it is one of the major components in Chinese five-spice powder.

APRICOT LEATHER   These sheets of dried apricot paste add flavor to some Egyptian beverages and can also be street snacks. They are available in stores selling Arab products.

ATA   This is a Yoruba-Nigerian term for the hot red chiles that turn up frequently in the cooking of that country. *Ata* can include all forms of chiles, both red and green. *See also* Chiles.

ATJAR PICKLE   This is a South African corruption of the Malaysian term *atjar* or the Indian *achards.* It refers to vegetables and unripened fruits that are preserved in a spiced oil mixture. Traditionally, the oil was fish oil, but today's tastes tend to prefer olive or vegetable oils.

AVOCADO *(Persea americana)*   Although native to Central or South America, this tree has been taken to Africa's heart, and its pear-shape fruit turns up in salads and appetizers throughout the tropical regions of the continent.

Avocados are readily available all year round. The most common variety, the Hass, is oval with a rough greenish-brown skin. Look for avocados that are heavy for their size and that yield only slightly to the touch. Purchase the avocados before they are too ripe, as they will readily ripen at room temperature.

BAMBARA GROUNDNUT *(Voandzeia subterranea)*   This African native has caused more than one unwary culinary historian to feel that they have found an African form of the American peanut. The plant, which takes its origins in western Africa, is the one that is referred to in Ibn Battuta's 1352 description of the food of the natives of Iwalatan, "They dig from the ground a crop like beans and they fry and eat it. Its taste is something like fried peas." The beanlike seeds are cultivated throughout the continent and are called *okboli ede* by the Ibo of Nigeria, and *nzama* or *njama* in Malawi. The Malawians say that anyone can sow the beans, but only those who have lost a child may "bury" or plant them. Food historian William Woys Weaver informs me that he has found traces of the use of the Bambara groundnut in the African-American diet of the southern United States, where it was called the goober pea. They are difficult to find, but they can be grown.

BANANA *(Musa spp.)*   The banana is perhaps the best-known of all tropical ingredients. The fruit of this giant grass that is a relative of the lily and the orchid bananas arrived on the African continent early. Plantations of bananas are mentioned as having existed in Eritrea in the sixth century. By 1336 they are found in Morocco, and in the fifteenth century they are mentioned as having grown in Senegal. Today they turn up in virtually all sub-Saharan corners of the continent, where they are found in wide variety, from the small green *matoke* of Uganda to the piles of familiar yellow ones that can be seen in the markets of Abidjan, Côte d' Ivoire.

No less popular than their smaller cousins, plantains are the cooking bananas of the continent and are roasted and pounded into mashes and even fermented to prepare beer in Tanzania and Uganda.

Bananas are readily available, although those in search of unusual varieties will have to journey to a specialty greengrocer. Plantains are a bit more difficult to find. Plantains are used in all stages of ripeness, because as they ripen their starch turns to sugar. Green ones are used for chips and occasionally mashes. Ripe ones are pounded into mashes and fried as Aloco (page 92) and in other dishes, and overripe ones are the basis for more than one dessert.

BAOBAB TREE *(Adansonia digitata)*   These low-spreading trees dominate the plains of tropical Africa and have taken on great importance in the mythologies of many countries. Many different parts of the baobab turn up on the table. The acid pulp is made into a cooling drink; the white, spongy fruit is edible; and the leaves are pulverized and used as a thickener for soups and stews under the Mandinka name of *laalo mbep*. The oral tale of the founder of the Mandinka dynasty, Sundiata Keita, tells how the crippled adolescent who would become the redoubtable leader was inspired to walk after a co-wife insulted his mother, who asked to borrow some baobab leaves because her crippled son couldn't pick them from the trees for her.

The slippery consistency that the leaves give to a dish have led to the Wolof expression in Senegal, *Addina du cheere wai des na ko laalo* (Life is not a bowl of millet couscous, so it must be seasoned with *laalo*).

BATON LELE (TWIRL STICK)   This is a small branch of a tree with several offshooting branches arranged in such a way that it can be used as a whisk for cooking. It is called a *mufraka* in Sudan and is used there for stirring up dishes that contain okra.

BISSAP ROUGE   See ROSELLE.

BITTER LEAF   Traditionally used in Nigerian cooking, these are fresh leafy greens that are prepared like spinach and appear in soups and in stews. They are washed with salt and rubbed to remove some of their bitterness before adding them to a dish.

Bitter leaf can be purchased fresh in some African markets or found prewashed, air-dried, and ready for use.

BLACK-EYED PEAS *(Vigna unguiculata* or *Vigna sinensis)*   Legumes are among the world's oldest crops. They have been found in Egyptian tombs, and turn up in passages in the Bible, and may have originated in North Africa. The black-eyed pea, with its distinctive black "eye," is often called a cowpea, with the latter term sometimes referring to a smaller variety. As there are over 7,000 different varieties, it often gets very confusing. The important thing to know is that they are used in everything from soups to fritters and can be purchased fresh, canned, or dried.

If you're fortunate enough to find fresh ones, try them. Select unblemished pods, and shell them as you would peas. The canned and dried ones will have to do for the rest of us.

NOTE: The canned ones are too mushy to use when preparing the bean fritters called *akara;* they will not hold together.

BLACK PEPPER   See PEPPER.

BROAD BEANS *(Vicia faba)*   These beans are believed to have originated in North Africa or the eastern Mediterranean and were used in much of Europe, as string beans are today, until the Spaniards brought the green bean back from South America in the sixteenth century. Fresh young beans can be eaten raw without their thick outer skin, but the more mature beans are eaten in soups and stews. An excellent source of folic acid, broad beans are also called fava beans from their Latin name and are a main ingredient in Egyptian ful.

Broad beans are readily available dried and canned.

BUTTERMILK   Traditionally, this is the milky, slightly sour liquid that separates from cream during the production of butter. Today in the United States adding bacteria to milk produces buttermilk. Buttermilk is readily available in the dairy cases of most supermarkets.

CALABASH   These gourds are eaten in some parts of the African continent. In most other areas, they are hollowed out and dried to make food containers ranging from dippers and ladles to serving bowls and dishes. Often they are decorated with burned-on or finely incised designs and become pieces of art in themselves.

CALABAZA *(Cucurbita* spp.*)*   It was long thought that these members of the squash family originated in Egypt, but recent studies indicate that this squash actually comes from Peru. A winter squash, calabaza, like its cousins the butternut and the acorn squash, which can be substituted for it in many dishes, is a frequent addition in the soups and stews of the continent.

Calabaza, which is increasingly available in supermarkets, is often called West Indian cooking pumpkin. Because of its size, it is rarely found whole but is usually sold in pieces. Look for pieces with bright-orange skin with no blemishes or dark marks.

CANARI   This is a French term for the terra-cotta vessel that is often used in the preparation of soups and stews. When baking, more typical terra-cotta cookers can replace them. When cooking over an open flame, you'll have to use a heavy cast-iron pot instead.

CARAWAY *(Carum carvi)*   One of the drugs mentioned in the Egyptian treatise on illness and healing known as the Ebers papyrus, caraway is the dried ripe fruit of a parsley relative that is native to western Asia. It turns up in North Africa in some of the spice mixtures and in South Africa in some of the dishes brought by the Dutch. The name *caraway* comes from the Arabic *karawiya.* The seeds are the most commonly used portion of the plant, but occasionally it is possible to find the fresh leaves, which have a mild flavor.

Caraway seed is best purchased whole in small batches and stored in airtight containers in a cool, dark place.

CARCADE   See ROSELLE.

CARDAMOM (GREEN/WHITE)   *(Elettaria cardamomum)*   One of the world's most ancient and highly prized spices, cardamom was used by the ancient Egyptians. Today it turns up in parts of northern and eastern Africa to flavor the coffee or the pots of tea that mark the hours of the day. To bring out the best flavor when cooking with cardamom, toast the seeds. Split open the pods, remove the seeds, and toast them in a dry skillet until they give off a rich aroma.

Purchase cardamom from spice sellers. As the loose seeds quickly lose their taste, get the whole green or white pods, seed them, and grind them yourself after toasting. Brown cardamom is not really cardamom but a less expensive relative.

CASSAVA *(Manhiot esculenta or Manhiot dulcis)*   Also known as manioc or yuca, this starchy tuber is a migrant to the African continent from South America. Its long, tuberous root and dull-green leaves turn up in the cooking of the continent. The tuber, which may be white, yellowish, or reddish, is cooked and eaten in many forms and is mashed into *fufu* in parts of West Africa. The tuber is also used to prepare cassava meal, known as *gari*, and cassava flour.

Cassava meal can be found in stores selling Latin American and Brazilian products, while fresh cassava tubers and cassava leaves can be found at greengrocers' shops in Latin American and West Indian neighborhoods. For the leaves, you may have to ask for *dasheen* or *malanga*. Cassava tubers should not show mold or have sticky spots and should smell fresh. Reliable merchants will often break them to show you that they are firm inside.

CHICKPEAS *(Cicer arietinum)*   This plant from the Middle East has been important in the culinary traditions of that area for millennia. The fruit of the plant, which are known as chickpeas, garbanzos, or ceci, have appeared on tables as hummus, and fried as appetizer snacks. Depending on the variety of chickpeas, they can range in color from light yellow to dark, almost blackish brown.

Chickpeas are readily available canned or dried. If purchasing dried beans, get them from a store where there is a fair turnover, as they tend to harden somewhat when they sit. Canned beans work well in most recipes but should not be used in those where texture is important.

CHILES *(Capsicum species)*　It seems difficult to believe that a scant twenty years ago there were very few chiles on the market outside the American Southwest and specialized ethnic markets. Now wherever you turn there are new types of chiles that are being touted and sampled. In many parts of the African continent, chiles are so much a part of the culinary heritage that it seems impossible to imagine that they are not indigenous. The chile of choice throughout much of West Africa is the habanero, followed closely by the bird chile and the cayenne chile. In most kitchens, the heat is regulated according to the preferences of the family, and cooks attempting to duplicate an "authentic" African heat should remember that heat is frequently moderated for individual taste. Chile-heads can make use of a simple chile that they then cut and add as a condiment (see Moctar's Chile, page 138).

　Whatever the use, use caution when handling searingly hot chiles if you are not familiar with them. Coat your hands with oil, or use rubber gloves and *do not touch your eyes* while handling chiles. You can also lower the heat of the chile while retaining its flavor by taking out the seeds and ribs. If using the chile in a slow-cooked dish, simply prick the chile with a fork and remove it when the desired heat is obtained.

CHINESE GUNPOWDER TEA　One of the green teas of China, this tea is said to get its name from its appearance—the tightly rolled leaves are thought to resemble gunpowder. This is the classic tea that is used for Thé Naa Naa Marocaine or for Thé Sénégalaise. It is available at specialty shops and via mail order.

CINNAMON *(Cinnamomum verum)*　This is the bark of a relative of the laurel tree. There are references to its use in Ancient Egypt, but this is under debate, as the spice is not recorded in its native Sri Lanka until the thirteenth century. Cinnamon turns up in Moroccan tajines and in some of the Indian cooking of the eastern and southern regions. The classic cinnamon quills are assembled, using the longest pieces of bark and rolling them daily until they dry into the familiar shape.

　Ground cinnamon, like most ground spices, is frequently adulterated with other, less expensive items. Purchase cinnamon by the quill—and be careful, because the stronger-tasting and coarser-looking cassia is frequently substituted.

CITRONNELLE　See LEMONGRASS.

CLOVES *(Eugenia caryophyllus/ Syzygium aromaticum)*　These unopened flower buds from a small evergreen tree native to Southeast Asia have become one of the world's most popular spices. By the second century, cloves had made their way to Africa and were traded in the spice market at Alexandria. In the eighteenth century, the French smuggled some seedlings to Mauritius and to Bourbon and broke the

Portuguese and then Dutch monopolies. From Mauritius, plants were conveyed to Zanzibar, and today Zanzibar and neighboring Pemba are still responsible for a large proportion of the world's cultivation (although no longer the 90 percent that their output represented in the 1930s).

Cloves should be purchased whole. Grind your own in a spice grinder if necessary. Store them in an airtight container in a cool, dry place.

COCONUTS *(Cocos nucifera)*   A fruit seed, like almonds, this nut is the fruit of a palm tree that can grow up to 100 feet high. The tree is thought to have originated in Melanesia or Southeast Asia, but it is now found through the tropical world. The coconut is an indispensable plant in much of the tropics, serving as everything from roofing to food. Tales from the Second World War in the South Pacific have it that coconut water, the liquid inside green, or water, coconuts, is so pure that it was used when blood plasma was unavailable. The meat is also said to be a laxative and a diuretic. While coconut is considered to be a good source of potassium and is high in fiber, the oil prepared from the nuts is the most highly saturated of all vegetable oils.

When confronted by that bin full of brown hairy coconuts in the supermarket, look for one with an uncracked shell and shake it to make sure that there is liquid inside. An unopened coconut will last for about four months, and once opened, the meat can be either covered with water and kept for a few days before use, or frozen. Coconut can be grated or flaked and is particularly good as a garnish when toasted in the broiler.

Coconut water is the liquid inside the coconut. To prepare coconut milk, grate 2 cups of coconut. Place it in a cheesecloth bag and infuse it in 1 cup coconut water, massaging the bag to make sure that all the coconut liquid has been extracted. The coconut milk can be used in a variety of dishes. A thinner coconut milk can be prepared by repeating the process with milk or water a second time.

CORIANDER *(Coriandrum sativum)*   This Mediterranean native is used for its leaves, which give the characteristic cilantro bite to dishes like Morocco's chermoula, or fish marinade. The seed is mentioned in the Ebers papyrus, and seeds have been found in the mummy wrappings of Egyptian pharaohs.

Fresh coriander leaves are readily available in greeengrocers' shops. They may sometimes be called by their Spanish name, *cilantro.* The seeds of the Moroccan coriander plant are more readily available than the sweeter Indian variety. Chop a bit of the root into a dish for intense coriander flavor. Fresh leaf coriander does not keep well and should be bought just prior to use and stored in the refrigerator wrapped in slightly damp paper towels or in a plastic bag. Seed coriander can be kept in an airtight container in a cool, dry place.

CORN *(Zea mays)*   This cereal grain is native to the Americas and was introduced to Africa in the sixteenth century by the Portuguese. It is an immigrant that has taken the African continent by storm. Familiar to most Americans as a summer supper side dish, corn turns up in many guises in the cooking of the continent. It is used as cornmeal or corn flour in many of the mashes and porridges and is roasted and served as one of the favorite roadside snacks virtually throughout the continent. Hominy, which is prepared from flint or dent corn, is served with a variety of additions in much of the South and East and is fermented to turn up as pastes in the West. Some forms of corn are called mealie in South Africa.

Corn is readily available in a variety of forms. Fresh corn is available year-round, though it is best in summer. Corn should be prepared and served as near to purchase as possible. The best corn ever is picked and cooked right away. Hominy is available canned or dried. Cornmeal is available in a number of degrees of coarseness and in either white or yellow form. Corn flour is finely ground cornmeal.

COUSCOUS   This is not a grain, as many think, but rather a pasta that can be prepared from several types of cereal grains. The most familiar is prepared from semolina. In Mali and Niger, couscous is also prepared from millet. This couscous is known as *tiere* in Senegal. Couscous is traditionally prepared in a couscoussière. The bottom part, which is known as the *gdra*, is used to prepare the stew. The colander-like top part—the *kskas* or *keskes*—is used to steam the couscous. The holes allow the steam to flavor the grains of couscous.

COWPEAS *(Vigna unguiculata* or *Vigna sinensis)*   These are relatives of the black-eyed pea. For some people, they are the smaller variety. Others simply use the terms interchangeably. *See* Black-eyed peas.

CUBEBS *(Piper cubeba)*   These small berries of a pepper relative are native to Java and Indonesia. They are similar in appearance to black pepper but with a distinctive "tail." Cubebs were used in medicine in ancient China and reached Africa and the West via Arab traders. The taste is aromatic, but with a characteristic bite that some liken to a turpentine-like aroma. In his *Theatrum Botanicum*, published in 1640, herbalist John Parkinson reports that the King of Portugal prohibited the sale of these aromatic berries in order to promote the sale of black pepper, over which he held a virtual monopoly. In Africa, the cubeb turns up (as do many unusual spices) in the ras al-hanout of Morocco (see page 68). More surprisingly, it turns up in dishes like the stews of Benin, where its use is so frequent it is referred to as *piment pays* (pepper of the country).

CUMIN *(Cuminum cyminum)*   Native to the Nile Valley, the spice gives a warm flavor to many of the spice mixtures of North Africa. In parts of the continent it is known by its Indian name, *jeera*, or by the Arabic, *kamoon.* The spice also gives many of the Cape Malay and Indian curries of eastern and southern Africa their distinctive taste.

In North Africa, cumin is frequently a part of spice mixtures, while in the Indian cooking of the continent it is toasted before use. Cumin seeds should be purchased in small batches and will keep well in an airtight container in a cool, dark place.

CURRY POWDER   Anyone knowledgeable about spices will tell you that there's no such thing as curry powder. Curry powders derive from prepared spice blends that were designed to go with particular dishes. The premixed blends were simply labor-saving. The Madras curry powder mixtures that are called for here usually contain saffron, ginger, turmeric, cumin, coriander, and chiles of several sorts. Madras curry powders are some of the hottest of the curry powders.

When purchasing a curry powder, look for a blend that is aromatic and purchase it in small quantities so you do not keep the spices too long. Better yet, prepare your own blend using this recipe:

5 dried bird chiles

2 teaspoons coriander seeds

½ teaspoon mustard seeds

½ teaspoon black peppercorns

½ teaspoon green peppercorns

¾ teaspoon fenugreek seeds

7 curry leaves

½ teaspoon ground ginger

1 tablespoon turmeric

Seed the chiles and place them and the whole spices in a heavy cast-iron skillet. Toast them over medium heat until they darken and perfume the air. Allow the spices to cool and then grind in a spice mill. Toast the curry leaves and grind them. Mix all the ingredients together and place in a jar. Cover tightly. You can personalize the recipe by adding more or less of the spices, as you like. You may consider adding cumin, cardamom, cloves, and cinnamon, among others.

DATES (*Phoenix dactylifera*)   Mentioned in the Bible, this fruit is a native of the Middle East and much prized in the northern part of Africa. Dates vary in texture and in sweetness. Indeed, bakers in Egypt used to be called workers in dates, because they used dates to sweeten some of their confections. Some of the more popular varieties of dates include the *medjool*, the *halawy*, the *Khadrawi*, and the *deglet noor.*

If you are able to purchase dates in bulk, look for plump ones that are not dried out or moldy.

EGUSI SEEDS *(Citrullus colocynthis)*   These are melon seeds that are used as a thickener for soups and stews in many parts of western Africa. They also add a slightly nutty flavor, but can be oily for some tastes.

Egusi seeds are available in African specialty markets. If you cannot find *egusi*, you can substitute shelled pumpkin seeds.

FANNER BASKET   This is a large flat basket that is used for winnowing grains in many parts of the continent.

FENUGREEK (*Trigonella foenum-graecum)*   This annual plant grows well in the area around the Mediterranean and was known to the Ancient Egyptians, who used it in embalming and to reduce fevers. The yellowish-brown seeds are used in Egyptian breads and turn up in the berbere spice mixture of Ethiopia as well as in the curry spice mixtures of the Indians of the African continent.

The seeds should be kept in an airtight container in a cool, dry place. Fenugreek seeds are difficult to grind and are better processed by first toasting them and then pounding them in a mortar.

FIGS *(Ficus carica)*   Natives to the Mediterranean Basin, figs have a history that stretches back to ancient times. Fig trees are long-lived and can survive for up to one hundred years. They are very nutritious, high in dietary fiber, and rich in calcium and iron. Fresh figs don't last long, however, and they are particularly valued because they can be easily dried. They were used by many Mediterranean cultures as sweeteners prior to the introduction of sugar and in parts of North Africa are roasted as a coffee substitute.

Dried figs are readily available, and fresh figs are available when in season. If purchasing fresh figs, look for plump ones with unbroken and unblemished skins. Dried figs should be firm and clean.

GARLIC *(Allium sativum)*   This "stinking weed" is one of the treasures of the food world. Thought to have originated in the Middle East, garlic was known to the Ancient Egyptians, who fed it to the builders of the pyramids in large quantities, as it was supposed to increase stamina. It was also used in embalming, though there are many who would claim that the pungency of the bulb is enough to raise the dead. Garlic is indeed pungent, and its fragrance makes some shy away from using fresh garlic cloves. *Garlic powder, garlic granules, and garlic salt are no substitute for fresh garlic.*

Garlic is easy to purchase, readily available, and simple to use. To crush a clove, simply whack it with the flat end of a chef's knife. For those who are absolutely garlic-phobic, you can get a bit of the flavor by impaling a peeled clove on the tines of a fork and stirring it through the food that is being prepared. Others can simply rejoice in the flavor it adds to any dish.

When purchasing garlic, look for heads that are heavy and firm. (Light ones may contain cloves that have dried out.) Garlic should be free from mold or damp. It will keep for several months.

GEBNA   This is an Egyptian soft cheese, which is often served as an appetizer with radishes, sliced cucumbers, scallions, tomatoes, and pita bread.

GHEE   It is the purest form of butterfat and has been used in the cooking of India for almost 10,000 years. Ghee is clarified butter and can be prepared at home by slowly simmering butter over a low flame for about 30 minutes and then skimming off the froth and removing the solids. The remaining ghee is fragrant and the clarifying stops the butter from going rancid.

Ghee can also be purchased at shops selling Indian ingredients.

GINGER *(Zingiber officinale)*   This rhizome has been cultivated in Asia for over 3,000 years. The Ancient Egyptians knew it; the Arabs brought it to East Africa in the thirteenth century; and the Portuguese introduced it into West Africa. An essential ingredient in much curry powder, ginger turns up on the continent in everything from ginger beers and other drinks to the ginger-spiced cookies of South Africa.

Purchase rhizome ginger when it is firm. It can be stored in the refrigerator wrapped in paper towels or in plastic bags. Dried ginger, which is used in desserts and in some spice mixtures, is best kept in an airtight container in a cool, dry place.

GRAINS OF PARADISE *(Aframomum melegueta)*   This relation of cardamom is a spice that is comparatively unused today. It turns up in Nigerian and Beninoise cooking and in Moroccan ras al-hanout (see page 68). This is ironic indeed, since the spice was once so popular that the entire coastal area from Guinea to Côte d'Ivoire was known as the grain coast in honor of the grains of paradise that were produced there and shipped to Europe. Even today, between the Guinea coast and northern Africa, there is a substantial trade in these grains, which are also known as Guinea pepper or Guinea grains. The small reddish-brown seeds are sold either in their seedpod or separately and have a pungent, peppery flavor.

Grains of paradise are not readily available in spice markets, but they can be occasionally found in herbalists' shops and are usually available in botanicas, as followers of New World variations of the Yoruba religion still use the spice—called *atare* in Yoruba—in many ways.

GREENS   There are myriad varieties of leafy greens on the African continent ranging from the *meloukhia* of the northern quadrant to the *brede* of Madagascar. Most of the local greens are not available in the United States. Spinach is the constant substitute, but with the appearance of such greens as dandelion greens and dasheen and more, you can now try other greens as substitutes, varying the cooking times, and see what tastes you like.

GUEDGE   These funky pieces of dried smoked fish are used to enhance the tastes of many Senegalese stews. Substitute any pungent smoked fish.

GUINEA HEN *(Numida meleagris)*   This omnivorous fowl with speckled plumage was known to the ancient world. The Romans named it the Numidian, or Carthage, hen because of its supposed origins.

   The meat, which is not much eaten in the United States, is popular in parts of Africa. Guinea fowl has lean meat, which is low in calories and in fat, needs to be basted when cooking, and is truly tasty.

HOMINY CORN   See CORN.

KANAKA   This is an Egyptian coffeepot in which the coffee is brewed with boiling water. Kanakas usually are brass, but some are silver.

KARKADEH   See ROSELLE.

KINKÉLIBA   The leaves of this plant are brewed into a tea by the Senegalese (page 349). It is supposed to calm and relax one.

LABNA   This is a semisoft Egyptian cheese that can be preserved in olive oil and spices or deep-fried.

LEMONGRASS *(Cymbopogon citratus)*   The outer leaves of this tall tropical grass are used in many parts of western Africa to brew a citrus-tasting tea known as *citronnelle,* which is taken after dinner or for stomach ailments.

   Citronnelle can be purchased in teabags in health-food stores. Fresh lemongrass stalks can be purchased in some supermarkets and greengrocers' selling Asian products. Look for thick, long stalks. Fresh lemongrass can be kept in plastic bags in the refrigerator or frozen and defrosted as needed. Dried lemongrass should be protected from humidity and kept in airtight containers.

LENTILS *(Lens esculenta* or *Lens culinaris)*   The seeds of this small, bushy plant are one of the world's oldest foods. Lentils are thought to have originated in the Middle East. They turn up in the cooking of the African continent in many of the dals brought by immigrants to the eastern coast from the Indian subcontinent. They have a long history on the continent, though, and have been found in the stomach content of predynastic bodies and in the underground galleries of the Step Pyramid at Saqqâra. They cook quickly and do not require the presoaking that many legumes do. Lentils are widely available in supermarkets and in health-food stores.

When buying lentils, look for places that sell them in bulk and have a good turnover. Select those that are not cracked or broken and that do not have little pinprick-like marks that may indicate insect damage.

LICORICE POWDER *(Glycyrrhiza glabra)*   The roots of this plant are ground into a powder, which is infused into a cooling drink by Egyptians.

Licorice root can be purchased at health-food stores and can be ground into a powder with a spice grinder.

LONG PEPPER *(Piper longum)*   This relative of the black pepper family is a long oval type of pepper that adds bite to some ras al-hanout mixtures (see page 68). The dry unripe berries of the species are about one inch long and look like stiff brownish-black catkins. They are more frequently found in the cooking of India and the Far East.

Long pepper can be found in North African spice markets and occasionally in health-food stores. They will keep if stored in an airtight container in a cool, dark place.

MANGOES *(Mangifera indica)*   Imported into Africa in the sixteenth century, this fruit is actually thought to be a native of India. Anyone who has ever been on the African continent during its varying mango seasons knows that the streets are perfumed with their fragrance and children vie with each other to see just how many they can eat. More often than not mangoes are eaten raw as dessert. They come to the tables heaped in straw baskets. They're cut along each side of the stone, then twisted open, scored, and savored by those of delicate manners. The rest of the world just sucks on them, prompting many a rude name.

Mangoes are also used in cooking and turn up in preserves and chutneys, and increasingly in pies and desserts.

There are numerous varieties of mango, some claim over a thousand, so choosing them by color or size can be a very risky business indeed. Select them instead when the skin yields slightly to the touch but is not too soft.

Mangoes are increasingly available at supermarkets and greengrocers'. If you can't find one, head to a Caribbean neighborhood.

MANGO TREE

MASHES   These are the starchy underpinnings of much of the cooking of the African continent. From the couscous of Morocco and the Maghreb, to the mealie pap of South Africa, passing through the *fufus* of the West and the *ugali* of the East, these dishes provide the starch that accompanies the meal.

MEALIE   See CORN.

MELEGUETA PEPPER   See GRAINS OF PARADISE.

MELOUKHIA (Corchorus olitorius)   This member of the hemp family is depicted on ancient Egyptian temple paintings and is still popular today in much of the northern African world, where young, deep-green leaf shoots are picked and prepared like spinach. *Meloukhia* is glutinous, as are many of the textures that are prized on the continent, and dishes prepared with it have a slippery consistency that many Americans find unpleasant. The leaves, though, are loved in Tunisia and Egypt, where they can be found fresh and dried in marketplaces.

   Meloukhia is available at shops selling Middle Eastern and North African products. It can be found frozen or dried. The fresh plant occasionally turns up, but the other types can be substituted.

MILLET *(Panicum miliaceum* and *Setaria italica)*   The term *millet* is used to refer to several cereal grains that are unrelated. While it is clear that one or more of the grains referred to as millet has long been in use on the African continent, it has been found at early archaeological sites. Scholars are still unsure as to the plant's origins. Millet is a very important grain in much of Africa, and some believe the plant originated on the continent, in the area near Ethiopia.

Easily cultivated and fast-growing, millet is drought-resistant and can survive in poor soil, but it does not like the cold and so remains, for most Americans, known only as the slender stalk that is placed in the parakeet's cage on a regular basis.

It is, however, a major grain on the African continent and is even made into couscous by natives of Mali, Niger, Senegal, and other countries. Millet has no gluten and so turns up in the flat breads that are prevalent in much of the northern quadrant of the African continent. It is also brewed into a number of millet beers, which have given folks a buzz for centuries. Millet is such an important grain on the continent that many other grains have been subsumed under the term. Teff, an Ethiopian grain, and the one that is classically used to prepare injera, is classified among the millets.

Millet and millet flour are available in health-food shops and some supermarkets. Look for the hulled, whole-grain form. Puffed millet is also occasionally found, but it cannot be substituted for the grain.

MINT (*Mentha* spp.) This aromatic herb is native to the Mediterranean area and much used in the cooking of the region. Perhaps the best-known example of the use of mint is the Thé Naa Naa Marocaine of Morocco that turns up in Senegal as Thé Sénégalaise, which uses spearmint to perfume pots of Chinese gunpowder tea.

There are over six hundred varieties of this easily cultivated perennial herb. If you should find that mint tea is something you crave, consider a pot of mint on the kitchen windowsill or a small patch of it outside the kitchen door. If your thumb is a color other than green, mint can be purchased both fresh and dried at supermarkets. For better-quality mint than those flakes that are packaged in tin canisters, head to an herbalist or a Middle Eastern or North African store and purchase the herb by the pound.

MORTAR AND PESTLE No kitchen on the African continent would be complete without at least one of these. From the massive wooden ones that are used to husk grain to the heavy brass *mehraz* that is used to grind spices and herbs in Morocco, these implements play a major part in the African cook's *batterie de cuisine*. Be sure that you have at least a small one in which to hand-grind spice mixtures. It may be in marble, in brass, or in heavy unglazed ceramic. Larger mortars are made by hollowing out tree trunks, and the rhythmic thunk-thunking of the tall pestles gives rhythm to many a woman's day in the more southern reaches of the continent.

BREAD AND ORANGE MERCHANTS

NAARTJIE *(Citrus reticulata)*   This is the South African version of a tangerine. Its slightly tart taste turns up in condiments and in the liqueur known as Van der Hum (page 352). They are not yet available in the United States and can be replaced by the ordinary tangerine or the tart clementine.

OKRA *(Hibiscus esculentus)*   The mucilaginous pod is the continent's culinary totem. From the *bamia* of Egypt to the *soupikandia* of Senegal, passing by the various *sauces gombos* and more, this pod is used in virtual continent-wide totality. It is native to Africa, and its origins are trumpeted by its names in a number of languages throughout the world. The American okra comes from the *twi* of Ghana, while the French opt for *gombo,* which harks back to the Bantu languages of the southern segment of the continent.

Whatever it's called, it is much prized in the continent of its origin, where the pod, which grows on tall bushes, is loved for its thickening properties. The slime that has made it the most maligned of vegetables in this country, outside of the South, is actually thought there to be a virtue. Cutting the pod increases okra's "sticking power" and some recipes from western Africa call for the pod to be minced into a gluey mass. The slime, though, can be limited, if not eliminated, by selecting small pods and leaving them whole.

Frozen okra is readily available and can be substituted when fresh is unavailable. Okra is still one of those vegetables that have not become "designer," so you may have to look for it in African-American neighborhoods and in greengrocers' and shops catering to Middle Eastern clientele. Select pods that are green in color; black stripes often indicate that the pods are fibrous. The okra should be tender, not soft, and without bruises or marks. If you're not using it right away, blanch it and freeze it for storage. Cooks should note that okra has a chemical reaction with cast-iron and copper pots, which affects the color, not the taste, of the pod. I once said that wherever okra points its green tip, Africa has passed; I still agree with myself.

ONIONS   These globes of delight originated in prehistoric times and were much prized by the ancient world. The Ancient Egyptians used them to pay tribute to their gods, and onion remains have been found in the tomb of the pharaoh Tutankhamen. The plant, which is thought to be native to the eastern Mediterranean, figured and still figures largely in the average workingman's diet. In pharaonic Egypt, the average workingman's lunch consisted of beer, onions, and bread. Onions today are popular throughout the continent as seasoning.

Onions are readily available in supermarkets and greengrocers'.

ORANGE-FLOWER WATER   Called *zhaar* in Morocco and *mazahir* in Arabic, orange-flower water is used to impart a subtle flavor to many North African dishes. In Morocco and the Maghreb, much of the orange-flower water that is consumed is home-distilled from fresh orange blossoms.

In the United States, the choices are the Lebanese version that is readily available in shops selling Middle Eastern items and the harder-to-find French variety that can be found at gourmet stores and some shops selling baking supplies. Orange-flower water will last virtually indefinitely, but it loses its potency and becomes slightly cloudy if left on a pantry shelf too long.

PALM OIL (RED/WHITE) *(Elaesis guineensis)*   Palm oil has fallen out of favor in the United States because of its high percentage of saturated fatty acid. In many parts of the African continent, though, the oil is prized and is at the basis of much of the cooking. In the area around the Congo River, *malafu ma n'amba,* as palm oil is called, is sacred. It is used to mark births, weddings, and funerals and is an important part of many ancestor cults. *Epo,* as the oil is called by the Yoruba of Nigeria, also has relgious symbolism, and many of the *apataki* or tales of the gods speak of it. Palm oil has long been used on the continent. Herodotus and Deodorus of Sicily report that it was used in the Egyptian mummification process.

There are two main types of palm oil. The more familiar red palm oil brings its distinctive taste and hue to dishes like Senegal's *soupikanya* and the *akara* of Nigeria. This red oil has even crossed the Atlantic to become one of the hallmarks of the cooking of Bahia, Brazil. The less familiar palm kernel oil is light tan and has an almost molasses-sweet smell. A seasoned version of the red type, called *zomi,* is also occasionally available.

Palm oil is available in shops selling African and Brazilian goods. Those who are concerned about health issues involving eating of excessive saturated fats can moderate their palm oil intake by diminishing the amount of palm oil used and replacing it with another vegetable oil or by eliminating it altogether. If you are using another vegetable oil, give it an orange tint by sautéing a few bits of achiote or annatto in the oil and allowing the oil to cool before proceeding with the recipe.

PEANUTS *(Arachis hypogae)*　This native of the New World is thought by many to have originated in Africa, because its popularity in North America harks back to the era of the slave trade. The peanut is not a nut at all. In fact it is a legume and closer to the black-eyed pea than it is to the almond. Peanuts were brought to Africa by Portuguese slave traders and spread only slowly. The Mandinka of western Africa still remember this and refer to the legume as *tiga,* a diminutive of the Portuguese word *manteiga,* meaning butter. The oil of the peanut was used for cooking.

Peanuts and, more important, peanut oil became a major commerce in colonial Senegal, and large oil factories were constructed there to process the legume. The peanut boom was such that the ports of Saint Louis and Dakar exported 100,000 tons of peanuts in 1898 and six times as much by 1931. A friend of mine always opined that there should be a statue somewhere in Senegal to George Washington Carver. To my knowledge, there is none.

Today, the boom has long since passed, but there are still mountains of peanuts harvested in places like Rufisque and processed into the peanut oil that fries foods in Senegal and France. Vendors on city streets still sell sand-roasted *guerte,* as the legume is known in Wolof, and tourists and natives alike scarf down vast quantities of peanut-butter stew known as *mafé* (page 255).

Roasted peanuts are readily available in shops, and raw peanuts are increasingly easy to find, particularly in the South, where they are much loved. If purchasing peanuts in the shell, be sure they are fresh, since peanuts are susceptible to aflatoxin, a fungus-caused mold.

PEPPER *(Piper nigrum)*　This spice is the most widely used in the West. In fact, it is so popular that in ancient times a market in Rome was named the Piper Horatorium for the main spice that was traded there. In other times, pepper was so highly prized that it was literally worth its weight in gold. While we English speakers get our word *pepper* from the Sanskrit *pippali,* the French get their *poivre* from the name of one of the early traders in the commodity. Pepper is perhaps one of the spices that have had the greatest influence on the history of the world. Desire to control the pepper trade sent Portuguese explorers around the Cape of Good Hope to India, and a desire to break the Portuguese monopoly on the trade routes prompted Columbus to venture out toward the west.

The pepper plant is native to the Malabar Coast of southwestern India, but today's pepper can come from Malaysia, Indonesia, or even Brazil. Pepper loses its pungency rapidly after it is ground, and for that reason, anyone who wants to use black or white pepper in cooking should have a pepper mill. It doesn't have to be the fancy baluster-sized thing that appears to grind out a few shreds in restaurants, it can simply be a serviceable, functioning grinder. *Use it.* You'll be surprised at the difference it makes.

Purchase pepper as you do all spices and herbs, in small amounts to ensure freshness. The larger the grain, the more expensive the pepper. Look for even-sized berries. Many consider the finest black pepper in the world to be India's Tellicherry pepper. Black peppercorns are the fermented, sun-dried berries of the pepper plant. White peppercorns are the ripe berries with the outer skin removed, which are then dried until they are cream-colored. Green peppercorns are the fresh berries. They are usually available either freeze-dried or in brine. Tree-ripened red peppercorns are virtually unavailable outside of pepper-growing countries.

The pink peppercorns that are sold in markets and that turn up in peppercorn mixtures are not pepper at all but the berries of a South American tree *(Schinus terebinthifolius)*. They should be used sparingly, as in large quantities they can be toxic.

PLANTAIN   See BANANA.

PRESERVED LEMONS   These aromatic lemons are an ingredient in much Moroccan cooking and can add zest to any number of dishes. They can also be used in everything from soups and stews to salads in ordinary cooking. Prepare them yourself (page 139), or find them in a shop that specializes in Middle Eastern foods.

PUMPKINS   See CALABAZA.

RAS AL-HANOUT   This spice mixture is the classic one for Moroccan cooking. Ras al-hanout means "top of the shop," and in the mixture each spice merchant concocts an aromatic mix that is his alone. The most complex of these mixtures are those from the city of Fez. These may have more than twenty ingredients, including the usual items, such as cardamom, clove, cinnamon, nutmeg, chiles, ginger, rose petals, allspice, black pepper, lavender blossoms, and turmeric, as well as such exotic ones as dung beetle eggs, Spanish fly, belladonna, chufa nuts, monk's pepper, long pepper, cubeb, grains of paradise, and more. You can prepare your own mixture using a much-simplified recipe (page 149) or purchase some ready mixed at a shop selling North African foods. If purchasing ras al-hanout, buy it unground and then enjoy trying to identify all the ingredients.

RED PEPPERCORNS   See PEPPER.

RICE (*Oryza sativa*)   Rice is one of the world's most important cereal grains, and one variant of the plant, *Oryza sativa*, originated in parts of Southeast Asia, where the wild grain is still growing today. Another variant, *Oryza glabberima*, originated on the African continent in the area of Sierra Leone and Liberia.

Rice was known to the Moors, who introduced it to the Spaniards in the eighth century. The food, which represents the world's second-largest food crop, is semiaquatic, and the United States owes its knowledge of rice culture to the African continent. The task system of cultivating rice that originated in Africa is the system that was used by enslaved Africans to create the Carolina rice industry.

In many parts of Africa, rice is the staple grain. Senegalese would be lost without their *thiebou dienn* or their *yassa* with white rice, and Jollof rice is a hallmark of the English-speaking West. Rice flour is also used in Benin, Nigeria, and other parts of western and southern Africa to prepare mashes.

Rice is readily available in many varieties. Select a short-grain or broken rice when preparing dishes like *thiebou dienn* and a long-grain for other dishes. Rice flour can be purchased at health-food shops.

ROSEBUDS   See ROSES.

ROSELLE (*Hibiscus sabdariffa*)   These are the flowers and leaves of the hibiscus relative known as sorrel in the Caribbean, as *bissap rouge* in Senegal, and as *karkadeh* or *carcade* in Egypt. The slightly acidic drink is spiced in a variety of ways.

Roselle can be purchased at health-food stores and at West Indian markets. If purchasing bulk roselle, look for pods that are not broken and dusty. As West Indian sorrel is traditionally a Christmas beverage, the pods are readily available in the winter season.

ROSES   These aromatic flowers find their way into the cooking of the continent. Rosebuds are an ingredient in ras al-hanout, while rose petals are used as a garnish on some desserts in North Africa. Rosewater, or rose-flower water, is used to perfume teas and other drinks and as a sophisticated addition to many dishes.

If using rosebuds or rose petals, be sure that the flowers involved have been cultivated for eating. Roses that are purchased at florists may have been sprayed with toxic pesticides. When purchasing rosewater, remember that while the water itself will last indefinitely, it will lose its aroma with time and may turn yellowish. Buy in small quantities. Also remember that the rosewater produced in Lebanon, like its orange-flower water counterpart, is not as fragrant as the French type.

ROSEWATER   See ROSES.

SESAME *(Sesamum indicum)*   This plant is thought by many to have originated in Africa. Known as *benne* in the Wolof language of Senegal, it has been used for millennia for its oil, which does not turn rancid in heat. Sesame is one of the plants that are listed in the Ebers papyrus of Ancient Egypt and turns up in the pastries of North Africa.

To get the most flavor from sesame, toast it before using it by placing the seeds in a heavy skillet over low heat and stirring constantly until they turn light brown. Watch carefully during this process because one glance away and you can end up with an inedible mass of burned seeds.

Sesame is readily available from health-food stores and spice merchants and via mail order.

SEVILLE ORANGE *(Citrus aurantium)*   The sour orange is thought to have originated in northeastern India and arrived on the African continent thanks to the Moors. When the Moors continued their conquest of the Mediterranean Basin, around 700, they took the orange with them to Spain, where it flourished in the towns of Moorish Andalusia, like Seville. There are several African variations of sour oranges, and the peel and pulp are used in the confection of sweets and beverages.

Sour oranges are somewhat difficult to find fresh, but the juice is available in specialty markets.

SHEA BUTTER *(Butyospermum paradoxum parkii)*   This tree, which is native to the western African grasslands, produces a small chestnut-sized fruit that is processed into a natural vegetable butter. The tree and its fruit are described by Ibn Battuta in the fourteenth century and then named by Mongo Park in the eighteenth. Park gives his name to the plant as well. The butter, known as shea butter in English and *karité* in French, has the advantage of being able to be stored year-round without salt. The name *karité* comes from the Fulani *karchi*, which in turn is a transliteration of the Arabic *gharti*. *Karité* is such a staple in parts of Mali that the Dogon have their own rituals surrounding its preparation. Some feel that *karité* has an unpleasant smell. Cooking the butter and allowing it to harden can attenuate this.

Shea butter is also an amazing emollient and is available in health-food stores. Be sure that you are purchasing food-grade shea butter, and not shea butter that has been processed for cosmetic use.

SMOKED SHRIMP (DRIED)   These smoked crustaceans are a pungent flavor addition to any dish to which they are added. While I've called them dried smoked shrimp, those from the area of the Gulf of Benin are so large that they would be more aptly named dried smoked prawns.

Dried smoked shrimp are found at markets selling Chinese ingredients, but for the truly pungent ones, try to find a market specializing in African ingredients. As they were originally smoked and sun-dried to preserve them for later use, they will keep for at least a month in an airtight container in a cool, dark place. When purchasing them, be sure thay they have no insects and are not desiccated.

SORREL   See ROSELLE.

SOURSOP (*Annona maricata*)   The shape of this South American tropical fruit has earned it the nickname of bullock's heart in some countries. Inside the spiny, leathery, dark-green skin, the pulp is white and creamy and slightly granular. This cousin to the cherimoya is generally eaten raw or in sorbets or creams.

Soursop are best selected for purchase when they yield slightly to the touch but remain firm. The skin should be dark green, not black, which indicates overripeness. While they can be ripened at room temperature, they should be consumed fairly soon after purchase, for they will not keep well.

Soursop can be found at specialty greengrocers'. Soursop nectar can be found in the Hispanic section of many supermarkets and at stores selling Hispanic products as *jugo de guanabana.*

SWEET POTATO (*Ipomoea batatas*)   Hopelessly confused with yams in the northern part of the Western Hemisphere, true sweet potatoes are the reddish-orange tubers that make regular appearances on the Thanksgiving table. The plant is native to Central America and not related to the potato or to the true yam. The sweet potato is a recent arrival in the cooking of the African continent and turns up in some dishes. On the mother continent, though, the true yam has primacy.

Sweet potatoes are available year-round. Select firm ones without soft spots. Refrigerating them will slightly alter their taste.

SZECHUAN PEPPERCORNS   See ANISE PEPPER.

TELLICHERRY PEPPER   See PEPPER.

TURMERIC (*Curcuma longa*)   When seen in its fresh form, it's not hard to believe that this Southeast Asian rhizome is a relative of ginger. The yellow of the powdered version of this plant is what gives curry powders their distinctive color. Turmeric has been used for millennia in south Asia and was brought to the African continent by Arab traders. It turns up in Morocco's ras al-hanout as well as in the curry mixtures of the eastern and southern parts of the continent.

Turmeric is usually found dried and powdered in the United States. If purchasing this type, do not depend on color as a guide to freshness, as different varieties have different intensities of hue. Buy in small quantities as with any spice and keep in an airtight container in a cool, dark place. If purchasing fresh turmeric, look for thick rhizomes without soft spots or cracks. Turmeric can be found in shops selling Indian ingredients.

UTAZI LEAVES (*Crongromena ratifolia*)   This pale leaf is one of the traditional flavorings for Nigeria's peppersoup. It has a bitter taste and is used sparingly. It can be used as a substitute for bitter leaf. This leaf is hard to locate, as is the bitter leaf for which it sometimes substitutes. You can use any bitter green instead, such as broccoli rabe leaves or arugula. In a pinch, spinach can be substituted.

WATERBLOMMETJIE   Indigenous to South Africa, these seedpods from a plant like a water lily taste like a cross between asparagus and artichokes. They are now being cultivated in the southwestern Cape region as well as in Switzerland. *Waterblommetjie* are available only in winter in the Cape region, but I hope their taste soon makes its way to the United States.

WATERMELON (*Citrullus lantanus*)   This melon is thought by many to be native to the African continent and have originated in the central section of the continent. It was consumed in Ancient Egypt and appears in tomb paintings. While watermelon is a summer treat for most Americans, in countries where water is polluted or in short supply, the melon, which is between 92 and 95 percent water, is a much-prized fruit.

Watermelons come in many sizes and shapes, ranging from small and round to ovals weighing up to 90 pounds. A South African melon known unfortunately as the Kaffir melon (*Kaffir* is the "N" word of South Africa) is very much like a rindless watermelon and may be one of its ancestors.

Watermelon should be purchased when the fruit is heavy and has a slightly paler spot on the bottom indicating that the fruit rested on it while ripening. A good resounding "thunk" will tell you if the fruit is full of water and ready to eat. Watermelon should be chilled after cutting and then eaten within a few days.

YAM (*Dioscorea* spp.)   This plant, which is one of the most widely consumed foods in the world, is thought by many to have an African origin. Archaeological evidence shows that yams were cultivated in parts of the continent more than 10,000 years ago, and archaeologists now feel that there was an early yam culture that rivaled the early cereal cultures on the continent. While true yams are often confused with sweet potatoes in the United States, they have their own identity in much of the rest of the world, where they are used in everything from soups to snacks. As new yams are propagated from cuttings of old ones, they are considered sacred in many parts of Africa. The Akan peoples of Ghana particularly have impressive yam festivals, where the new yams are taken out and paraded through the streets and celebrated with singing, dancing, and, of course, feasting. In Guinea, they are so much a part of the diet that the word *yam* is a synonym for the verb "to eat." The word has crossed the Atlantic and is found as the verb *nyam* among the Gullah-speaking peoples of the Sea Islands and in Jamaica.

There are many different types of yams, varying from those that have light-brown skin to those that are hairy and almost black. The interior flesh of the tuber varies as well and can range in color from pristine white to almost purple. Yams grow to be larger than potatoes or sweet potatoes, so they are often sold in pieces. The buyer should look for ones that show no signs of mold or spoilage. Yam flour is also an ingredient in many West African mashes and is simply dried yam that has been pulverized into a flour.

Many varieties of yams are increasingly available at supermarkets and greengrocers' in Hispanic and West Indian neighborhoods. Yam flour is available at shops selling African ingredients.

YAM FLOUR   See YAM.

YETE   This dried smoked mollusk is much prized in Senegal, where it is used to season many stews like *thiebou dienn.*

MAIL=ORDER SOURCES

◎◎◎

An African meal is a dining experience that begins at the moment you open the kitchen door and ends when you leave. Everything from food to music, place settings to condiments is a part of the whole. Give your meal a touch of the continent with suitable music and a suitable setting. Check the world-music section of the larger record shops like Tower and Virgin and HMV or mail-order from a catalogue. Look for serving baskets, trays, dishes, and tablecloths at local museums specializing in the wares of the continent. I found wonderful Ethiopian baskets in the gift shop of New York's Museum of African Arts.

Although I have attempted to list a substitution whenever the traditional ingredient is not readily available, this is not always possible. Some you may have to get by mail. Also, readers who live outside of major metropolitan areas may not have access to greengrocers' or spice shops selling ingredients used in African cooking. For this reason, I have included a brief list of some places that can help you. Call first and always begin with a small order. Here are some of the places that I use.

Adriana's Caravan
409 Vanderbilt Street
Brooklyn, NY 11218
800-316-0820
Cubebs, melegueta pepper, palm oil, pili pili
peppers, and more. The catalogue offers over 400 spices.

African Heritage Foods
D.B.A. Country Cottage Savories
P.O. Box 497
Jefferson Valley, NY 10535
914-228-1584
This company offers three sauces and one shake based on
the spice mixtures of Ethiopia. Afri-Q is a good substitute
for Ethiopia's berbere.

Almacenes Shango
661 Madison Avenue
New York, NY 10029
212-722-4275
This shop is actually a botánica, but they sell some
ingredients, like melegueta pepper, that have a ritual as
well as culinary use.

Aphrodisia Products
262 Bleecker Street
New York, NY 10014
212-989-6440

Classic Taste Harissa
Trade Mart Kitchen
2100 North Stemmons Freeway
Dallas, TX 75207
800-553-3784
The company offers a variety of chile pastes and sauces, including a very good Tunisian-style harissa.

Fauchon
26, place de la Madeleine
Paris, France 75008
47-42-60-11
A range of spices including their own brand of ras al-hanout.

Frieda's by Mail
P.O. Box 58488
Los Angeles, CA 90058
800-241-1771
www.Frieda.com
Exotic fruits and vegetables from the folk who brought you the kiwi. Catalogue available.

K. Kalustyan
123 Lexington Avenue
New York NY 10016
212-685-3451
These folk have been around for decades and know what they're doing. Catalogue available. They have a wide range of spices and products from Arab and Indian cuisines.

J. Martinez and Company
3230A Peachtree Road NE
Atlanta, GA 30305
888-642-JAVA
Estate-packaged coffee from around the world including Kenya AA.

Penzeys, Ltd.
P.O. Box 933
Muskego, WI 53150
414-679-7207
This company offers over 250 spices and spice blends by catalogue.

Stern's US
598 Broadway, 7th Floor
New York, NY 10012
212-925-1648
Music to dine by from all around the continent is available from this major importer of worldbeat tunes.

T-Salon and Emporium
11 East 20th Street
New York, NY 10003
212-358-0506
A variety of teas from around the world, including some from Kenya and the South African rooibos tea from the Mariage Frères in Paris.

Vineyard Sound Herbs
P.O. Box 1664
Vineyard Haven, MA 02568
508-696-7574
This small shop offers a wide variety of hard-to-find and unusual spices and spice blends, including Nigerian ginger and cubebs.

Zamaani
2111 Holy Hall Street
Houston, TX 77054
713-790-0012
Sometimes you need the proper place setting. This small company sells a line of table accessories that are handmade on the continent.

Zingerman's
422 Detroit Street
Ann Arbor, MI 48104
313-769-1625
Great olive oils from around the globe.

West African Grocery
524 Ninth Avenue
New York, NY 10018
212-695-6215
This store, unfortunately, does not do mail-order, but it's important enough to merit a stop if you're in the New York City area. They have everything from the ordinary to the super exotic, from frozen giant Nigerian snails and packaged bitter leaf to dried bat. It's a must.

TASTES

of a

CONTINENT

PREPARING SHEA BUTTER

APPETIZERS

◎◎◎

A Continent of Nibblers

From the Cape to Cairo, Mombasa to Monrovia, people walk through the streets of the African continent with their hands full and their mouths moving. They may be nibbling on a simple ear of grilled corn or working their way through a paper roll filled with almonds or melon seeds, but nibblers they are. Appetizers, in the European context, are virtually unknown in the traditional diet, but many of the street nibbles and the savory vegetable dishes can serve as appetizers in a European-style menu.

GEBNA MAKLEYAH
Fried Cheese *(Egypt)*

AKARA
Bean Fritters *(Nigeria)*

AKARA AWON
Okra and Bean Fritters *(Nigeria)*

AKARA IJESHA
(Nigeria)

AKARA EGUSI
(Nigeria)

CHEESE AKARA
(Nigeria)

SAVORY PORRIDGE FRITTERS
(East Africa)

SWEET PORRIDGE FRITTERS
(East Africa)

PORRIDGE FRITTERS II
(East Africa)

ALL-PURPOSE FRITTER BATTER
(All Africa)

ALOCO
Fried Plantains *(Côte d'Ivoire)*

SAVORY ALOCO SAUCE
(Côte d'Ivoire)

PLANTAIN CRISPS
(Ghana)

DODO-IKIRE
Fried Plantain *(Nigeria)*

BEIGNETS DE SARDINES
Sardine Fritters *(Algeria)*

FÈVES SÈCHES FRITES
Fried Fava Beans *(Algeria)*

BRIK AUX CHAMPIGNONS
Mushroom Brik *(Algeria)*

CRABMEAT APPETIZER
(Côte d'Ivoire)

COCONUT CRISPS
(All Africa)

DITHOTSE
Roasted Pumpkin Seeds *(South Africa)*

✳

The Night Market in Cotonou

Cotonou, Benin, is in the deep heart of market country. Every four days, the large Dan Tokpa spreads its stands out along the side of the river and beckons buyers and sellers from as far east as Ghana and as far west as Nigeria. The Adjara market, located an hour outside of town, opens on a different four-day schedule and entices purchasers with an array of products produced by the Yoruba people. The Yoruba language and ethnic group cross the border into southwestern Nigeria in one of colonialism's many geographical "uh-ohs." These are both megamarkets, defining spots for the commerce of the Gulf of Benin, in which the market women proudly reign as empresses over the stalls set up in public spaces.

I've shopped in the Tokpa, as it is affectionately known to the natives of Cotonou, and I've journeyed to the edge of the country to purchase Yoruba specialties like my handmade mortar and pestle from the Adjara. My favorite market in Cotonou, though, is the night market. Like many of my favorite travel adventures, I discovered it by accident. It was evening and my friend Theodora was rushing home to prepare dinner. As we bustled down the sandy streets of the capital, we suddenly stopped and parked. I followed curiously as her rapid steps took us through an archway that we had passed on several occasions without my noticing. As we entered and my eyes adjusted to the darkness, I was thrilled to see that the small oil lamps that appeared on each stand were prepared from used condensed-milk tins and looked exactly like those in night markets in Haiti. The rich aroma of boiling palm oil perfumed the air. Women dressed in brightly colored wrappers and head ties stood by their pots offering fried tidbits and leaves full of steamed delights. We purchased some *akasa*, fermented corn paste wrapped in leaves, and some of the *akara* that had been perfuming the air with their fragrance. I wanted to stay and watch the women as they turned pieces of chicken on grills and deftly prepared sauces in multicolored enameled bowls. Theodora, though, for whom this magic was just quotidian, made her purchases, and allowed me a few minutes to gaze, and savor, then we went out through the archway and back into the street.

MARKET FOOD IN DAHOMEY (BENIN)

GEBNA MAKLEYAH
◎◎◎

FRIED CHEESE (EGYPT)

Two different types of cheeses, labna *and* gebna, *are prepared by modern Egyptians—*labna *by straining salted yogurt into a creamy consistency,* gebna *by pressing salted curds and allowing them to dry and harden over a two- or three-day period. Ancient Egyptians could have prepared both versions. In fact, two jars from the First Dynasty tomb of Hor-aha contained a residue from something that appears to be mighty like cheese. In this version, I've replaced the traditional cheese with feta.*

SERVES 4 TO 6

Place the cheese, flour, egg, salt, and pepper in a bowl and mix well with your hands. Roll the mixture into 1-inch balls. If it's too loose, add a tiny bit more flour. If it's too dry, add a bit of the liquid from the feta cheese. Heat oil for deep frying to 375 degrees in a heavy Dutch oven or deep fryer. When the oil is hot, add the cheese balls a few at a time and fry until they are golden brown. Remove with a slotted spoon and drain on absorbent paper. Serve warm with lemon wedges and triangles of pita bread.

1 cup finely crumbled firm feta cheese, or other firm mild cheese such as farmer cheese
1 tablespoon flour
1 egg
Salt and freshly ground black pepper, to taste
Olive oil for deep frying
Lemon wedges and pita triangles, for serving

Sweet rice is

eaten quickly.

—SIERRA LEONE

AKARA

◎◎◎

BEAN FRITTERS (NIGERIA)

These white-bean fritters define Nigerian cooking for many people. Traditional in western Nigeria, they have crossed the nation's borders and the Atlantic Ocean to become one of the defining dishes of the African-Atlantic world. Frying in deep oil, a traditional West African cooking technique, is one of the hallmarks of the food of the African-Atlantic world.

These Nigerian bean fritters turn up in Brazil as the ubiquitous acarage, using black-eyed peas. They are found throughout the Caribbean, and there's even a recipe for acara in the kosher cookbook of Curaçao's Mikwe Israel Synagogue, one of the Western Hemisphere's oldest!

There are several different types of Nigerian akara. The most common and best-known is the white bean and palm oil akara.

If you are wary of red palm oil because of cholesterol considerations, you can mix the oil for frying half-and-half with polyunsaturated oil or change the cooking oil entirely. For one time only, though, I would suggest to one and all that they attempt the akara *the traditional way. If the oil is truly hot, the fritter will not absorb much and the taste is unique.*

The beans must be cleaned the day before and soaked overnight.   SERVES 6

2 cups dried Great Northern beans

Oil for deep frying, preferably red palm oil (see Note)

1½ cups cold water

½ teaspoon finely minced habanero chile, or to taste (see Note)

1 small onion, finely minced

Salt, to taste

Prepare the beans by picking over them to remove any impurities and broken or bad beans and soaking them overnight in water to cover. The next day, remove the skins from the beans by rubbing them between your hands. Heat the oil for frying to 375 degrees in a heavy Dutch oven or a deep fryer. Place the prepared beans in a meat grinder or food processor and pulse until you have a smooth paste. Place the paste in a large bowl. Beat the bean paste with a wooden spoon to aerate it, and gradually add the water. Continue to beat while adding the water. Use only enough water to make a mixture that will fall easily from the spoon. Add the chile and onion and season to taste with salt. Continue to stir so that all ingredients are well mixed. When ready, spoon the *akara* up by the tablespoonful and drop a few at a time into the hot oil. Fry for 2 minutes on each side, or until golden brown. Drain on absorbent paper. Serve hot.

NOTE: See Glossary (page 55) for information on chiles and Glossary (page 66–67) and Mail-Order Sources (page 74) for information on red palm oil.

Variations

AKARA AWON

◉◉◉

OKRA AND BEAN FRITTERS (NIGERIA)

Here okra is added to the basic akara *mixture before frying.*

Wash and top and tail the okra, discarding any blemished or hard pods. Place the okra pods in the bowl of a food processor and pulse until they are finely minced. Alternatively, you can mince the okra pods with a sharp knife, but the pods will get slimier and slimier as you cut. When the okra is minced, add it to the *akara* ingredients and proceed as for regular *akara*.

6 fresh okra pods

AKARA IJESHA

◉◉◉

(NIGERIA)

The Ijesha are one of the groups of the Yoruba people. For the Ijesha akara, *only enough water is added to the beaten bean mixture to allow it to become a paste. It should be thick. Ijesha* akara *are traditionally fried in red palm oil and are dropped by the handful or from a large wooden spoon into the hot oil. The Ijesha* akara *may incorporate other ingredients, but they must be large.*

AKARA EGUSI

◎◎◎

(NIGERIA)

Equal parts of ground egusi *(page 59) and half-ground Great Northern beans are used. After the mixture is prepared, the* akara *is deep-fried in palm oil, drained, and served hot.*

CHEESE AKARA

◎◎◎

(NIGERIA)

This is a Nigerian twist on the cheese puff. Add about ¼ cup grated cheddar cheese to the basic akara *batter and decrease the amount of water slightly. This will be a thicker* akara *batter than the traditional one, closer in texture to Akara Ijesha.*

SAVORY PORRIDGE FRITTERS
◎◎◎

(EAST AFRICA)

There is a tradition of deep frying in oil throughout the continent, and fritters are culinary hallmarks. While rice and corn, beans and bananas prevail in much of the western part of Africa, in the east, fritters are also a way to use up any of the left-over mashes or porridges that traditionally support the soupy stew that may be a main course. SERVES 6

Heat the oil for deep frying to 375 degrees in a heavy cast-iron Dutch oven or a deep fryer. Mix the porridge, onion, parsley, and chile together in a medium bowl. In a separate bowl, beat the eggs and the milk. When the oil is hot, take a tablespoon of the porridge mixture, dip it in the beaten egg mixture, and drop it into the hot oil. Proceed with the remaining porridge a few tablespoonfuls at a time and fry for 2 minutes on each side, or until lightly browned, then drain on absorbent paper. Serve hot with a spicy sauce such as Savory Aloco Sauce (page 93).

Oil for deep frying

3 cups leftover porridge (see Note)

⅔ cup minced onion

2 tablespoons minced parsley

Minced fresh chile, to taste (see Note)

2 eggs

¼ cup milk

NOTE: Porridge is simply a term used for the starchy mashes that accompany a main meal; it may be the cornmeal mash that is called *ugali* in Kenya and *tuo* in Nigeria (page 287) or any of the other mashes. This recipe can also be used with any of the western African mashes like the cassava porridge known in Benin as *eba* (page 285).

For information on chiles, see the Glossary (page 55) and Mail-Order Sources (page 74).

Variations

SWEET PORRIDGE FRITTERS

◎◎◎

(EAST AFRICA)

Mix the leftover porridge with 2 tablespoons of dark brown sugar, or sugar to taste. Fry as for the savory fritters and serve with a dusting of brown sugar.

PORRIDGE FRITTERS II

◎◎◎

(EAST AFRICA)

Some leftover mashes are too stiff to be spooned up, but that doesn't save them from the fritter fondness of the East Africans. The mashes are sliced into pieces and then seasoned and fried like their looser cousins. You will need to refrigerate the porridge for at least several hours before you can use it for these fritters.   SERVES ABOUT 6

Oil for deep frying
1 cup roasted peanuts
2 eggs
Six 4-inch-square pieces of thick porridge, about ½ inch thick (see Note)

Heat the oil in a heavy cast-iron Dutch oven or a deep fryer until it is 375 degrees. While the oil is heating, pulverize the peanuts in a food processor until they are finely minced. Place the ground peanuts in a bowl. Beat the eggs in a small bowl. When the oil is hot, first dip the pieces of porridge into the egg batter, then dredge them in the ground peanuts and place them in the oil a few at a time. Fry for about 2 minutes on each side, or until golden brown. Drain on absorbent paper and serve hot.

NOTE: While the porridge or mash is still warm, place it in a baking pan and smooth out the top. Cover and refrigerate for several hours or overnight.

ALL-PURPOSE FRITTER BATTER

◎◎◎

(ALL AFRICA)

Fritters using fritter batter are eaten around the continent, and there are a variety of different ways to prepare the batters. This all-purpose fritter batter eliminates the need to worry about the variations for whatever you would like to make into fritters. The batter can be used for sweet ingredients if you substitute 1 tablespoon of brown sugar for the salt and pepper.

MAKES ABOUT 1½ CUPS BATTER

Mix the flour, salt, and pepper together in a medium-sized bowl. Make a well in the middle and break the eggs into the well while beating the mixture. Continue to beat, adding the milk, until the mixture has become a uniform, thick paste. Cover the bowl with a dampened cloth and allow it to rest for 12 hours. When the batter is ready, prepare the fritters according to the fritter recipe directions.

1 cup flour
Salt and freshly ground black pepper,
*   to taste*
2 eggs
½ cup milk

SELLING FRITTERS

ALOCO

◎◎◎

FRIED PLANTAINS (CÔTE D'IVOIRE)

This treat has become so popular in western Africa that it has even given its name to impromptu markets that spring up along the sides of roads in the evening. There, women set up a tray and a burner and fry the aloco *for sale. In the French-speaking world, these markets are known as* alocodromes. *One of my favorite* alocodromes *in West Africa is located near the night market at Cocody in Abidjan, Côte d'Ivoire. There, in a market lit by twinkling kerosene lanterns, it is possible to purchase not only* aloco *but also* poulet braisé, *grilled chicken served with a tomatoey barbecue sauce,* Maïs Grillé *(grilled ears of corn, page 178), and other street foods.*

These West African night food markets have an allure all their own and students, singles, and even families venture to eat, sitting on small wooden stools illuminated only by flickering lanterns, the air perfumed with the aroma of wood smoke and frying palm oil. Others prefer to bring the aloco *home wrapped in a calabash or an enameled bowl wrapped in a brightly colored piece of cloth known as a* pagne. *You can't bring the aroma of the night market home, but you can still enjoy the* aloco.

SERVES 8 TO 10

8 firm ripe plantains

3 cups palm oil

3 cups peanut oil

Peel the plantains and cut them crosswise into ½-inch rounds. Pour the palm oil and the peanut oil into a deep fryer or into a heavy Dutch oven and heat it to 375 degrees. Fry the plantain slices a few at a time until they are golden on the outside but still soft on the inside. Drain the *aloco* on absorbent paper and serve warm. *Aloco* may be served either sweet or savory. If sweet, sprinkle the finished *aloco* with sugar. (Pure cane brown sugar is most authentic, if you can get it.) If you want savory *aloco*, try serving them with the following hot sauce.

SAVORY ALOCO SAUCE
◎◎◎

(CÔTE D'IVOIRE)

MAKES ABOUT ¼ CUP

Grind the chile and the onions together in a food processor until you have a thick paste. (You may need a teaspoon of water to get it started.) Heat the oil in a heavy skillet, add the paste, and cook over medium heat for 5 minutes, stirring constantly, until the sauce is completely warmed. Salt to taste and serve warm with the *aloco*.

1 teaspoon minced habanero chile, or to taste (see page 55)
2 small onions
3 tablespoons palm oil or peanut oil
Salt, to taste

PLANTAIN CRISPS
◎◎◎

(GHANA)

Snacking seems to be a favorite West African pastime, whether at night markets or when simply strolling down a country road. Snacks also turn up at outdoor dance halls like Accra's famous Tip Toe. There, in the seventies, it was possible to hear some of the country's best high-life music while drinking large bottles of beer and munching on yellow plantains that were sliced and served as chips.

SERVES 6

3 large firm yellow plantains
Peanut oil for deep frying
1 tablespoon ground ginger
1 tablespoons cayenne pepper
Salt, to taste

Peel the plantains and cut them into thin rounds using a sharp paring knife or a mandoline. Heat the oil for deep frying to 375 degrees in a deep fryer or heavy Dutch oven. When the oil is hot, fry the plantain slices a few at a time. Drain the crisps on absorbent paper and continue until they are all fried. Mix the ginger, pepper, and salt together in a brown paper bag. Add the plantain crisps and shake to coat all the crisps. Serve warm with drinks. (If the ginger is too pungent for you, try a mixture of chile powder and salt.)

DODO-IKIRE
◎◎◎

FRIED PLANTAIN (NIGERIA)

This snack is as popular as potato chips in many parts of Nigeria. There are an infinite number of versions that can be found in almost all Nigerian cookbooks. In this one, the overripe plantain is sliced lengthwise, but it can also be diced and formed into small balls. SERVES 4

Heat the oil for deep frying to 350 degrees in a Dutch oven or deep fryer. Peel the plantains and cut them lengthwise into strips. Mix the salt and the minced chile together in a small bowl. When the oil is ready, dredge the plantain strips in the spice mixture, then fry for 2 minutes on each side, or until golden brown. Drain on absorbent paper and serve warm or at room temperature.

Palm oil for deep frying
2 overripe but firm plantains
Salt, to taste
Minced fresh chile, to taste
  (see page 55)

MOUNTAINS OF PEANUTS

BEIGNETS DE SARDINES

◎◎◎

SARDINE FRITTERS (ALGERIA)

These easy-to-make fritters are popular snacks in Algeria among the pied noir, *as the French settlers were called. They often appeared as Algerian tapas known as* khemia, *along with other nibbles like marinated olives, grilled chickpeas, and mini-brochettes.*

You can make these with any small firm-fleshed fish. If you can find whitebait, they are perfect as fritters. Simply wash them quickly in water and lemon juice, dredge in the batter, and fry. You don't have to worry about cleaning them, as you can eat all of them.

SERVES 8 TO 10

Olive oil for deep frying
1 pound fresh sardines, beheaded and
   cleaned
Salt and freshly ground black pepper,
   to taste
All-Purpose Fritter Batter (page 91)
Lemon wedges, for serving

Heat the oil for deep frying to 375 degrees in a deep fryer or heavy Dutch oven. With a sharp paring knife, remove the sardine spines and spread the sardines flat. Dredge the flattened sardines in the fritter batter and fry on each side for 3 minutes, or until browned. Serve hot with lemon wedges.

FÈVES SÈCHES FRITES
◎◎◎

FRIED FAVA BEANS (ALGERIA)

The fava bean is popular throughout North Africa, where botanists think it originated. The Ancient Egyptians cultivated these beans, which are also called broad beans. In fact, these beans were the only variety of legume of the Vicia genus known to Europeans until the Spaniards brought green beans back from the Americas. In this recipe, the dried beans are reconstituted, split, and deep-fried for a crunchy snack that is also served as a khemia, *or tapas.*

You can prepare chickpeas the same way. You may wish to use a bit of cumin or cayenne pepper as the seasoning. The beans need to soak overnight before cooking.   SERVES 8

Pick over the dry beans, place them in a bowl with cold water to cover, and allow them to sit overnight. When ready, heat the oil for deep frying to 375 degrees in a heavy Dutch oven or deep fryer. Drain the beans, split them in two with your fingers, and dry them well. Fry them for 5 minutes, then remove and drain on absorbent paper. Season with salt and pepper and serve warm.

1 pound dried fava beans
Olive oil for deep frying
Salt and freshly ground black pepper,
   to taste

BRIK AUX CHAMPIGNONS
◎◎◎

MUSHROOM BRIK (ALGERIA)

Although the brik *seems to have originated in Tunisia, where it is one of the classic appetizers, it has migrated to parts of eastern Algeria on the Tunisian border. There, the dough used is not the semolina-based* ouarka (warka) *of the Tunisian* brik *and Moroccan bastilla, but rather one that is similar to the filo or phyllo dough that I use here.*

SERVES 6

Vegetable oil for deep frying
½ pound mushrooms, sliced
4 cloves garlic, minced
1 small onion, minced
2 tablespoons olive oil
2 tablespoons minced flat-leaf parsley
Salt and freshly ground black pepper,
*   to taste*
2 teaspoons flour
12 sheets of filo

Heat the vegetable oil for deep frying in a heavy Dutch oven or deep fryer to 375 degrees. While the vegetable oil is heating, sauté the mushrooms, garlic, and onion in the olive oil in a heavy skillet for 15 minutes. When the mushroom mixture is cooked, add the parsley and seasonings, place the mixture in the bowl of a food processor, and pulse until puréed. Stir the flour into the purée to thicken it, being sure that it is well mixed. Separate the filo into sheets, place a tablespoon of the *brik* mixture on a sheet, and fold it into a packet 4 by 5 inches. Fry the packets for 2 to 3 minutes, or until golden brown, in the vegetable oil. Drain on absorbent paper and serve warm as an appetizer.

CRABMEAT APPETIZER

◎◎◎

(CÔTE D'IVOIRE)

This is really a crab salad and can serve as either an appetizer or a light entrée. It is clearly a modern invention, but one that nonetheless speaks to the continuing evolution of the cooking of the continent.

SERVES 4 AS AN APPETIZER, 2 AS AN ENTRÉE

Combine the crabmeat, pineapple, mayonnaise, and *pili pili* sauce in a bowl, cover with plastic wrap, and chill for 1 hour. When ready to serve, divide into portions and spoon into the pineapple boats. Decorate each with a sprig of mint and serve.

3 cups flaked crabmeat
2 cups fresh pineapple chunks
2 tablespoons mayonnaise
(for homemade, see page 146)
Dash of Pili Pili Sauce (page 145),
or to taste
4 Pineapple Boats (page 302)
4 sprigs fresh mint, for garnish

COCONUT CRISPS

◎◎◎

(ALL AFRICA)

These small toasted slices of coconut are an expatriate invention—wonderful as an accompaniment to drinks. When the bits of toasted coconut are cut into smaller pieces, they're perfect for dusting on the top of curries or sprinkling over desserts.

SERVES 8 TO 10

1 brown coconut, shelled and peeled

Open a brown coconut by baking it in a 350-degree oven for 10 minutes, then whacking it soundly with a hammer on its "fault" line. Take out the coconut meat, reserving the liquid for other uses. Remove the brown rind from the meat and pare the coconut into long thin strips with a potato peeler or paring knife. Place the pieces on a cookie sheet and brown them under the broiler for about 5 minutes, or until they are lightly toasted. Watch them carefully, as they go from lightly toasted to charred black in the blink of an eye. Serve warm with drinks.

DITHOTSE
◉◎◉

ROASTED PUMPKIN SEEDS (SOUTH AFRICA)

Among many of the traditional cultures of Africa, nothing goes to waste in the food chain. Entrails are eaten with delight, small larvae are consumed with gusto, and the seeds and leaves of plants form the basis for many favored dishes. So it is with these pumpkin seeds. Traditionally they are eaten to accompany sauces or porridges, but they can also be eaten as a snack or served with drinks. If you use melon seeds, you will have the snack known in Nigeria as egusi, *which is also used in other recipes.* MAKES 2 TO 3 CUPS

Wash the seeds and remove any pumpkin that may remain on them. Heat a heavy cast-iron skillet and add the wet seeds. Cook over medium heat for about 5 minutes, or until the seeds are hot enough to pop open. Salt to taste and serve warm.

Seeds from 1 large pumpkin, butternut squash, or calabaza

Salt, to taste

SALADS AND SOUPS

Small Bowls and Side Dishes

Many of the dishes of the African continent—from the couscous on the north to the sauce that is spooned over the mealie pap in the south—could be defined as soups. There are also classic soups, like the fast-breaking *harira* that is the first meal eaten during Ramadan by many of the continent's Muslims, and soups that are being created by new cooks and chefs. Salads are a relatively recent addition to the African menu, unless they are the traditional small plates of North Africa.

Salads

SALADES VARIÉES
Various Salads *(Morocco)*

SLATA FEL FEL
Grilled Bell Pepper Salad *(Morocco)*

GRATED CARROT SALAD
(Morocco)

COOKED CARROT SALAD
(Morocco)

ORANGE AND RADISH SALAD
(Morocco)

SALADE DE COURGETTES AU CARVI
Zucchini Paste with Caraway *(Morocco)*

SALADE DE CONCOMBRE À LA MENTHE
Minted Cucumber Salad *(Algeria)*

SALATIT FASULYA KHADRA
String Bean and Onion Salad *(Egypt)*

SALADE D'AUBERGINES
Eggplant Salad *(Algeria)*

SALADE DE LAITUE À L'ANANAS
Pineapple and Lettuce Salad
(Democratic Republic of Congo)

AVOCAT FARCI
Stuffed Avocados *(Côte d'Ivoire)*

AVOCAT VINAIGRETTE
Avocado with Vinaigrette Dressing *(Cote d' Ivoire)*

COLONIAL SALAD *(NIGERIA)*

AVOCADO AND PAPAYA SALAD
(Kenya)

TOMATO AND OKRA SALAD
(Nigeria)

YAM SALAD
(Nigeria)

ROOIBEET SLAAI
BEET SALAD *(South Africa)*

Soups

GREEN MEALIE SOUP
(South Africa)

CHICKEN PEPPERSOUP
(Nigeria)

NWO-NWO
Peppersoup II *(Nigeria)*

OKRA SOUP
(Sierra Leone)

NKATENKWAN
Chicken Peanut Soup *(Ghana)*

✳

The muezzin has done his virtuoso number on the last call to prayer of the day and the prayer rugs have been rolled up. The gates have been pulled down on the boutiques and the little boys are no longer buzzing around tourists like mosquitoes. The *guerrab*, or water sellers, no longer flash their smiles for photos. The Djema el Fna, or Square of the Dead, the most lively place in the city of Marrakesh, is transforming itself from the daytime haunt of tourists into the suppertime spot for those who want to taste some of Morocco's best street food. The strong men now perform their acrobatic feats to the glow of hurricane lamps, and the storytellers' crowd gathers around the flickering glow of camping lanterns. The Gnaouia musicians still sing their haunting chants. Night falls.

In another corner of the square, the food stalls are setting up for the evening. Where during the day they had sold oranges and fresh juices, they now transform themselves into mini-restaurants complete with long tables covered in oilcloth and a variety of choices for the diner. There are brochettes of lamb, small pieces of meat grilled over charcoal braziers and served with fresh hunks of dense chewy bread. Others will sip a bowl of rich soup thick with pasta and filled with the tastes of spices. There are almond sellers and those with huge mounds of dried fruit: dates, figs, and more. The night darkens and the tales continue and for those who wish, the stroll is transformed into an ambulatory dinner theater with almonds as an appetizer, the hot foods the main course, and the dates and figs and perhaps a mandarin orange or two as dessert.

SALADS

SALADES VARIÉES

VARIOUS SALADS (MOROCCO)

Traditionally, many small plates of vegetables and salads come to the table as the first course in a Moroccan banquet. These dishes may include cooked carrots dressed with a savory marinade (page 109), mixtures of orange and grated radish (page 110), marinated tomatoes, slices of eggplant (page 114), or grilled bell pepper salad (page 107). Many hostesses pride themselves on the number of small plates they serve, and at times the variety of small salads seems endless. The dishes are a vegetarian's delight and many would constitute wonderful vegetable side dishes if served alone. At times, I confess, I wish that the main course were just more of these small plates. A combination of them would make a perfect (albeit nontraditional) summer meal. Usually, these salads are served room temperature, not cold, though I find that some have more zing if slightly refrigerated.

SLATA FEL FEL

◎◎◎

GRILLED BELL PEPPER SALAD *(MOROCCO)*

The bell peppers in this salad can be cut into small cubes or into strips. Red and green peppers are usual, but you can add further variety by using orange, yellow, or even purple ones.

SERVES 4

Roast the bell peppers by placing them on the rack of a broiler and turning them slowly until they are completely charred. When done, peel the skin off with a sharp paring knife. It is easier to peel the peppers if you place them in a brown paper bag for a few minutes after roasting. Cut the peppers into ½-inch strips lengthwise and place them in a glass salad bowl. Mix the remaining ingredients together and pour the marinade over the peppers. Cover with plastic wrap, let sit for I hour, then stir and serve.

½ pound sweet red and green bell peppers
1½ tablespoons extra-virgin olive oil
1 tablespoon freshly squeezed lemon juice
½ teaspoon cumin
1 teaspoon minced flat-leaf parsley
Salt and freshly ground back pepper, to taste

Let no one uproot the

pumpkin in the old

homestead.

—EAST AFRICAN SAYING

GRATED CARROT SALAD
◎◎◎

(MOROCCO)

Orange-flower water, a staple in the cabinet of anyone who loves the tastes of the Maghreb, is the secret that gives this salad its delicate flavor.
SERVES 4

6 medium-sized carrots

2 navel oranges

2 teaspoons freshly squeezed orange
   juice

2 teaspoons confectioners' sugar

2 teaspoons orange-flower water
   (see Note)

Salt, to taste

Wash and scrape the carrots. Using the medium-shredding disk of a food processor or a hand grater, grate the carrots into a glass salad bowl. Peel the oranges and segment them, removing all the pith and membrane and reserving 2 teaspoons of the juice. You can segment the oranges easily if you remove all the white pith from the orange with a sharp paring knife and then, holding the orange in one hand, run the knife around each segment inside the membrane. Do this over a small bowl to catch the juice. Add the orange segments to the salad bowl. Mix the remaining ingredients and the reserved orange juice together in a small bowl and pour it over the carrot and orange segments. Mix the salad well, cover with plastic wrap, and refrigerate for 1 hour. Stir before serving. Serve chilled.

NOTE: See Glossary (page 66) and Mail-Order Sources (page 74).

COOKED CARROT SALAD
◎◎◎

(MOROCCO)

When it's carrot season in Morocco, carrots turn up on the table in all possible manners. This small plate uses cooked carrots and is an ideal way to serve up a bumper crop. SERVES 8

Wash the carrots, scrape them, and slice them into ¼-inch-thick rounds. Bring the water to a boil in a heavy 3-quart saucepan. Add the carrots and the garlic, cover, and cook for 15 minutes, or until the carrots are fork-tender but not mushy. Drain the carrots and place them in a glass salad bowl. Mix the remaining ingredients together in a small bowl, then pour over the salad and toss well. Cover with plastic wrap and set aside for 30 minutes to allow the flavors to mix. Serve at room temperature.

8 medium-sized carrots
1 cup water
1 clove garlic
½ teaspoon paprika
½ teaspoon ground cumin
2 tablespoons extra-virgin olive oil
2 tablespoons red wine vinegar
1 tablespoon minced flat-leaf parsley
Salt and freshly ground black pepper,
to taste

ORANGE AND RADISH SALAD
◎◎◎

(MOROCCO)

Radishes are very popular in North Africa. They were eaten in pharaonic Egypt and turn up as garnishes, nibbles, and salad ingredients virtually throughout the region. Here the zip of radish is paired with the sweetness of orange and orange-flower water.

SERVES 4 TO 6

1 bunch large red globe radishes

4 large navel oranges

2 tablespoons freshly squeezed orange
 juice

1½ teaspoons orange-flower water
 (see Note)

1 teaspoon confectioners' sugar

1 teaspoon freshly squeezed lemon juice

Wash the radishes, cut off the green tops and the roots, and grate the radishes into a glass salad bowl. Peel the oranges and segment them (see page 108), reserving 2 tablespoons of the juice. Place the orange segments in the bowl with the grated radish. Mix the remaining ingredients and the reserved orange juice together in a small bowl and pour the marinade over the radish and orange mixture. Cover with plastic wrap and set aside for 30 minutes so that the flavors mix. Serve at room temperature.

NOTE: See Glossary (page 66) and Mail-Order Sources (page 74).

SALADE DE COURGETTES AU CARVI

◎◎◎

ZUCCHINI PASTE WITH CARAWAY (MOROCCO)

This salad is a more like a paste or dip. Scoop it up with toasted triangles of pita bread.   SERVES 4 TO 6

Wash the zucchini and cut them into 1-inch slices. Place them in a heavy saucepan with the water, cover, and cook, stirring occasionally, for about 10 minutes, or until all the water has evaporated and the zucchini is soft. Place the zucchini in a mortar along with the remaining ingredients and pound until you have a thick paste. (Alternatively, you can put the cooked zucchini and remaining ingredients in the bowl of a food processor and pulse until you have a paste, but the consistency will not be the same.) Adjust your seasonings and serve at once.

1 pound zucchini
½ cup water
1 large clove garlic
½ teaspoon caraway seeds
3 tablespoons extra-virgin olive oil
1 tablespoon freshly squeezed lemon juice

SALADE DE CONCOMBRE À LA MENTHE
◎◎◎

MINTED CUCUMBER SALAD (ALGERIA)

Similar to the tzatziki *of Greece, this easy-to-prepare salad is a perfect cooler during the dog days of summer. I always have the ingredients on hand, and more often than not have a bit already made in the refrigerator.* SERVES 4

1 large European or seedless hothouse
   cucumber
½ cup plain yogurt
2 tablespoons minced fresh mint
1 clove garlic, minced
Salt and freshly ground black pepper, to
   taste

Cut the cucumber into thin slices and place them in a medium-sized glass salad bowl. Mix the remaining ingredients together and pour them over the cucumber slices. Cover with plastic wrap and chill for 1 hour. Serve chilled.

THESE ARE KOLA NUTS

I'm a curious person. If I've read about something or heard of it and the opportunity comes to sample it, nine times out of ten I'll try it—at least a bit. Such was the case with kola. I'd seem small piles of them lined up on woven trays for sale by vendors on the street and been told that the reddish multipart kernels were the famous kola that men chewed. I was also told that proper young ladies would never think of chewing kola and that they would never, under any circumstances, accept kola from someone who was not a close friend of the family. Well, all the admonitions were enough to get me going. On my next trip out, I returned with a small leaf in which were three kola nuts. Once back in my room, I took a small nibble, momentarily confusing them with betel and hoping they wouldn't stain my teeth and leave me open to ridicule. They were just bitter. A second nibble confirmed that kola addiction was not in my future. Now I just smile and nod when listening to my friends warn their daughters of the evils of kola. They should just let them try some; I'll take odds they'll never want any more.

SALATIT FASULYA KHADRA

◎◎◎

STRING BEAN AND ONION SALAD (EGYPT)

I'm not exactly sure when string beans arrived in Egypt. Onions are another matter; it seems as though they've always been there. According to Herodotus, the builders of Kufu's pyramids were paid in onions and radishes. In this recipe, the onions are not the traditional white onion, but red onion, a more recent arrival.   SERVES 6 TO 8

Bring the water to a boil in a medium-sized saucepan. Trim and wash the beans, remove any blemished ones, place them in the boiling water, and cook for about 5 minutes, or until they are tender but still slightly crisp. Drain the beans, place them in a glass salad bowl, and allow them to cool. Place the onion slices in a small bowl, cover them with the lemon juice, and allow them to soak for 30 minutes. When ready to serve, add the onions to the string beans, drizzle them with olive oil, season with salt and pepper, and serve at room temperature.

1 quart water

2 pounds string beans

2 large red onions, thinly sliced

1 tablespoon freshly squeezed lemon
   juice

1 tablespoon olive oil

Salt and freshly ground black pepper, to
   taste

SALADE D'AUBERGINES
◎◎◎

EGGPLANT SALAD (ALGERIA)

Eggplant is the king of North African vegetables; it appears in everything, even dressed with mint and yogurt in salads such as this one.   SERVES 4

4 small eggplants
1 tablespoon olive oil
1 cup plain yogurt
1 clove garlic, minced
1½ tablespoons chopped fresh mint
   leaves
Mint sprigs, for garnish

Peel and slice the eggplants and sauté them in the olive oil over medium heat until fork-tender. Drain them on absorbent paper. Meanwhile, mix the remaining ingredients together in a glass or crockery salad bowl. Add the eggplant slices, mix well, cover with plastic wrap, and chill for 1 hour. Serve chilled, garnished with mint sprigs.

SALADE DE LAITUE À L'ANANAS

◎◎◎

PINEAPPLE AND LETTUCE SALAD
(DEMOCRATIC REPUBLIC OF CONGO)

Although pineapples are native to the New World, many of the world's pineapples are grown in parts of Africa, notably Côte d'Ivoire. There, the pineapples that are not exported to European markets turn up in all sorts of dishes. This salad, unusual in the cooking of western Africa, is perhaps one of the simplest uses pineapples are put to. The secret is a ripe, sweet pineapple and good fresh homemade mayonnaise. SERVES 4 TO 6

Peel the pineapple, reserving the juice. Core it and cut it into small pieces. Wash the lettuce, separate it into leaves, and tear each leaf into bite-sized pieces. Place the pineapple and the lettuce in a large glass salad bowl. Add the mayonnaise and 2 teaspoons of the reserved juice and mix the ingredients together so that the lettuce and pineapple pieces are lightly coated. Chill for 30 minutes. Serve chilled.

½ ripe fresh pineapple
1 medium head Boston lettuce
3 tablespoons mayonnaise
   (for homemade, see page 146)

AVOCAT FARCI

◉◉◉

STUFFED AVOCADOS (CÔTE D'IVOIRE)

When it's avocado season in Côte d'Ivoire, the small eggplant-hued globes that are Ivoirian avocados turn up everywhere. I re-
member that, on my first solo trip to that country, I arrived at about the same time as the avocado harvest. I stayed at the then
new Hôtel Ivoire and spent my time going from restaurant to restaurant sampling the different dishes that were made with the
buttery smooth avocados. This dish, which can also be prepared with crabmeat or flaked tuna fish, was served as an appetizer.
It also makes a perfect light summer lunch. SERVES 6

3 cups cooked peeled miniature shrimp
    (about 100 per pound)
2 cups minced fresh pineapple
3 medium to large ripe avocados
1 tablespoon freshly squeezed lime juice
6 Boston lettuce leaves for serving
Classic Vinaigrette (page 134), to taste

Mix the shrimp and pineapple together in a medium-sized bowl. Cover with plastic wrap and chill for 1 hour. When ready to serve, cut the avocados in half lengthwise and remove the pits. Rub a bit of the lime juice on the avocado meat to make sure that it does not discolor. Place the avocado halves atop the lettuce leaves on individual saucers and mound them full of the shrimp and pineapple mixture, dripping some over the side. Drizzle vinaigrette over the pineapple and shrimp and serve immediately.

AVOCAT VINAIGRETTE
◎◎◎

AVOCADO WITH VINAIGRETTE DRESSING (CÔTE D'IVOIRE)

While this would seem at first to be as French as a stroll down the Champs Elysées, it should be remembered that many of the avocados served in France come from places like Côte d'Ivoire. When it's avocado season in Abidjan, the administrative capital, avocados with a simple vinaigrette dressing come to the table in many westernized homes and the city's restaurants.

SERVES 1

Split the avocado lengthwise in half with a sharp knife and remove the pit. Place the halves on a plate and rub the lemon wedge over the avocado meat to prevent it from discoloring. Drizzle the dressing over the avocado and serve immediately.

1 small ripe Hass avocado

1 lemon wedge

3 tablespoons Classic Vinaigrette
  (page 134)

COLONIAL SALAD
◎◎◎

(NIGERIA)

Miss Williams' Cookery Book, *published in Nigeria in the late 1950s, gives several suggestions for salad ingredients and even includes a diagram to demonstrate how to arrange them. Miss Williams notes that salads are not a traditional Nigerian dish, but rather a dish from Europe that is growing in popularity among Nigerians. Some of her advice still rings true today. She suggests, among other things, that the ingredients be arranged as "tastefully and colourfully" as possible and that "neatness and daintiness are the success of a good salad." Following her dictums, I have created Colonial Salad in honor of Miss Williams' original salad.*

SERVES 6 TO 8

2 small heads Boston lettuce

1 small bunch watercress

1 cup shredded red cabbage

2 cups diced cooked sweet potato

2 cups diced cooked yam

4 medium carrots, scraped and grated

3 ripe medium tomatoes, sliced

1 can oil-packed albacore tuna, drained

1 (3¾-ounce) can sardines, drained

2 cups cooked Great Northern beans

2 avocados, diced

¼ cup diced dried smoked shrimp, pulverized in a food processor (optional) (see Note)

Classic Vinaigrette (page 134), to taste

Arrange all the ingredients except the avocados, shrimp, and vinaigrette neatly on a large platter, making sure that the finished salad will provide pleasure for the eye as well as for the mouth. Cover with plastic wrap and chill for 1 hour. When ready to serve, dice the avocado. The optional smoked shrimp can be sprinkled on top of the beans. Serve the vinaigrette in a sauce-boat. Allow your guests to select the items that appeal to them and then add dressing to their taste.

NOTE: See Glossary (page 70) and Mail-Order Sources (page 74) for dried smoked shrimp.

Avocado and Papaya Salad
◎◎◎

(KENYA)

Salads, in the Western sense, are recent additions to the African table. But they are catching on, and home cooks and chefs alike are making abundant use of the variety of vegetables and greens available. This salad, inspired by one from Kenya's colonial period, uses avocado, papaya, and grapefruit. The original version called for, among other things, a half cup of mayonnaise.

SERVES 4

Peel the avocados and the papaya and remove the pits and seeds. Cut the fruit into 1-inch pieces and mix them together in a medium-sized bowl. Peel the grapefruit and with a sharp knife, segment it, removing the thin membrane from each segment. Cut the segments in half and add them to the avocado and papaya mix. Wash the lettuce, break it into leaves, and pat dry. Arrange the lettuce leaves on a platter and mound the mixture atop them. Prepare vinaigrette by whisking the lemon juice, olive oil, and salt and pepper together in a small bowl. Drizzle the dressing over the salad and serve immediately.

2 large avocados
1 small papaya
1 ruby-red grapefruit
1 small head Bibb lettuce
1 tablespoon freshly squeezed lemon juice
2 tablespoons extra-virgin olive oil
Salt and freshly ground black pepper, to taste

TOMATO AND OKRA SALAD
◎◎◎

(NIGERIA)

This is an unusual use of the pod that is so popular on the African continent. This salad will taste best if you use only fresh young okra pods the size of your little finger.

SERVES 4

1 pound okra

3 large ripe tomatoes, peeled, seeded, and coarsely chopped

1 small head Boston lettuce

¼ cup Classic Vinaigrette (page 134)

2 teaspoons Chile Oil (page 138), or to taste

Wash and top and tail the okra, discarding any blemished or hard pods. Cook the okra as for boiled okra (page 198). Drain it and allow it to cool. Prepare the tomatoes. Wash the lettuce, break it into leaves, pat dry, and arrange the leaves on a large platter. Mound the okra on top of the lettuce and top with the chopped tomatoes. When ready to serve, dress the salad with vinaigrette to which you have added 2 teaspoons of chile oil.

YAM SALAD

◎◎◎

(NIGERIA)

This is the West African answer to the potato salad of the American South. The traditional African yam (not sweet potatoes, please!) is used. As with American potato salad, you can doll this one up with everything from diced red and green bell peppers to European additions like minced sweet pickled gherkins, thinly sliced celery, and chopped hard-boiled eggs.

SERVES 4

Mix all the ingredients together in a large bowl, cover with plastic wrap, and refrigerate for 1 hour to allow the flavors to mingle. Serve chilled. The salad can be served from a bowl or arranged on a bed of lettuce on a decorative platter.

1 pound Boiled Yams (page 279), diced

2 large onions, minced

1 small red bell pepper, cored, seeded, and minced

1 small green bell pepper, cored, seeded, and minced

¼ cup mayonnaise (for homemade, see page 146)

ROOIBEET SLAAI

◎◎◎

BEET SALAD (SOUTH AFRICA)

This is a European dish that has made the translation to the South African table. In this dish, I have called for canned beets, but fresh beets—boiled, peeled, and thinly sliced—can be used as well.

SERVES 4 TO 6 AS A CONDIMENT

One 1-pound can sliced red beets
2 medium onions, thinly sliced and
*   treated (see Note)*
2 tablespoons red wine vinegar
Salt and sugar, to taste

Place the beets and the onions in a medium-sized glass salad bowl. Mix the vinegar and seasonings together and pour them over the beets, making sure that the vegetables are well covered. Cover the bowl with plastic wrap and refrigerate for 2 hours. Serve chilled.

NOTE: Treat the onions by slicing them thinly and rinsing them with cold water, while separating them into rings.

SOUPS

Soups are generally not a part of the traditional menu in most of western Africa because so many of the main dishes are really soupy stews. Most African soups can become main dishes with the addition of a few more pieces of meat and an accompanying starch. With increased health consciousness, though, soups have become light meals and are eaten more and more frequently.

GREEN MEALIE SOUP

◎◎◎

(SOUTH AFRICA)

C. Louis Leipoldt was an Afrikaner gourmet, writer, and poet who was noted for his appreciation of the cooking of the Cape region. While I'm not sure that I would have agreed with his politics, I do like his green mealie soup, of which this is my own variation.   SERVES 6 TO 8

Cut the corn from the cob and place it in a stockpot with the water and the wine. Prepare a bouquet garni by tying the thyme, parsley, bay leaf, mace, and peppercorns in a small square of cheesecloth. Add the bouquet garni to the pot and cook over medium heat for 5 minutes, or until the corn is tender. Remove the corn, put it through a food mill, and return it to the pot. Add the chicken stock and simmer the soup over low heat for 30 minutes. Adjust the seasonings, add a pinch of sugar, and serve hot.

1 dozen ears fresh corn

1 quart water

1 cup white wine

½ teaspoon minced fresh thyme

1 teaspoon minced parsley

1 bay leaf

1 blade mace

6 black peppercorns

1 cup chicken stock

Pinch of sugar

CHICKEN PEPPERSOUP
◎◎◎

(NIGERIA)

Peppersoup is a popular Nigerian favorite and can be prepared with chicken, fish, goat, mutton, game, or organ meats. It should be fiery hot with spices.   SERVES 6 TO 8

3-pound chicken, cut into serving pieces

¼ cup freshly squeezed lemon juice

4 cups water

1 onion, minced

2 cloves garlic, minced

2 tablespoons minced dried bird chiles,
    or to taste (see Note)

Salt, to taste

4 cups chicken stock

¼ cup Peppersoup Spice Mixture
    (page 153)

2 tablespoons minced dried smoked
    shrimp (see Note)

2 tablespoons chopped fresh mint

Mint sprigs, for garnish

Wash the chicken pieces, rub them with lemon juice, and place them in a large stockpot with the water, onion, garlic, and minced chiles. Salt to taste and bring to a boil over high heat. Lower the heat to medium and simmer for 30 minutes. Add the chicken stock and the spice mixture and continue to cook for an additional 30 minutes, or until the chicken is well cooked. Stir in the shrimp and mint and continue to cook for an additional 10 minutes. Serve hot in soup bowls, garnished with a few sprigs of fresh mint.

NOTE: See Glossary for chiles (page 55) and dried smoked shrimp (page 70), both available through mail order (page 74).

NWO-NWO

◉◎◎

PEPPERSOUP II (NIGERIA)

This is the most popular of the Nigerian peppersoups. Prepared with goat meat or mutton (lamb stew meat may be substituted), it is consumed in great quantities by beer and palm wine drinkers, as it is reputed to help ease the pains of the morning after the night before. It is traditionally served in earthenware soup pots. SERVES 6 TO 8

Have the butcher cut the goat meat into small pieces, leaving the bones in. Wash the goat meat and place it in a stockpot with the water, onion, garlic, and chiles. Season with salt and bring the soup to a boil over high heat. Lower the heat to medium and simmer for 45 minutes. Add the spice mixture and the stock and cook for an additional 15 minutes, or until the meat is tender. Stir in the shrimp, mint, and *utazi*. Adjust the seasoning and cook for 5 minutes more, then serve hot in soup bowls.

NOTE: See Glossary for chiles (page 55), dried smoked shrimp (page 70), and *utazi* leaves (page 72), all three available through mail order (page 74).

2 pounds goat (or lamb) for stewing

6 cups water

1 onion, minced

1 clove garlic, minced

2 tablespoons minced dried bird chiles (see Note), or to taste

Salt, to taste

2 tablespoons Peppersoup Spice Mixture (page 153)

2 cups beef stock

2 tablespoons minced dried smoked shrimp (see Note)

1 tablespoon chopped fresh mint

1 tablespoon chopped utazi leaves (see Note)

OKRA SOUP

◎◎◎

(SIERRA LEONE)

From the bamia *of Egypt to the* tchingombo *of the Bantu regions, okra is revered for its ability to thicken a soup or stew. There is something about okra's slipperiness that makes many Americans despise the green pod. But its digestibility and mucilaginous qualities make it one of the African continent's favorites. This dish from Sierra Leone uses only a few pods but demonstrates okra's ability to thicken soup.*   SERVES 4

1 pound stewing beef

1 tablespoon vegetable oil

1 large onion, thinly sliced

*Salt and freshly ground black pepper,
    to taste*

3½ cups beef stock

8 small okra pods

2 small eggplants, sliced

*3 tomatoes, peeled, seeded, and coarsely
    chopped*

Cut the beef into small cubes. Heat the oil in the bottom of a large stockpot and brown the beef. Add the onion and the seasonings and cook for 10 minutes, stirring occasionally. Add the stock and bring the soup to a boil over high heat. Lower the heat and simmer, covered, for 30 minutes, or until the beef is almost cooked. Wash and top and tail the okra, discarding any blemished or hard pods. Add the eggplant, tomatoes, and okra and simmer for an additional 15 minutes, or until the vegetables are soft. Remove the vegetables with a strainer and put them through a food mill. Return the puréed vegetables to the pot. Adjust the seasoning and continue to cook for 5 minutes, or until the soup has thickened. Serve hot.

NKATENKWAN

◎◎◎

CHICKEN PEANUT SOUP (GHANA)

Chicken groundnut soup is a Ghanaian classic. It can also be prepared with fish. In that case, bring the water to a boil before adding the fish, then proceed.   SERVES 6 TO 8

Place the peanuts in a food processor and pulse them until you have a thick paste. Wash the chicken pieces and place them in a large stockpot with the water or chicken stock. Bring to a boil, then add the seasonings, tomatoes, and onion. Lower the heat and simmer, covered, for 35 minutes. When the onions are soft, remove them and the tomatoes with a slotted spoon, put them through a food mill, and return them to the soup. Add the water to the peanut paste and gradually stir it into the soup. Continue to simmer over low heat for 15 to 20 minutes, or until all the flavors have mixed well. Serve hot with *fufu* (page 284).

1 cup shelled and skinned roasted
  peanuts
1 quart water or chicken stock
3-pound chicken, cut into pieces
Salt and ground red chile, to taste
3 large tomatoes, peeled, seeded, and
  coarsely chopped
1 large onion, thinly sliced
1 tablespoon water

CONDIMENTS

Hot Stuff and Palate Coolers

Condiments are the name of the game on the continent generally, from the harissa of Tunisia to the *pili pili* sauce of Angola to the peppersoup mix of Nigeria. Many of them are fiery hot and dense with the taste of chile pepper, but some, like the chutneys and the *atjars* of the south, give subtlety to dishes. The heat that they bring frequently necessitates cooling down and so some of the side plates offer a cool, refreshing taste.

KHALATA LLI-L-SALATA
Salad Dressing *(Egypt)*

SALSIT KHALL BI-L-TOON
Garlic Dressing *(Egypt)*

CLASSIC VINAIGRETTE
(West Africa)

NIT'IR QIBE
Spiced Butter *(Ethiopia)*

HARISSA
Chile Paste *(Algeria)*

QUICK HARISSA
Chile Paste *(Tunisia)*

MOCTAR'S CHILE
(Senegal)

CHILE OIL
(West Africa)

PRESERVED LEMONS
(Morocco)

LIME ATJAR
Lime Pickle *(South Africa)*

ATJAR
Pickling Marinade *(South Africa)*

WORTEL SAMBAL
Carrot Sambal *(South Africa)*

KOMKOMER SAMBAL
Cucumber Sambal *(South Africa)*

PICKLED OLIVES
(West Africa)

PILI PILI SAUCE
(West Africa)

MAYONNAISE
(All Africa)

MAYONNAISE PILI PILI
Hot Mayonnaise *(Côte d'Ivoire)*

MOROCCAN SPICE MIXTURE
(Morocco)

DUKKAH
Egyptian Spice Mixture *(Egypt)*

WEST AFRICAN SPICE MIXTURE
(West Africa)

PEPPERCORN MIXTURE

ATA
Chile Sauce *(Nigeria)*

HOT SAUCE
(West Africa)

TRADITIONAL PEPPERSOUP SPICE MIXTURE
(Nigeria)

PEPPERSOUP SPICE MIXTURE
(Nigeria)

HILDAGONDA'S BLATJANG
(South Africa)

POIRES À L'AIGRE-DOUX
Sweet and Sour Pears *(Tunisia)*

APRICOT CHUTNEY
(South Africa)

✻

A Spice Market in Mombasa

Mombasa, Kenya's eye to the East on the Indian Ocean, is a city of contrast. While the rest of Kenya is culturally situated in Africa, parts of the old town of Mombasa seem to have been lifted from the Arabian Peninsula or transplanted from North Africa. Nowhere is this felt more strongly than in the twisting, turning alleyways where women covered from head to toe in black *buibuis* scurry from doorway to doorway like so many ravens.

This is the stronghold of the Swahili culture that can be seen all along the eastern coast of Africa. The markets of old Mombasa reflect this as well and are fragrant with the scent of spices from the dhow trade that brings the small lateen-sailed vessels from Yemen, Arabia, and even as far as India with the prevailing winds. Antiques shops boast sturdy vessels of hammered brass and thick iron-bound chests that look as though they could contain a king's ransom. It was in one such place that I found my spice box. The lingering fragrances that it captured impelled me to find a spice shop.

The shop was small and narrow and filled from rafters to floor with burlap sacks and baskets full of spices. The fragrance was one that I would have expected in Cairo or Fez, not in Kenya. It was dense with cumin and rich with curry powders, a touch of chile for heat and a wafting scent of mint. The aromas were wonderful. I attempted to match them to the ones that remained in my brass box with its seven compartments. There was a hint of garlic, a touch of caraway, the orange-yellow stain of turmeric. The search became a puzzle for the vendor, who rose to the occasion and presented me with small packets of just what I needed. As a parting package, and to signal that he'd enjoyed the fun as much as I had, he gave me a packet of a tea spice that was rich with a spicy blend and fragrant with black pepper. I've never been able to find one like it again and I'm not at all sure I can find my way back to the shop. Who knows? Perhaps I'll have as much fun trying to duplicate my last bit of tea spice with another merchant as I had filling my spice box with the merchant in Mombasa.

KHALATA LLI-L-SALATA

◎◉◎

SALAD DRESSING (EGYPT)

MAKES 3 TABLESPOONS

Place all the ingredients together in a small nonreactive bowl and whisk them until they are well mixed. Pour over whatever salad you select.

1 tablespoon olive oil

1 tablespoon freshly squeezed lemon juice

2 teaspoons cider vinegar

Salt and freshly ground black pepper,
    to taste

1 clove garlic, crushed

Pinch of cumin

Red pepper flakes, to taste

PAPAYA TREE

SALSIT KHALL BI-L-TOON
◎◎◎

GARLIC DRESSING (EGYPT)

This very tangy dressing is used on greens and on vegetables in Egypt. I've mellowed it out a bit by using cider vinegar instead of the tart distilled vinegar that is traditionally used. It's simple to prepare and adds a definite kick to whatever you serve it with. Just be sure that all your guests are lovers of the "stinking weed."   MAKES 2 TABLESPOONS

10 to 15 cloves garlic
Salt, to taste
1 tablespoon cider vinegar

Crush the garlic with the salt in a mortar and pestle or food processor until it is smooth. Add the vinegar a bit at a time and blend until you have an unctuous paste.

CLASSIC VINAIGRETTE
◎◎◎

(WEST AFRICA)

This is the classic recipe for vinaigrette. The French always say that vinaigrette requires a spendthrift for oil and a miser for vinegar. I would add: and someone creative to ring in the changes. You can personalize your vinaigrette with the addition of everything from a dash of sesame oil to a bit of minced garlic to a pinch of your favorite fresh herb or a change of oil or vinegar. Use this recipe as a starting point.   MAKES ABOUT ¾ CUP

3 tablespoons red wine vinegar
1 tablespoon balsamic vinegar
½ teaspoon Dijon-style mustard
Pinch of sugar
Salt and freshly ground black pepper, to
   taste
9 tablespoons extra-virgin olive oil

Combine all the ingredients except the olive oil in a small glass bowl and beat well with a fork or wire whisk. Gradually drizzle in the olive oil, making sure that all the ingredients are well mixed. Serve at once in a sauceboat or drizzle over the salad and toss.

NIT'IR QIBE

◎◎◎

SPICED BUTTER (ETHIOPIA)

A wide variety of cooking oils are used around the African continent. The Indians use ghee in their cooking, the Senegalese peanut oil, the Nigerians red palm oil. In Ethiopia a spiced clarified butter called nit'ir qibe *is used to season a range of dishes.*

MAKES 1 CUP

Toast the turmeric, cardamom, fenugreek, cinnamon, nutmeg, and clove by placing them in a heavy skillet over low heat, stirring occasionally, for 3 to 5 minutes, or until they are fragrant and roasted. Place the butter in a heavy saucepan and melt over low heat, stirring occasionally. Do not let the butter brown. When it is completely melted, bring it to a boil and skim off all the white foam. Mix the onion, garlic, and ginger together and add the mixture to the butter, along with the toasted spices. Continue to simmer gently over low heat for 20 minutes. Remove from the heat and allow it to stand until the spices settle. Then strain the *nit'ir qibe* into a large container, cover, and store in a cool place.

NOTE: See Glossary (page 59) and Mail-Order Sources (page 74) for fenugreek.

½ teaspoon turmeric

¼ teaspoon cardamom seeds

⅛ teaspoon ground fenugreek (see Note)

1 piece of stick cinnamon, ½ inch long

⅛ teaspoon freshly grated nutmeg

1 clove

1 pound unsalted butter, cut into small pieces

2 tablespoons chopped onion

1½ tablespoons minced garlic

2 teaspoons minced fresh ginger

HARISSA

◎◎◎

CHILE PASTE (ALGERIA)

This condiment is a must for those who love North African food. While harissa is available both in cans and in tubes, nothing has quite the taste of a homemade one. There are as many different recipes for harissa as there are cooks in North Africa, so this Algerian pied noir *version is just an outline. Improvise and come up with one of your own.*

MAKES ABOUT 1 CUP

½ pound fresh hot red chiles

1 head garlic

5 teaspoons caraway seeds

5 teaspoons coriander seeds

5 teaspoons cumin

1 tablespoon salt, or to taste

¼ cup extra-virgin olive oil

Slit the chiles open with a sharp paring knife and remove the seeds. Wash the chiles and allow them to drain for 1 hour in a colander. Peel the garlic and place it in the bowl of a food processor with the chiles. Place the caraway, coriander, cumin, and salt in the bowl of a spice mill and pulverize them to a fine powder. Add the seasonings to the food processor and pulse until you have a thick paste, drizzling in the olive oil a bit at a time. When ready, stir to make sure that the seasonings are well mixed, then spoon into a large jar. Pour a layer of olive oil over the top to preserve the harissa. Refrigerate. When ready to serve, spoon the harissa up through the olive oil.

QUICK HARISSA

◎◎◎

CHILE PASTE (TUNISIA)

Harissa is considered to be the national condiment of Tunisia. One cosmopolitan friend of mine so craves it that she begs for "care packages" of it when she cannot find it in her local supermarket. This quick version is most assuredly not authentic, but it will do in a pinch if you don't have time to prepare a batch of the real thing. MAKES ³/₄ CUP

Place the cayenne pepper in a small bowl. Place the remaining seasonings in the bowl of a spice mill and pulse until you have a fine powder. Add the powder to the cayenne pepper and drizzle in the olive oil, stirring constantly, until you have a thick paste. Place the harissa in a small jar and float a layer of olive oil on the top. Refrigerate. Use sparingly.

½ cup cayenne pepper

2 tablespoons cumin

1 tablespoon caraway seeds

1 tablespoon coriander seeds

1½ tablespoons olive oil

MOCTAR'S CHILE
◎◎◎

(SENEGAL)

Moctar Ndongo of Senegal, my late African suma mak *(big brother), was always served a small saucer with his meal. The saucer contained one habanero chile. Before eating he would carefully cut the chile in half and then quarters and proceed to cut the quarter into tiny pieces, which he would then sprinkle over whatever he was going to eat. While the amounts of chile that Moctar used were staggering to me, I heartily subscribe to his method, as it allows people to season the food to the heat that they desire. This, then, is not really a recipe, but a tribute to someone who was generous to me at the beginning of my trips down Africa's culinary roadways.*
SERVES 4 TO 6 OR MORE

1 habanero chile
1 saucer

This is an activity best accomplished by whoever is the resident chile head. This person gets custody of the saucer and carefully minces the habanero. The diners then each take as much as they wish. Alternatively (but this method lacks the ceremonial aspect), the chile can be minced in a food processor.

CHILE OIL
◎◎◎

(WEST AFRICA)

This simple preparation enhances the heat of several West African dishes. It's a quick way to preserve hot chiles and a way to add small amounts of fire to any dish.
MAKES 1 CUP

1 cup peanut oil
6 fresh bird chiles, or to taste (see
*   page 55)*

Place the chiles in the oil in a fancy cruet and allow them to rest for 1 week, until they have flavored the oil. Add a drop or two of the oil to your usual cooking oil for a special zap.

PRESERVED LEMONS

◎◎◎

(MOROCCO)

These lemons lend their unique flavor to many of my favorite Moroccan dishes. The soft skin of the lemon and the squishy flesh cannot be duplicated by anything. Pickled lemons are simple to prepare and will keep virtually indefinitely, if they last that long in your home. They don't in mine. The trick is to remember that the lemons must be covered with the lemon juice.

MAKES 6 PRESERVED LEMONS

With a sharp knife, slice the lemons into quarters, leaving the stem end intact so that the lemons will hold together. Rub 2 teaspoons of the salt into the flesh of one lemon, then re-form it and place it in a Mason jar. Continue the process with the remaining lemons until all have been processed. Press down on the lemons as you add them to the jar to release their juices. Then fill the jar with lemon juice to cover the lemons, leaving a bit of air space before sealing. Let the lemons cure in a cool space for about a month. When ready to serve, remove them from the jar, rinse, and add to your favorite Moroccan dish.

6 large lemons
¼ cup sea salt
Freshly squeezed lemon juice, if
necessary

A too modest man

goes hungry.

—ETHIOPIAN PROVERB

LIME ATJAR

◎◎◎

LIME PICKLE (SOUTH AFRICA)

Like preserved lemons in the North, in the cooking of Morocco, lime atjar *is a primary table condiment in the Malay food of South Africa.*

This recipe must be prepared eleven days before use.

MAKES 1 1/2 PINTS

12 limes
1 quart water
1 tablespoon kosher salt
1 pint Atjar marinade (opposite page)
⅓ cup mustard seeds
2 bay leaves

Wash the limes. Cut them into quarters with a sharp knife, discarding only a bit attached at the stem end. Place the limes in a large deep nonreactive bowl, cover them with the water and salt, and allow them to stand for 4 days at room temperature. Remove the limes and arrange them in sterilized canning jars. Bring the *atjar* marinade to a boil and add the mustard seeds and bay leaves. Pour the pickle mixture over the limes, seal, and refrigerate. Allow the pickles to sit for 1 week, then serve. They are eaten, skin and all, with southern African curries and other dishes.

ATJAR

◉◉◉

PICKLING MARINADE (SOUTH AFRICA)

Atjar, *a marinade for pickles, was brought to South Africa by the Cape Malay people, who are reputed to be some of that country's best cooks. It owes much of its taste to the achars of the Indian subcontinent, as witnessed by the use of fenugreek, turmeric, and curry.*

MAKES 1 PINT

Place the anchovy fillets and oil and the garlic in the bowl of a food processor and pulse until you have a thin liquid paste. Pour the paste into a small saucepan. Add the other ingredients and bring the *atjar* to a boil over medium heat. The *atjar* is ready to use for the Lime Atjar *(opposite page)* and similar recipes.

NOTE: See Glossary (page 59) and Mail-Order Sources (page 74) for fenugreek.

3 flat anchovy fillets and the oil from
   the can
3 cloves garlic
1 teaspoon ground fenugreek
   (see Note)
1 teaspoon turmeric
1 teaspoon minced habanero chile, or to
   taste (see page 55)
3 tablespoons Madras-type curry
   powder
1 pint vegetable oil

WORTEL SAMBAL
◎◎◎

CARROT SAMBAL (SOUTH AFRICA)

Here carrots are cooked in a spicy marinade to form a thick paste, the sweetness of the carrot contrasting with heat of the spices.

SERVES 6 TO 8

1 pound carrots, peeled and trimmed

2 green cardamom pods

1 dried hot red chile

1 tablespoon minced fresh ginger

1 clove garlic, minced

1 teaspoon sea salt

1½ cups sugar

½ cup water

¾ cup distilled white vinegar

Grate the carrots on the large holes of a hand grater or by putting them through the medium-shredding blade of a food processor. Remove the seeds from the cardamom pods and grind them into a powder in a spice mill along with the dried chile. Place all the ingredients except the vinegar in a 3-quart nonreactive saucepan, bring to boil, and cook, stirring occasionally, for 30 minutes. Add the vinegar, lower the heat, and cook for an additional 30 minutes, or until thick. Be sure to stir well so that the sambal doesn't stick to the bottom of the saucepan. When the sambal is a thick paste, spoon it out of the saucepan into a bowl. Cover it with plastic wrap and refrigerate for at least 1 hour. Serve chilled with curries and grilled meats.

KOMKOMER SAMBAL

◎◎◎

CUCUMBER SAMBAL (SOUTH AFRICA)

This sambal is a table condiment to accompany the spicy Cape Malay foods of South Africa. It is eaten after the food to cleanse the palate. Perhaps because no oil is used, it refreshes the diner—although a fair amount of hot chile is used as an ingredient. This cucumber sambal may be served as a salad as well. In that case, it becomes komkomer slaai, *and the cucumbers are thinly sliced instead of being grated.*   SERVES 6

Grate the cucumbers on the large holes of a hand grater into a glass salad bowl. Sprinkle them with the salt and let them stand for 2 hours, then drain them, pressing out all the liquid. Add the remaining ingredients and mix well. Cover with plastic wrap and chill for 1 hour. Serve chilled.

3 medium-sized fresh cucumbers, peeled and seeded

1 teaspoon sea salt

1 tablespoon cider vinegar

1 clove garlic, finely minced

1 teaspoon finely minced jalapeño chile (see page 55)

PICKLED OLIVES
◎◉◎

(WEST AFRICA)

During the 1960s yet another group of travelers hit the African continent and brought changes in matters culinary. This time they were neither missionaries nor colonizers, but rather young men and women from the campuses of the United States, traveling to the continent under the banner of the Peace Corps. They too had their cooking hints and knew how to make do when WAWA struck (WAWA is an acronym for West Africa Wins Again!). This is a trick that they used to transform the canned olives that they could occasionally get into something special.　　SERVES 6 TO 8

1 pound picholine or other green olives

3 cloves garlic, slivered

1 bay leaf

2 fresh hot chiles, or to taste (see page 55)

1 tablespoon dried oregano

¼ cup extra-virgin olive oil

¼ cup vegetable oil

Drain the olives, then make a small incision in each one. Place the olives in a sterilized jar with the remaining ingredients and close tightly. Keep the olives in a cool, dark place for 3 days. Serve with drinks.

PILI PILI SAUCE
◎◎◎

(WEST AFRICA)

This condiment is found on tables throughout western Africa and is combined with other ingredients to form cocktail sauces and mayonnaise (see page 146). Here is the basic recipe.

MAKES 2 CUPS

Mix all the ingredients together in a small bowl. Pour into a sterilized jar that can be tightly covered. Store in the refrigerator and serve with everything from grilled meats to sandwiches.

4 large tomatoes, peeled, seeded, and
   coarsely chopped
¼ cup minced onion
2 cloves garlic, minced
1 habanero chile, minced, or to taste
   (see page 55)
1 tablespoon prepared horseradish

STREET FOOD

MAYONNAISE
◎◎◎

(ALL AFRICA)

If you've never tasted homemade mayonnaise, you've missed a special treat. Whisk some up in a bowl or a blender. You'll never go back. The taste of the olive oil will change the taste of the mayonnaise. For an interesting and thoroughly West African twist on mayonnaise, add a few drops of red palm oil to the olive oil as you drizzle it into the egg.

MAKES ABOUT 1 1/2 CUPS

2 large eggs yolks
Salt, to taste
½ teaspoon dried mustard
Pinch of sugar
Pinch of cayenne pepper
4 teaspoons freshly squeezed lemon juice
1½ cups extra-virgin olive oil
1 teaspoon hot water

Place the egg yolks, salt, mustard, sugar, and cayenne and 3 teaspoons of the lemon juice in the bowl of a blender or food processor and mix on slow speed for 10 seconds. Gradually increase the blender speed while slowly drizzling in the olive oil. As the mixture begins to thicken, continue to add the oil, alternating it with a mixture of 1 teaspoon hot water and the remaining lemon juice. Chill and serve. Do not keep, but remake as necessary.

NOTE: Raw eggs carry the risk of salmonella. Foods prepared with raw eggs should not be served to the very young, the very old, or anyone with an impaired immune system.

MAYONNAISE PILI PILI

◉◉◉

HOT MAYONNAISE (CÔTE D'IVOIRE)

It was my fortune to be in Côte d'Ivoire soon after the opening of the Hôtel Ivoire. It was a marvel that drew numerous visitors, both foreign and Ivoirian, to eat in the six restaurants and just walk through the lobby. The coffee-shop restaurant in the basement took the name of the spicy mayonnaise that is served with some of their dishes.   MAKES 1 CUP

Mix the ingredients together and use on cold salads and anywhere that mayonnaise might be called for. This mayonnaise gives a special zing to chicken salad or coleslaw and is great with seafood cocktails.

1 cup freshly made mayonnaise
    (page 146)
1 tablespoon Pili Pili Sauce
    (page 145)

MOROCCAN SPICE MIXTURE

◉◉◉

(MOROCCO)

This is a mixture that I use at home that brings some of the flavors of Morocco to everyday cooking. I use it on roasted lamb (page 247) and on grilled lamb chops. It also works with chicken or fish that's going under the broiler.
    MAKES SLIGHTLY MORE THAN ¼ CUP

Place all the ingredients together in a spice mill or a mortar and pulverize until coarsely ground. This mixture will keep for several weeks in a tightly closed container.

1½ teaspoons coriander seeds
1 tablespoon cumin seeds
½ tablespoon caraway seeds
3 tablespoons dried mint leaves
3-inch piece stick cinnamon

DUKKAH
◎◎◎

EGYPTIAN SPICE MIXTURE (EGYPT)

This spice mixture is a staple in Egyptian households. Bread is usually dipped into olive oil and then the spices, or sometimes just into the spices. It is eaten at breakfast, as an appetizer, or as a snack at any time. The number of varieties is endless. Dukkah is usually made in large quantities and stored in jars. This recipe will make only a small amount, but you can simply expand the proportions for more. You should also improvise with the amounts of each spice to personalize your mixture.

MAKES 1 ¹/₂ CUPS

¼ cup coriander seeds
¼ cup unsalted peanuts
1 tablespoon cumin seeds
2 tablespoons sesame seeds
2 tablespoons dried chickpeas
½ cup salt
2 tablespoons dried mint leaves
1 teaspoon black peppercorns

Roast the coriander seeds, peanuts, cumin, and sesame seeds separately by placing them in a heavy skillet over medium heat and stirring them with a wooden spoon until they release a full aroma. Times will vary per spice; your nose should be your guide. When all the seeds are roasted, place all the ingredients in a mortar and pound until the seeds are finely crushed. You can use a food processor, but be careful not to allow the mixture to become a paste. Pour the mixture into a jar and seal tightly. It will keep for several weeks at room temperature.

WEST AFRICAN SPICE MIXTURE

◉◉◉

(WEST AFRICA)

The heat of West African cooking and the flavors of many of the region's traditional seasonings come together in this fiery mix, which is good on grilled meats or in stews. Be careful. A tiny dab will do you.

MAKES ABOUT 3 TABLESPOONS

Place all the ingredients together in the bowl of a spice grinder or a mortar and pulvarize until you have a fine powder. Use sparingly. This will keep for several weeks in a tightly closed container.

NOTE: See Glossary (page 57) and Mail-Order Sources (page 74).

1 tablespoon Peppercorn Mixture (page 150)

½ tablespoon Nigerian ground ginger or regular ground ginger

½ tablespoon grains of paradise (see page 60)

½ teaspoon red pepper flakes

1 teaspoon cubebs (see Note)

Pinch of powdered dried habanero chile

PEPPERCORN MIXTURE

◎◎◎

This is a mixture that uses a few traditional African spices to add an extra je ne sais quoi *to your pepper mill.*

MAKES ABOUT ³/₄ CUP

¼ cup Tellicherry peppercorns
   (see Note)
¼ cup Muntok white peppercorns
   (see Note)
2 tablespoons freeze-dried green
   peppercorns (see Note)
1 tablespoon pink peppercorns
   (see Note)
1 tablespoon Jamaican allspice berries
1 tablespoon cubebs (see Note)

Mix all the ingredients together in a bowl and then place them in your pepper mill. Any leftover mixture can be stored in a tightly closed jar for several months.

NOTE: See Glossary (pages 67 and 68) for peppercorns and page 57 for cubebs, and Mail-Order Sources (page 74) for both.

PREPARING PALM OIL

ATA

◎◎◎

CHILE SAUCE (NIGERIA)

This sauce is a Nigerian classic that turns up as an addition to everything from mayonnaise to salad dressing. It is also used individually as a sauce to spice up beans, fried plantains, boiled and mashed yam, and other bland dishes.

MAKES ABOUT 1 1/2 CUPS

Cook the onion and garlic in the oil in a heavy skillet for 5 minutes, or until they are lightly browned. Place the chopped tomatoes and the chiles in the bowl of a food processor and pulse until they are a thick paste. Add the paste to the skillet along with the remaining ingredients and cook over low heat for 15 minutes, or until most of the liquid has evaporated and the mixture is almost dry. Adjust the seasonings and allow the mixture to cool. The *ata* can then be spooned into plastic bags and refrigerated or frozen until ready to use.

1 small onion, minced

2 cloves garlic, minced

3 tablespoons peanut oil

¼ pound ripe tomatoes, peeled, seeded, and coarsely chopped

¼ pound fresh hot chiles

1½ tablespoons tomato paste

½ teaspoon dried thyme

½ teaspoon hot Madras curry powder

Salt, to taste

HOT SAUCE
◎◎◎

(WEST AFRICA)

This all-purpose hot sauce can be served with Akara (page 86–88) or with almost anything that can use a dash of liquid fire. The heat and the taste will depend on the type of chile you use. I prefer a mix of habanero and bird chiles, but pili pili chiles are good as well.   MAKES ABOUT 1 1/2 CUPS

3 tablespoons peanut oil

1 medium onion, chopped fine

Minced habanero chile, to taste (see page 55)

2 minced fresh bird chiles, or to taste (see page 55)

½ cup tomato paste

½ cup water

Salt and freshly ground black pepper, to taste

Heat the oil in a heavy skillet and fry the onion until it is browned. Add the minced chiles. Combine the tomato paste and the water and add it to the mixture. Let the sauce simmer over low heat for 5 minutes. Add salt and pepper to taste, let cool to room temperature, and serve.

TRADITIONAL PEPPERSOUP SPICE MIXTURE

◎◎◎

(NIGERIA)

This mixture of spices provides the seasoning in Nigeria's famous (or is that infamous?) peppersoups. The traditional ingredients that are called for are only available in stores selling Nigerian or African products. I have included this recipe so that you can see the world of new tastes that are yet to be discovered.

Mix all the ingredients together and grind them in a mortar and pestle or in a spice mill. Store the peppersoup spices in a tightly closed clean glass jar.

1 tablespoon atariko
1 tablespoon uda
1 tablespoon gbafilo
1 tablespoon ground ginger
1 tablespoon uyayak
1 tablespoon rigije

PEPPERSOUP SPICE MIXTURE
◎◎◎

(NIGERIA)

Now, if the traditional recipe for peppersoup spices reads like Martian, here's an alternative that was invented by homesick Nigerians. Anise pepper is also known as Szechuan or Sichuan pepper and can be found in ethnic or gourmet food stores. Also see Mail-Order Sources, page 74. MAKES ABOUT ¹/₂ CUP

1 tablespoon anise seeds

1 tablespoon coriander seeds

1 tablespoon cumin seeds

1 tablespoon allspice berries

1 tablespoon ground ginger

1 tablespoon fennel seeds

1 tablespoon anise pepper

1 tablespoon dried tamarind pulp
   (see Note)

1 teaspoon whole cloves

Mix all the ingredients together in a bowl. Place them in a spice mill and pulse until they are pulverized. Spoon the peppersoup spice mixture into a clean glass jar and cover tightly. While the peppersoup spice mixture will keep virtually indefinitely, the spices will lose their bite over time, so it is better to make a small batch at first and then increase the amount made as you use it more often.

NOTE: Tamarind pulp is available in Asian, Indian, and West Indian stores and through mail order (page 74).

HILDAGONDA'S BLATJANG
◎◎◎

(SOUTH AFRICA)

Hildagonda Duckitt was a very practical South African lady who was born in 1840 on a farm called Groote Post near Darling in the Cape region of South Africa. She was active in the social life of the Constantia area and began to collect the recipes of her native region while she was in her teens. One thousand copies of her cookbook, entitled Hilda's "Where Is It?" of Recipes, *were published in March 1891. The book, which is arranged in alphabetical order, is a presentation of Cape, Indian, and Malay dishes and preserves, and also includes a compendium of directions for polishing furniture and cleaning silk and a collection of home remedies for the sick. There were 28,000 copies in print by March 1914. One of my prized African cookbooks is a pristine copy of the 1914 edition in which I found the recipe that inspired Hildagonda's* blatjang, *a Cape Malay condiment.*

MAKES ABOUT ¹/₂ CUP

Remove the seeds and membranes from the chiles and place them in the bowl of a food processor. Pulse until you have a thick paste. Peel the onions, prick them with a fork and cook them in the microwave on high power for 2 to 3 minutes. Quarter them and add along with the remaining ingredients to the bowl of the food processor. Pulse until you have a thick paste. Serve as a condiment with grilled meats and Cape Malay dishes. Prepare this fresh each time, as it does not store well.

2 fresh hot red chiles
2 medium onions, peeled
2½ tablespoons freshly squeezed lemon juice
2 tablespoons almond paste
1 tablespoon apricot jam
2 teaspoons minced dried apricots
3 small cloves garlic
2 bay leaves

Poires à l'Aigre=Doux
◎◎◎

SWEET AND SOUR PEARS (TUNISIA)

These pears almost have the taste of my grandmother's, but I can assure you that she never got close to Tunisia in her lifetime. While Grandma Jones's pickled pears accompanied roasts and holiday dishes, these are traditionally used to accompany boiled meats and tajines. You can use this same process with melon or apples to create your own sweet-and-sour side dishes.

The pears must be started three days ahead.   SERVES 6 TO 8

2 pounds Seckel pears
2 quarts apple cider vinegar
4 sticks cinnamon (each 3 inches long)
6 whole cloves
2 cups confectioners' sugar

Peel the pears and place them in a saucepan with water to cover. Bring the water slowly to a boil and cook the pears until they are fork-tender but still firm. Drain the pears and place them in a large canning jar or crock. Place the remaining ingredients in a nonreactive saucepan and bring them slowly to a boil, stirring occasionally. When the mixture comes to a boil, pour it over the pears and allow them to marinate for 24 hours in the crock, refrigerated. Pour off the liquid into a nonreactive saucepan and bring it to a boil once again. When it is boiling, pour it over the pears again. Do this a total of three times, marinating for 24 hours each time, until the pears are impregnated with the essence of the liquid. Allow the pears to come to room temperature, seal the jar, and refrigerate. Serve the pears to accompany tajines or along with any roast, the way my Grandma Jones did.

APRICOT CHUTNEY

◎◎◎

(SOUTH AFRICA)

The chutneys, sambals, and atjars *of South Africa are part of that country's inheritance from the immigrants from India and Southeast Asia. This one uses the apricots that grow in the orchards that surround Capetown.*

MAKES APPROXIMATELY 2 CUPS

Place the dried apricots in a medium-sized bowl with water to cover. Allow them to soak for 1 hour, then drain them, reserving ¼ cup of the soaking liquid. Place the soaked apricots, fresh apricots, garlic, chiles, and ginger in the bowl of a food processor and pulse until you have a thick paste. Place the paste in a saucepan with the reserved water and the remaining ingredients and stir to mix well. Bring the mixture to a boil, then lower the heat and cook for about 30 minutes, stirring occasionally, or until the chutney thickens. Remove the chutney from the heat and spoon it into sterilized jars. The chutney will keep for a few days in the refrigerator. If you are going to make larger batches of the chutney, sterilize and process in a water bath according to proper canning procedure.

1½ cups dried apricots

4 fresh apricots, pitted

1 clove garlic, minced

3 fresh bird chiles, or to taste (see page 55)

1 thumb-sized piece fresh ginger

½ cup apple cider vinegar

½ cup sugar

VEGETABLES

◎◎◎

Lots and Lots of Leafy Greens

That the traditional African diet is basically vegetarian comes as a surprise to many (though anthropologists and scholars have commented on this for centuries). The range of greens is wide; *meloukhia* in the north and all manner of leafy greens in the western and eastern sections. Eggplant leaves, pumpkin leaves, bitter leaf, and others known only as *utazi* and *ukazi* all go into the pot and are transformed into rich stews. Vegetables range from the pumpkins and gourds that were eaten in pre–Columbian Exchange Africa to the corn, hominy, bell peppers, chiles, and tomatoes that go into most pots today. Those looking at the recipes of the continent quickly learn that Africa is an unheralded vegetarian paradise.

◎◎◎

KOSA MA'LIYA
Fried Zucchini *(Egypt)*

AWIRMA MASHWIYA
Baked Pearl Onions *(Egypt)*

MASHED EGGPLANT À LA ZEINAB
(Sudan)

FRIED EGGPLANT
(Kenya)

BATTER-FRIED EGGPLANT
(South Africa)

PUMPKIN FRITTERS
(South Africa)

CURRIED CABBAGE
(Kenya)

GESMOORDE KOOL
Braised Cabbage *(South Africa)*

IKELEKO
Samp *(South Africa)*

UMNGQUSHO
Samp and Cowpea Stew *(South Africa)*

SAMP AND TOMATOES
(Kenya)

IBHAQOLO IBANGQA
Corn on the Cob *(South Africa)*

CURRIED CORN
(Kenya)

MAÏS GRILLÉ
Grilled Corn *(All Africa)*

ABROW NE KOKOSI
Boiled Corn with Coconut *(Ghana)*

ABROW NE NKATE
Corn with Peanuts *(Ghana)*

ABROW NE ASE
Boiled Corn and Beans *(Ghana)*

IRIO
Stewed Vegetables *(Kenya)*

BOILED CALABAZA
(Kenya)

SAUTÉED CALABAZA
(Kenya)

CALABAZA AND TOMATOES
(Kenya)

SPINACH AND CALABAZA
(Kenya)

CAPE MALAY CALABAZA
(South Africa)

NKATE
Boiled Peanuts *(Ghana)*

NDIZI
Spicy Plantains *(Kenya)*

BOLI-BOPA
Grilled Plantains with Peanuts *(Nigeria)*

CURRIED VEGETABLES
(South Africa)

SMOOR TOMATOES AND ONIONS
(South Africa)

TOMATES FARCIES AUX ANCHOIS
Anchovy-Stuffed Tomatoes *(North Africa)*

GERBRAAIDE PATATS
Baked Sweet Potatoes *(South Africa)*

YEQEY SIR QIQQIL
Boiled Beets *(Ethiopia)*

YE'ABESHA GOMEN
Collard Greens *(Ethiopia)*

ZELBO GOMEN
Boiled Kale *(Ethiopia)*

STEAMED OKRA
(All Africa)

BAMIA MASLOUKAH
Egyptian-Style Boiled Okra *(Egypt)*

BAMYA ALICH'A
Ethiopian-Style Okra *(Ethiopia)*

BAMIA
Sweet and Sour Okra *(Egypt)*

SAUCE GOMBO
Okra Sauce *(Benin)*

STEAMED SPINACH
(All Africa)

OULA'ASS FEE EL FORN
Baked Whole Rutabaga *(Egypt)*

FUL MEDAMES
Egyptian-Style Broad Beans *(Egypt)*

BEIGNETS DE CHOUFLEUR
Cauliflower Fritters *(Algeria)*

✳

The Farm Market in Constantia

I've visited many parts of the African continent, and anyone who knows me knows that I'm never as happy as when I am walking through an open-air marketplace. I've strolled the endless rows of vendors in the Dan Tkopa in Benin. I've wandered through the souks of Fez and the spice markets of Cairo. South Africa, though, was a different sort of Africa—one where the First World met up with the Third World and where the stalls and the sights were at the same time familiar and different.

The road to Constantia took me out of Capetown, and while we were gliding along a superhighway, I was conscious that not far away antelopes were cavorting in the park that ran alongside the road. The houses looked like many of the step-gabled ones I'd seen in the Netherlands and on the other side of the Atlantic, in Curaçao.

The farm stand in Constantia was an indoor/outdoor venue that looked more like those I'd shopped at on drives in the United States, but there all similarity ended. The stand boasted the most wonderful array of products from the temperate and tropical zones: Plump fresh apricots lined up next to magnificent mounds of potatoes, strawberries I could snack on as we rode. The wonderfully fresh greens made me long for a kitchen. There were all manner of preserves, from the *meebos* or dried apricot and passion-fruit paste that is traditional to the cooking of the Cape to spicy chutneys and Cape gooseberry jams. The shelves overflowed. There was sea salt scented with black pepper and celery named for the Khoisan peoples who were some of the original inhabitants of the region, and new products like *rooibos* tea (which, I was assured, had no caffeine), and *waterblommetjie,* the water-blooming plants that turn up in a lush, rich Cape Malay soup. The cornucopia of South African bounty made me understand why the land had been selected as a provisioning post by the Dutch centuries ago. The multiplicity of ingredients and the varying cultures that they represented let me know that whatever difficulties this nation may encounter politically, the foods do come together on the table.

KOSA MA'LIYA
◉◉◉

FRIED ZUCCHINI (EGYPT)

While it is thought that wild squashes may have originated in Central America, the zucchini is Italian in origin. This summer squash is also much loved by peoples living in the Mediterranean Basin, however, and the Egyptians are no exception. Sautéed, rolled, stuffed with various ingredients, zucchini turns up on tables around the country. Perhaps one of the favorite ways of preparing it is fried.　SERVES 4 TO 6

Peel and slice the zucchini, place it in a colander, sprinkle it with salt, and allow it to sit for 1 hour. Preheat the oil for frying to 375 degrees in a heavy Dutch oven or deep fryer. Pat the zucchini slices dry on absorbent paper. Use one slice to test the oil to make sure that it is hot enough, then fry the zucchini a few slices at a time. Allow the slices to drain on absorbent paper, then transfer them to a serving dish. Drizzle the garlic dressing over the zucchini and mash with a fork. Cover with plastic wrap and refrigerate for 30 minutes. Sprinkle the parsley over the top of the dish and serve.

1 pound large zucchini
Oil for deep frying
2 tablespoons Garlic Dressing
　(page 134)
1 tablespoon minced parsley, for garnish

Awirma Mashwiya

◎◎◎

BAKED PEARL ONIONS (EGYPT)

Onions have a long history in Egyptian cooking. The onion was used in Ancient Egypt to pay tribute to the gods. Those who labored on the building of the pyramids were likely to find them in their lunch pails along with bread, beer, and radishes. Onion remains have even been found in the tomb of King Tutankhamen. Pyramid texts from the Old Kingdom speak of onions as being like white teeth. Ancient onions were smaller and milder than our present species and are probably best approximated by the small pearl onions that are used in this traditional recipe.   SERVES 4

1 pound pearl onions

Preheat the oven to 350 degrees. Place the onions in an ovenproof bowl and bake them for 1 hour. Remove them from the oven, peel off the skins, and serve hot.

Good millet is known

at the harvest.

—KENYAN PROVERB

MASHED EGGPLANT À LA ZEINAB
◎◎◎

(SUDAN)

I spent about a year begging my friend Debbie Mack, who spent several years living in the Sudan, for recipes from that country. Finally, she gave me a copy on a tattered piece of paper dated 6/17/80. On it, amid to-do notes of reports long since rendered and undecipherable jottings in Arabic, was a variation of this recipe. SERVES 4 TO 6

Wash the eggplant, peel it, and slice it lengthwise into ½-inch-thick slices. Place the slices in a bowl and sprinkle with the salt. Weight them by placing a plate on top of them and then adding a heavy can or two to press it down. Allow them to sit for 2 hours. (This will help the eggplant to expel some of its liquid and bitterness.) Discard the liquid and pat the eggplant dry with paper towels. Heat the oil in a heavy skillet and fry the eggplant slices, a few at a time, for 5 minutes, turning once. Place the cooked slices in a serving dish. When all the slices are fried, mix the remaining ingredients together and pour them over the eggplant slices. Mash with a fork and serve warm with wedges of pita bread.

2 pounds eggplant

2 teaspoons salt, or to taste

2 tablespoons olive oil

¼ teaspoon ground coriander

1 tablespoon freshly squeezed lemon juice

2 tablespoons crunchy peanut butter

Salt and red pepper flakes, to taste

FRIED EGGPLANT

◎◎◎

(KENYA)

Eggplants are sometimes called garden eggs in some English-speaking parts of Africa. African eggplant can vary in size and color. Most are small and purplish, although there is even a small green variety. This dish is a simple one that doesn't depend too much on the special taste of Africa's eggplants, so you can make it using the large eggplants that are found in almost any supermarket. In Kenya, these fried eggplant pieces are sometimes added to meat stews.   SERVES 6

2 medium eggplants, peeled and cut into 1- to 2-inch slices
¼ cup peanut oil
Salt and freshly ground black pepper, to taste

Place the eggplant slices in a medium-sized saucepan with water to cover. Bring to a boil, cover, lower the heat, and cook for 5 to 7 minutes, or until the eggplant is soft. Drain the eggplant slices. Heat the peanut oil in a heavy skillet. Pat the eggplant slices dry with absorbent paper and fry them in the oil for 2 to 3 minutes, turning once, so that they are brown and crisp. Drain on absorbent paper, season with salt and pepper, and serve hot.

BATTER=FRIED EGGPLANT
◎◎◎

(SOUTH AFRICA)

Eggplant is eaten virtually all over the continent. In South Africa it goes by the name brinjal. Brinjal *is the anglicization of the Hindu* baingan. *Here it is fried in a savory batter.*

SERVES 4

Wash the eggplants and cut them into 1-inch slices. Place them in a bowl, sprinkle them with the salt, and allow them to sit for 15 minutes to render some of their liquid and bitterness. Heat the oil for frying in a heavy skillet over high heat and prepare a batter by mixing together the remaining ingredients. When ready to fry, drop the eggplant slices, a few at a time, into the batter, making sure that they are well coated, and fry, turning once, for 3 to 5 minutes on each side. Drain on absorbent paper and serve hot.

2 large eggplants
¼ teaspoon salt
½ cup vegetable oil for frying
2 cups flour
½ teaspoon baking powder
1 teaspoon ground cumin
1 teaspoon ground coriander
1 teaspoon hot chile powder
1½ cups water
1 tablespoon vegetable oil

PUMPKIN FRITTERS
◎◎◎

(SOUTH AFRICA)

The early Dutch settlers brought many of their culinary habits with them from the cold north to the more temperate climate of the region surrounding Capetown. Pumpkin was one of the tastes that lingered on their palates. In South Africa the flat white Boer pumpkin is traditionally used, but the more readily available calabaza, or West Indian cooking pumpkin, can be substituted. Acorn squash can also be used in a pinch.

Make cinnamon sugar by mixing two parts sugar and one part ground cinnamon. It can be kept in a tightly sealed jar for months.

SERVES 8 TO 10

5 cups cooked calabaza
2 cups grated raw calabaza
1 teaspoon baking powder
½ cup flour
⅛ teaspoon ground cinnamon, or
    to taste
Pinch of salt
1 egg
Vegetable oil for deep frying
Cinnamon sugar, for dusting

Place the cooked pumpkin in a mixing bowl, mash it with a fork, and set it aside. Blanch the grated pumpkin by briefly dipping it in boiling water. Drain it and add it to the mashed pumpkin. Add the baking powder, flour, ground cinnamon, salt, and egg to the mixture and beat until it is smooth.

Heat the oil for deep frying in a heavy Dutch oven or deep fryer to 375 degrees. When hot, drop in the batter a tablespoonful at a time. Be careful not to place too many in the oil at once, as this will slow down the cooking time. Cook the fritters until golden brown on each side, turning once. Drain on absorbent paper. Place the fritters on a platter to serve and sprinkle with cinnamon sugar. Serve warm.

CURRIED CABBAGE

◎◎◎

(KENYA)

Kenya's coast has long traded with the countries to the east. In season, the port of Mombasa is dotted with the lateen sails of the dhows that ply the Indian Ocean. The influence of Arabia and the East is felt in the spices that are available in the market and in the taste of curry that lingers in many of the dishes, like this curried cabbage. SERVES 4 TO 6

Cut the cabbage into 1-inch slices and separate the leaves into pieces. Place the cabbage in a heavy skillet with the water and cook, covered, over medium heat for 20 minutes, or until the cabbage is fork-tender. While the cabbage is cooking, melt the butter in a second skillet and sauté the onions until they are translucent. Add the flour and the curry powder, stirring to make sure they are well mixed. Cook for 2 to 3 minutes, then add the milk and continue to cook until the sauce is smooth. When the cabbage is cooked, drain it and place it in a serving dish. Pour the curry sauce over it and serve hot.

1 medium cabbage
½ cup water
2 tablespoons butter
3 large onions, coarsely chopped
1 tablespoon flour
1 tablespoon hot Madras curry powder
½ cup milk

GESMOORDE KOOL
◉◉◉

BRAISED CABBAGE (SOUTH AFRICA)

The cabbage of northern Europe rounds the Cape of Good Hope to meet up with the ginger and chile of the East in this braised cabbage dish.

3 tablespoons butter

2 medium onions, thinly sliced

1 clove garlic, crushed

1 minced fresh bird chile, or to taste
   (see Note)

2 slices fresh ginger

1 medium cabbage, shredded

Place 2 tablespoons of the butter in a heavy skillet and heat it until it foams. Add the onion slices, crushed garlic, chile, and ginger and cook, stirring occasionally, until the onion is lightly browned. Add the shredded cabbage and the remaining 1 tablespoon of butter and cook for 10 to 15 minutes over low heat, or until the cabbage is soft. Serve hot.

NOTE: See Glossary (page 55) and Mail-Order Sources (page 74).

IKELEKO

◉◉◉

SAMP (SOUTH AFRICA)

Samp, or coarsely ground hominy corn, is a popular dish in South Africa, where it goes under many names. It is called ikeleko in Xhosa, setampo in Sotho, and matutu in Venda. It is traditionally prepared by pounding corn kernels in a mortar or on a grinding stone and then winnowing away the chaff. Ikeleko is traditionally served with a pat of butter or other fat added to the dish prior to serving. It usually accompanies meat dishes.

In this recipe, the samp needs to soak for 24 hours before preparation.

SERVES 4 TO 6

Wash the samp and pick through it to make sure that there are no stones or other impurities. Place the samp in a large saucepan with water to cover and allow it to sit for 24 hours. When ready to prepare, drain the samp and add the 6 cups fresh water. Bring the samp to a boil over medium heat, then lower the heat and simmer, covered, for about 1½ hours, or until soft. Drain any remaining water. Season with salt to taste and serve hot.

NOTE: Canned samp, which is carried by many supermarkets, can be substituted in any recipe calling for cooked samp. In Hispanic markets, samp is known as pozole.

3 cups samp (white hominy corn) (see Note)
6 cups water
Salt, to taste

UMNGQUSHO
◎◎◎

SAMP AND COWPEA STEW (SOUTH AFRICA)

This is another Xhosa variation on the South African culinary theme of samp, with additional ingredients. The cowpea is indigenous to the African continent. If you cannot find cowpeas, the larger black-eyed pea or any other bean can be substituted. The samp and cowpeas need to soak overnight before preparation.   SERVES 6 TO 8

2 cups samp (white hominy corn) (see Note)
1 cup dried cowpeas

Soak the samp and beans overnight in water to cover. When ready to cook, drain them and add fresh water to cover. Bring to a boil over high heat, then lower the heat to low and allow them to simmer, covered, for 1½ hours, or until they are cooked and most of the water has been absorbed. Drain and serve hot.

VARIATION: Reduce the amount of cowpeas to ¾ cup. Just prior to serving, add ½ cup coarsely chopped roasted peanuts.

NOTE: Canned samp, which is carried by many supermarkets, can be substituted in any recipe calling for cooked samp. In Hispanic markets, samp is known as pozole.

SAMP AND TOMATOES

◎◎◎

(KENYA)

Samp, the large-grained hominy that is called pozole in Mexico, makes an appearance in the cooking of the African-American South and in some of the dishes of sub-Saharan Africa. Samp is very popular in these areas because preserving corn as hominy is one of the simplest ways to keep it for long periods. This method was transported from the New World to the Old World along with the corn. The result is dishes like this Kenyan recipe for samp and tomatoes. SERVES 6

Heat the oil in a heavy saucepan, add the onion slices, and cook them until they are lightly browned. Add the remaining ingredients and cook, stirring occasionally, for 10 minutes. Serve hot.

NOTE: Canned samp, which is carried by many supermarkets, can be substituted in any recipe calling for cooked samp. In Hispanic markets, samp is known as pozole.

1 tablespoon peanut oil

2 medium onions, thinly sliced

6 medium-sized ripe tomatoes, peeled, seeded, and coarsely chopped

2 cups cooked samp (white hominy corn) (see Note)

Salt, to taste

IBHAQOLO IBANGQA

◎◎◎

CORN ON THE COB (SOUTH AFRICA)

Corn on the cob did not exist on the African continent prior to the Columbian Exchange, but you'd never know that from the amount of corn that is consumed in South Africa. The corn served in most areas of Africa tends to be more like the field corn from the United States, so we benefit by using the sweet corn that is at its prime in the summer months. Mealie, as corn is known in South Africa, comes to the table in all forms, from freshly harvested and on the cob to samp. This dish, which is called lehlabula la lefela *in Pedi and* infuto *in Zulu and Swazi, is familiar to most Americans as a summer dinner ac-companiment. For more zing, season your corn with a mixture of chile powder and salt.* SERVES 6

6 large ears fresh corn
Butter, salt, and chile powder, to taste

Bring 2 quarts of water to a rolling boil in a heavy saucepan or Dutch oven. Strip the corn of its green husks and its silk and place the ears in the boiling water. Cook for 5 minutes. Serve hot and season to taste with butter, salt, and chile powder.

CURRIED CORN
◎◎◎

(KENYA)

Although corn is a New World vegetable, it has been taken to the heart of much of Africa. It turns up in a variety of ways throughout the continent, from South Africa's mealies to East Africa's ugalis to West Africa's maïs grillé. Kenya, in eastern Africa, offers a cornucopia of cultures and cuisines to those who venture there, from the simple dishes of the Kikuyu to the complex curries and biryanis of the coastal Swahili culture. This dish is what happens when Africa's love of corn meets the spices of Kenya's coast.

If corn is not in season, you can use an equal amount of defrosted frozen corn.

SERVES 6 TO 8

Place the butter in a heavy saucepan and heat over medium heat until foaming. Add the onion and the garlic and cook, stirring occasionally, until they are lightly browned. Add the curry powder, stirring to make sure that the onions and garlic are well coated with the curry butter. Add the corn and continue cooking. Combine the cornstarch and coconut milk in a small bowl and add them to the saucepan along with the remaining ingredients, stirring well to distribute the liquid evenly. Lower the heat and cook, stirring occasionally, for 7 minutes, or until the coconut milk is almost all absorbed.

1 tablespoon butter

1 medium onion, coarsely chopped

1 clove garlic, minced

½ teaspoon hot Madras curry powder

5 cups fresh corn cut from the cob

½ teaspoon cornstarch

1 cup coconut milk (see page 56)

2 medium tomatoes, peeled, seeded, and coarsely chopped

Salt and freshly ground black pepper, to taste

MAÏS GRILLÉ

◎◎◎

GRILLED CORN (ALL AFRICA)

I am not sure where I first saw grilled corn being sold on the side of the road, but I know it made an impression on me. I will always remember the vendor, a woman fanning the coals in her brazier with a rattan fan while she deftly turned the corncobs with few twists of her fingers. The corn that was sold was a tough, mature ear, but the taste was enough to remind me of summer barbecues gone by. This dish is a street food nibble in Africa, not part of a meal, but if you use young ears, it will work just fine as a vegetable accompaniment as well.

If you really like things hot, season with a mixture of salt and powdered habanero chile.   SERVES 6

6 ears fresh corn
Salt and cayenne pepper, to taste

Heat the broiler or warm up the barbecue grill to cooking temperature. Remove the silk and husks from the corn. Place the corn on the grill and cook, turning it with tongs every few minutes so that it doesn't char, for 10 minutes, or until lightly toasted. Season and serve hot.

ABROW NE KOKOSI

◎◎◎

BOILED CORN WITH COCONUT (GHANA)

This dish is served in all parts of Ghana. It is called afiko *in Ga,* ebrow na kube *in Fante,* abodakple ene *in Ewe, and* abrow ne kokosi *in Twi. The corn used traditionally is dried corn that is soaked and cooked until soft. Here I have substituted fresh corn for a slightly different taste. See page 100 for instructions on how to shell a coconut and extract the meat. You will not need an entire coconut. Save the rest for Coconut Crisps (page 100) or use it grated in other dishes.*

SERVES 6

Place the corn in a medium-sized saucepan. Add the coconut milk and cook for 5 to 7 minutes, or until the corn is tender. Add the coconut pieces and stir to make sure that they are evenly distributed throughout the dish. The *abrow ne kokosi* can be served hot or at room temperature.

4 cups fresh corn cut from the cob
1 cup coconut milk (see page 56)
3 cups ½-inch cubes fresh coconut

ABROW NE NKATE

◎◉◎

CORN WITH PEANUTS (GHANA)

What's good with coconut is also good with peanuts for the Ghanaians. This dish can be prepared two ways. One version uses raw peanuts that are cooked with the corn; this version uses roasted peanuts.   SERVES 6

4 cups fresh corn cut from the cob
1 cup water
2 cups roasted unsalted peanuts

Place the corn and the water in a medium saucepan and cook for 5 minutes over medium heat. Add the peanuts and continue to cook for an additional 2 to 3 minutes, or until the corn is done. This dish can be served warm or at room temperature.

―――――――――――――――――――――――――

G IS FOR GNAOUIA

It's impossible to miss them, with their distinctive tasseled hats and their clanking cymbals. They are the Gnaouia, or *gnawa*, a religious brotherhood of dark-skinned Moroccans whose ancestors hail from the sub-Saharan parts of the continent. They are fixtures in the Djema el Fna (Square of the Dead) in Marrakesh, and their music has captivated more than one Western musician. I had been charmed by their acrobatic dancing, but when I was told that Gnaouia is simply a corruption of the word Ghana, I became mesmerized by them, fascinated by their history and their past.

The Gnaouia are the descendants of black Africans who journeyed across the Sahara to the north. They took their name from the empire of Ghana, the eleventh-century seat of sub-Saharan learning that fell at about the same time that the great Moroccan dynasties were forming. The Gnaouia brought with them not only their learning and their mysticism, but also their food. Their influence is felt throughout the Maghreb. In Tunisia today, there is a category of food known as Gnaouia food. It is slippery and rich with the greens known as *meloukhia*. The name persists also in many of the dishes prepared with okra. In fact, the slimy pod has even taken their name. In most of the country, it is simply known as *gnaouia*.

―――――――――――――――――――――――――

ABROW NE ASE
◎◎◎

BOILED CORN AND BEANS (GHANA)

Ghana's final entry into the corn sweepstakes is a dish that is not dissimilar to the American succotash, though the beans used here are black-eyed peas. The dish is traditionally served with the corn on the cob broken into small pieces. I have used fresh corn cut from the cob and canned black-eyed peas to make this a quick recipe that works as a busy weeknight vegetable side dish or a vegetarian entrée. SERVES 6 TO 8

Combine the corn, the black-eyed peas, and the water in a medium saucepan and cook, uncovered, over medium heat for 5 minutes. Season with salt and pepper to taste and serve hot.

4 cups fresh corn cut from the cob

2 cups drained canned black-eyed peas

1 cup water

Salt and freshly ground black pepper, to taste

IRIO

◉◉◉

STEWED VEGETABLES (KENYA)

This Kenyan dish is similar to the Ghanaian abrow ne ase *(page 181). White potatoes and greens (here spinach) are added to the dish.*

SERVES 6

1 cup fresh or frozen corn kernels
1 cup cooked kidney beans
4 medium potatoes, peeled and cut into
   ½-inch cubes
1 pound spinach, washed and chopped
Salt and freshly ground black pepper,
   to taste

Place all the ingredients in a large stockpot with water to cover. Bring to a boil over low heat and cook until the potatoes are fork-tender. Drain and serve hot. The diner mashes the ingredients together before eating.

BOILED CALABAZA
◎◎◎

(KENYA)

This squash is eaten in many ways throughout East and West Africa and is in such general use that it's hard to believe that members of the squash family originate in the Americas. Gourds and melons, though, have been eaten in Africa for millennia, and many of the recipes that today call for members of the squash family probably were originally prepared with some form of melon or gourd. This is one of the simplest ways to prepare and savor calabaza.   SERVES 4 TO 6

Peel the calabaza and cut it into ¾-inch cubes. Place them in a heavy saucepan with water to cover. Bring to a boil, lower the heat, and simmer for about 10 minutes, or until the calabaza is fork-tender. Season with salt and pepper to taste and serve hot with the butter.

1 pound calabaza (see page 53)
Salt and freshly ground black pepper,
   to taste
1 tablespoon butter

LUNCHEON WITH A QUEEN

There's a story about the seventeenth-century Mbundu queen Nzinga recounted in the sixth book of the *Descrição Histórica dos Três Reinos do Congo, Matamba e Angola,* by João Antonio Cavazzi de Monte-cuccolo, originally published in 1687. In it, he describes a lunch at Nzinga's court. The queen, in her usual manner, was seated on a mat surrounded by her ladies and ministers. Her meal was served in vessels of clay, although she owned silver ones as a mark of her status. When the food was served, it was hot, and the guests ate with their hands, passing the food between their left and right hands until it cooled off. Cavazzi once counted eighty different dishes being served. On another occasion, Nzinga asked him to share a dish of small rodents complete with their fur. When he demurred, Nzinga said, "Europeans, you don't know what's good." When Nzinga drank, all those present clapped their hands or touched their fingers to their feet to say that she should enjoy what she was drinking from her head to her toes. She ate in great pomp, and the leftovers were fed to the rest of the court.

SAUTÉED CALABAZA

◎◎◎

(KENYA)

Although it goes by the name of pumpkin, most of the pumpkin used in the cooking of Africa is similar to the Latin American calabaza. If you cannot get calabaza at your greengrocers' or supermarket, substitute butternut squash, which is similar in texture and taste. Don't use American pumpkin.   SERVES 6

1¼ pounds calabaza, peeled and cut
　　into ¾-inch cubes
3 tablespoons peanut oil
2 medium onions, minced
Salt and freshly ground black pepper, to
　　taste

Place the calabaza pieces in a saucepan with water to cover and cook for 10 minutes, or until fork-tender. Remove the calabaza pieces, peel them, and mash them with a potato masher. Heat the peanut oil in a heavy skillet, add the onion, and cook until lightly browned. Add the calabaza to the cooking onions, mashing it down with the back of a fork. Cover the skillet and cook for 3 to 5 minutes, or until it forms a brown crust on the bottom. Uncover and stir, breaking up the crust, then mash, cover, and cook again. Repeat mashing and cooking until all the calabaza is brown like the bottom crust. You may have to add a bit more oil if the skillet gets too dry. Season with salt and pepper to taste and serve hot.

CALABAZA AND TOMATOES
◎◎◎

(KENYA)

Here the calabaza meets up with tomatoes for a vegetable dish that is delicious and colorful. This dish can be transformed into a main dish, with the addition of a few pieces of meat, as can many of Africa's vegetable dishes. SERVES 6

Place the calabaza cubes in a medium-sized saucepan with water to cover and cook for 10 minutes, or until they are tender but not falling apart. Drain well. Heat the peanut oil in a heavy skillet, add the onion slices, and cook until they are lightly browned. Add the tomato and cook, stirring occasionally, for 3 minutes. Add the calabaza, sugar, and salt and stir well. Cook, uncovered, without stirring, until the liquid is all absorbed and the bottom forms a brown crust. Serve hot.

1 pound calabaza, peeled and cut into ¾-inch cubes

1 tablespoon peanut oil

2 large onions, sliced

6 large ripe tomatoes, peeled, seeded, and coarsely chopped

Pinch of sugar

Salt, to taste

SPINACH AND CALABAZA
◎◎◎

(KENYA)

This dish is easy to prepare from either raw ingredients or their precooked varieties. Since there are already recipes in this book for boiled calabaza and steamed spinach, I will give you the method that uses the cooked ingredients rather than giving the basic cooking again.

SERVES 6

2 cups cooked spinach (see page 202)
2 cups cooked calabaza (see page 183)
2 tablespoons peanut oil
2 medium onions, sliced
Salt, to taste

Coarsely chop the spinach. Push the cooked calabaza through a potato ricer. Heat the oil in a skillet and cook the onion slices until they are lightly browned. Add the spinach and calabaza, season with salt to taste, and cook, uncovered, without stirring, over low heat for 5 to 7 minutes, or until a brown crust is formed at the bottom. Serve hot.

CALABAZAS TO MARKET

CAPE MALAY CALABAZA

◎◎◎

(SOUTH AFRICA)

Pumpkins and gourds were eaten on the African continent long before the Europeans arrived. This recipe using the West Indian cooking pumpkin, or calabaza, is similar in composition to our candied sweet potatoes, but with the South African twist of minced dried apricots. If calabaza cannot be found, you can substitute butternut or acorn squash for a similar taste.

SERVES 4

Preheat the oven to 350 degrees. Rub the inside of an ovenproof casserole with a bit of oil or spray it with cooking spray to prevent sticking. Add the calabaza, apricots, and orange juice. Sprinkle with the brown sugar and cinnamon and dot with butter. Cover with aluminum foil and bake for 30 minutes, or until the calabaza is fork-tender. Serve hot.

1 pound calabaza, peeled and cut into
    ¾-inch cubes
¼ pound dried apricots, minced
½ cup freshly squeezed orange juice
1 teaspoon brown sugar
½ teaspoon ground cinnamon
1 tablespoon butter

NKATE

◎◎◎

BOILED PEANUTS (GHANA)

Peanuts have a complicated place in the African culinary repertoire. While Africans did use groundnuts of some sort, most notably the Bambara groundnut, prior to the Columbian Exchange, the nut of preference is now certainly the peanut. Peanuts migrated from Africa to the United States during the period of the Slave Trade, forever confusing many who think that peanuts are African in origin. They are from the New World, but they have certainly taken over the minds and hearts, and stomachs, of much of Africa.

One of the ways that peanuts are eaten is simply boiled. I am particularly intrigued with this, as I remember my father doting on raw peanuts when he could find them and my paternal grandmother growing her own in her small garden spot near the projects in which she lived. I have even found boiled peanuts served at a ceremony for the caboclo *(native Brazilian spirits) in a Candomblé house in Bahia, Brazil, and in many guises in African cooking. Here, then, is a simple Ghanaian recipe for boiled peanuts. If you don't grow your own peanuts, and cannot find raw ones at your greengrocers', mail-order them from one of the sources in the section starting on page 74.* SERVES 4 TO 6

3 pounds raw peanuts in their shells (see page 67)

Place the peanuts in a large saucepan with water to cover and boil, covered, for 1 hour, or until the peanuts are soft. Drain the peanuts. Eat them as a snack or serve them with boiled ears of corn on the cob that have been cut into 2-inch pieces.

NDIZI

◎◎◎

SPICY PLANTAINS (KENYA)

In some parts of Kenya plantains are called matoke. *Here the* matoke *are cooked in ghee (clarified butter) and seasoned with chile and cilantro.*

SERVES 6

Peel the plantains and slice them into 1-inch pieces. Place them in a bowl with the lemon juice and lukewarm water to cover for 3 minutes. Heat the ghee in a heavy skillet and fry the onions, cilantro, and chile until the onion is translucent. Add the plantains and the beef stock and cook, uncovered, for 30 minutes. Serve hot. You can drain the plantains or use the cooking liquid as a sauce.

8 medium plantains (see page 51)

2 tablespoons freshly squeezed lemon juice

1 tablespoon ghee (see page 60)

2 onions, thinly sliced

1 teaspoon minced fresh cilantro

¼ teaspoon minced fresh bird chile, or to taste (see page 55)

2 cups beef stock

BOLI - BOPA
◎◎◎

GRILLED PLANTAINS WITH PEANUTS (NIGERIA)

Some of West Africa's street snacks make perfect vegetable side dishes for Western-style meals. This roadside favorite from Lagos, Nigeria, combining grilled plantains and salted peanuts, is a perfect example. SERVES 4

4 medium-ripe plantains (see page 51)
1 cup roasted salted peanuts

Preheat the broiler. Using a sharp paring knife, peel the plantains and place them on a rack under the broiler. Broil them for 5 to 7 minutes, turning them to make sure that they are cooked through. When they are done, cut them into chunks and serve with the roasted peanuts.

VARIATIONS: This dish can be served without the peanuts. Instead, serve the plantains in a sauce of 2 tablespoons red palm oil that has been warmed and seasoned with ground chiles and salt to taste.

You can also cook the plantains on a grill. Brush them lightly with 2 teaspoons olive oil, place on the grill, and proceed as in the recipe.

CURRIED VEGETABLES

◎◎◎

(SOUTH AFRICA)

Indian influences are felt widely in South African cooking. In the region around Capetown, however, the major culinary force is that of the Cape Malay. This group of people take their tastes in curry from the milder curries of Southeast Asia, as shown in this dish of curried vegetables.   SERVES 8

Heat the oil in a large heavy saucepan and pan-fry the potatoes for 5 minutes, or until they are golden brown. Drain the potatoes on absorbent paper and set them aside. Add the butter and onions to the saucepan and cook the onions for 5 minutes, or until they are soft and slightly brown. Add the tomatoes and spices and simmer, covered, over low heat for 15 minutes. Add the potatoes, cabbage, carrots, and cauliflower and cook for an additional 15 minutes. Finally, add the peas and cook for 3 minutes, or until the vegetables are tender. Serve hot with white rice.

7 tablespoons sunflower oil

8 small Yukon Gold potatoes, peeled
   and coarsely chopped

2 tablespoons butter

2 large onions, thinly sliced

2 large ripe tomatoes, peeled, seeded,
   and coarsely chopped

1 teaspoon minced fresh ginger

2 teaspoons minced garlic

1 small green jalapeño chile, minced,
   or to taste

1½ tablespoons mild curry powder

½ small head cabbage, shredded

8 carrots, peeled and cut into julienne
   strips

3 cups cauliflower florets

2 cups fresh or frozen peas

SMOOR TOMATOES AND ONIONS
◎◎◎

(SOUTH AFRICA)

In this tomato and onion mixture, the addition of a bit of sugar makes all the difference. It brings out the sweetness of the tomato and softens its natural acidity. The resulting dish can be transformed into a main dish with the addition of pieces of leftover fish or meat.
SERVES 4

2 tablespoons vegetable oil

1 large onion, thinly sliced

2 large ripe tomatoes, peeled, seeded, and coarsely chopped

1 small green jalapeño chile, minced, or to taste (see page 55)

1 tablespoon sugar, or to taste

Salt, to taste

Heat the oil in a heavy saucepan and cook the onion slices over medium heat for 5 minutes, or until they are soft and slightly brown. Add the tomatoes and chile and cook over low heat for 20 minutes, stirring occasionally, to make sure that the flavors mix. Add the sugar and salt and serve hot.

TOMATES FARCIES AUX ANCHOIS
◎◎◎

ANCHOVY-STUFFED TOMATOES (NORTH AFRICA)

This twist on stuffed tomatoes combines the traditional flavors of sun-ripened tomatoes with the anchovy, one of the favorite fish of the Mediterranean region.

SERVES 4 TO 6

Core the tomatoes and remove the seeds. Lightly salt the insides of the tomatoes and allow them to drain over a colander for a few minutes, until they have drained off some of their liquid. Mix the anchovies, bread crumbs, shallots, salt, pepper and 3 tablespoons of the Parmesan cheese together to make the stuffing.

Preheat the broiler. When the tomatoes have completely drained, stuff them and place them in a greased broiler-proof pan. Sprinkle some of the remaining cheese on top of each tomato. Put them under the broiler and cook until the cheese on top has melted and formed a brown crust. Serve hot as an appetizer or side dish.

8 ripe but firm tomatoes
Salt, to taste
8 salted anchovy fillets, chopped
½ cup fresh bread crumbs
2 shallots, minced
Freshly ground black pepper, to taste
5 tablespoons grated Parmesan cheese

GERBRAAIDE PATATS
◎◎◎

BAKED SWEET POTATOES (SOUTH AFRICA)

In South Africa, the potatoes of choice for this dish are the yellow-fleshed ones that they call borie patat. *They are tradition-ally served with barbecued meats and salads at a* braai (barbecue).　　　SERVES 4

4 large sweet potatoes
2 tablespoons vegetable oil

Preheat the oven to 350 degrees. Wash the sweet potatoes well, dry them, and slather them with the vegetable oil so that their skins will crisp slightly while they bake. Prick them with a fork so that they don't explode while cooking. Place them in the oven and cook for 45 minutes to 1 hour, until they are fork-tender. Serve hot.

YEQEY SIR QIQQIL
◎◎◎

BOILED BEETS (ETHIOPIA)

The popular root vegetable is given a simple but delicious preparation in this Ethiopian dish.　　　SERVES 4 TO 6

6 beets
¼ cup freshly squeezed lemon juice
¼ cup extra-virgin olive oil

Wash the beets thoroughly and remove the beet tops, reserving them. You can use them for juice or use them as cooked greens. Place the beets in a heavy saucepan with water to cover, bring to a boil, lower the heat, and simmer, covered, for 40 minutes, or until the beets are fork-tender. When ready, peel the beets and cut them into thin slices. Prepare a dressing from the lemon juice and olive oil, drizzle it over the beets, and mix well. Serve hot.

YE'ABESHA GOMEN
◎◎◎

COLLARD GREENS (ETHIOPIA)

The abundant use of leafy greens is one of the hallmarks of the food of the African continent in general. Here, the familiar collard green, which has become emblematic of African-American cooking, is given an Ethiopian twist in a dish that can be served either warm or at room temperature.   SERVES 4 TO 6

Wash the greens thoroughly. Remove any discolored spots and cut out any thick woody stems. Place the greens in a heavy saucepan with 1 cup of the water, cover, and bring to a boil. Lower the heat and cook for 20 minutes, or until the greens are tender. When ready, drain the greens, reserving the liquid, and cut them into small pieces.

In a heavy skillet, heat the oil and cook the onions until they are lightly browned. Add the greens, the reserved and remaining 1 cup water, the garlic, and the ginger and cook, uncovered, until almost dry. Add the chiles and cook for an additional 5 minutes. Serve either warm or at room temperature.

1 pound collard greens
2 cups water
3 tablespoons olive oil
1 cup chopped red onions
½ teaspoon minced garlic
¼ teaspoon minced fresh ginger
Salt, to taste
3 medium Anaheim chiles, cut into
   thin strips (see page 55)

ZELBO GOMEN
◉◉◉

BOILED KALE (ETHIOPIA)

Kale, a nonheading member of the cabbage family, has been cultivated for more than 2,000 years. Although not usually thought of with the other leafy greens so popular on the African continent, it too takes an Ethiopian turn in this dish.

SERVES 4 TO 6

1 pound kale
2½ cups water
¾ cup red onions
3 tablespoons olive oil
1 tablespoon minced garlic
1 tablespoon minced fresh ginger
1 teaspoon minced jalapeño chile, or to
    taste (see page 55)
Salt and freshly ground black pepper,
    to taste

Wash the kale in cold water, making sure to remove all the grit. Cut out any discolored spots and remove any woody stems. Tear the kale into small pieces and place it in a heavy saucepan with the water. Bring the kale to a boil over medium heat, then add the remaining ingredients and stir well. Lower the heat and cook, covered, for 25 minutes, or until the kale is tender. Serve hot or at room temperature.

STEAMED OKRA

◎◎◎

(ALL AFRICA)

From north to south, east to west, okra gets its culinary due. This slippery pod turns up in soups and stews. It is fried and baked. Sometimes it leaves all pretense aside and appears at the table simply boiled and seasoned with a squeeze of fresh lemon juice (which, incidentally, cuts some of the slime for which it is reviled in much of the rest of the world). I said in my cookbook Iron Pots and Wooden Spoons: Africa's Gifts to New World Cooking, *wherever okra points its green tip, Africa has passed. It is so emblematic of the cooking of Africa and the African diaspora that I have it engraved on my professional stationery.*

SERVES 4

Wash and top and tail the okra, discarding any blemished or hard pods. Place it in a heavy saucepan. Add the water, cover, and cook over medium heat for 5 minutes, or until the okra is fork-tender. Add the lemon juice, stir, drain, and serve hot.

1 pound fresh young okra pods
1 cup water
1 teaspoon freshly squeezed lemon juice

BAMIA MASLOUKAH

◎◎◎

EGYPTIAN-STYLE BOILED OKRA (EGYPT)

Here is a simple yet flavorful Egyptian version of okra in all its splendor. Long live the mucilaginous pod!
Select small pods the size of your little finger with no blemishes. Remember that the more you cut okra, the slimier it gets.

SERVES 6

1½ pounds fresh okra pods
1 tablespoon vegetable oil
1 medium onion, minced
2½ cups beef stock
1 teaspoon freshly squeezed lemon juice

Wash and top and tail the okra, discarding any blemished or hard pods. Heat the oil in a heavy saucepan and sauté the onion until it is translucent. Add the okra and cook it for 3 minutes, stirring constantly. Add the stock, cover, and cook for an additional 10 minutes, or until the okra is fork-tender. Add the lemon juice and serve hot.

BAMYA ALICH'A

◎◎◎

ETHIOPIAN-STYLE OKRA (ETHIOPIA)

Okra is celebrated Ethiopian-style in this dish. Traditionally, the okra is soaked overnight and drained to rid it of some of its slime. I've cut down on cooking time and some of the slippery quality by using only the smallest okra pods and then cutting them only once.

SERVES 4 TO 6

Wash and top and tail the okra, discarding any blemished or hard pods. Split each pod in half lengthwise. Heat the oil in a medium saucepan and cook the onions until they are light brown. Add the tomatoes and bring the mixture to a boil. Lower the heat, add the garlic, ginger, and cardamom, and stir well. Add the okra, cook, uncovered, over low heat for 20 minutes, then add the chiles and continue to cook for 5 minutes. Adjust the seasoning and remove from the heat. Serve hot or at room temperature.

4 cups young okra pods

¼ cup olive oil

1½ cups minced red onions

2 cups coarsely chopped seeded peeled ripe tomatoes

2 teaspoons minced garlic

2 teaspoons minced fresh ginger

½ teaspoon ground cardamom

2 jalapeño chiles, minced, or to taste (see page 55)

BAMIA

◎◎◎

SWEET AND SOUR OKRA (EGYPT)

This Egyptian recipe adds a bit of honey and a squeeze of lemon. It goes well with grilled meats.

SERVES 4 TO 6

1 pound small okra pods

2 tablespoons olive oil

1 tablespoon honey

*Salt and freshly ground black pepper, to
   taste*

*1 tablespoon freshly squeezed lemon
   juice*

½ cup water

Wash the okra and pat it dry with paper towels. Top and tail it, discarding any blemished or hard pods. Heat the olive oil in a heavy saucepan and sauté the okra in the oil for 3 to 5 minutes, turning each pod once. Add the honey, salt, pepper, lemon juice, and water. Cover, lower the heat, and simmer for 15 minutes, adding more water if necessary. Serve hot.

SAUCE GOMBO

◎◎◎

OKRA SAUCE (BENIN)

This is a simple vegetarian version of a West African sauce. With the additions of crabmeat, dried smoked shrimp, and more, it can be transformed into a main dish, Sauce Aimée (page 222). Here, though, is the purest version—super-low in calories and delicious when served over rice or a mash.   SERVES 4

For a slightly different taste, add a few cubebs to your seasoning.

Wash and top and tail the okra, discarding any blemished or hard pods. Place the okra, tomatoes, chile, and water in a heavy saucepan and bring to a boil. Lower the heat to medium and simmer, covered, for about 10 minutes, or until the okra is fork-tender. Remove the chile when the dish is hot enough for your taste. Season with salt and pepper and serve hot over rice or a mash.

1 pound fresh okra

2 medium-sized ripe tomatoes, peeled, seeded, and coarsely chopped

1 habanero chile, pricked with a fork

1 cup water

Salt and freshly ground black pepper, to taste

YAMS AND PLANTAINS

STEAMED SPINACH
◎◎◎

(ALL AFRICA)

The word for spinach in French, épinard, even derives from the word for spinach from the Moorish Arabic of Andalusia— isbinah. *No one is quite sure where spinach originated, but Persia and Tibet have been proposed. While it is not the green of choice in much of Africa, as it prefers a more temperate climate, spinach is frequently substituted for other greens. Here, then, is a basic spinach recipe for use when cooked spinach is required. As spinach diminishes greatly when cooked, you'll need at least a pound per person.* SERVES 4

4 pounds fresh leaf spinach (not from the plastic bag, please)
2 tablespoons water

Wash the spinach thoroughly. It is usually sandy and there is nothing worse than a mouthful of grit. Place the spinach in a large heavy pan with the water. Cover and cook over low heat for 5 minutes, or until the spinach is tender. Serve hot with Pili Pili Sauce (page 145), Ata (page 151), Hot Sauce (page 152), or a small dab of harissa (page 136 or 137).

OULA'ASS FEE EL FORN
◎◎◎

BAKED WHOLE RUTABAGA (EGYPT)

Rutabagas are the result of a cross between members of the Savoy cabbage family and the turnip family; they were developed by the Scandinavians in the Middle Ages. Rutabagas have made their way to the African continent along with their older cousin, the turnip, and appear in soups and stews. In this unusual side dish, the whole root is placed in the oven and baked.

SERVES 4 TO 6

Preheat the oven to 375 degrees. Scrub the rutabaga with a steel vegetable brush to remove the wax with which they are usually coated. Wash it, pat it dry with absorbent paper, pierce it with a knife, wrap it in foil, and put it in the oven. Bake for 50 to 60 minutes, or until fork-tender. When done, slice and serve hot with the seasonings and butter.

1 rutabaga (1½ pounds)
Salt and freshly ground black pepper,
    to taste
1 tablespoon butter

FUL MEDAMES
◎◎◎

EGYPTIAN-STYLE BROAD BEANS (EGYPT)

This dish is the national dish of Egypt, consumed in the mansions of the rich and the huts of the poor. Traditionally, ful was sold on street corners and in snack shops. Large copper vats called edra *were used to cook the beans. The sellers would take their pots to the* hamman, *or bathhouses, and leave them to simmer overnight on the embers of the fires that heated the water. Today, most of the pots are aluminum, but the love of beans lingers on.*

Beans were eaten in pharaonic Egypt, and this dish is pre-Islamic and pre-Ottoman. There are myriad variations on the ful theme as well as several different ways of spelling it, including ful, fuul, *and* fool. *No matter how it's spelled and no matter how it's served, the dish is an African classic.*

The beans need to soak overnight before cooking.

SERVES 4 TO 6

2 cups dried Egyptian broad beans or dried Italian fava beans

4 cups water

6 cloves garlic, or to taste

1 teaspoon sea salt, or to taste

1 tablespoon freshly squeezed lemon juice

¼ cup olive oil

1½ tablespoons minced parsley

GARNISHES
Radishes
Hard-boiled eggs
Scallions
Pita bread, cut into wedges and toasted

Wash the beans and pick them over, removing any discolored ones or stones. Place the beans in a large stockpot with the water and allow them to soak overnight. The next day, add more water, enough to cover, and bring the beans to a boil over medium heat. Lower the heat, cover, and simmer the beans for 2 hours, or until they are tender. You may need to add more water. If so, add only boiling water or the beans will toughen.

While the beans are cooking, mash the garlic and the sea salt together in the bowl of a mortar or a food processor. Mix the lemon juice, olive oil, and parsley together and add to the garlic mixture. When the beans are cooked, drain them, reserving 1 tablespoon of the cooking liquid. Add the garlic mixture and the 1 tablespoon reserved cooking liquid to the beans and stir to combine. Serve warm with the garnishes arranged on a platter. Each person is served a plateful of ful and adds the garnishes of his or her choice.

BEIGNETS DE CHOUFLEUR

◎◎◎

CAULIFLOWER FRITTERS (ALGERIA)

Fritters are found all over the African continent. In fact, they are one of the hallmarks of African cooking no matter where it is found in the world. These tasty pieces of batter-dipped cauliflower are seasoned with lemon juice. I add just a tiny bit of cumin to give them a little flavor zap. SERVES 6

Wash the cauliflower and separate it into florets. Blanch the florets by cooking them in boiling water for 10 minutes, or until fork-tender but not soft. Drain and dry well.

Heat the oil for deep frying to 375 degrees in a heavy Dutch oven or deep fryer. While the oil is heating, prepare a batter from the eggs, flour, and seasonings. When the oil is hot, dip the cauliflower pieces in the batter, then fry them until they are golden brown. Drain them on absorbent paper and serve hot with the lemon wedges and a few sprigs of parsley as garnish.

1 head cauliflower
Olive oil for deep frying
3 eggs
1 tablespoon flour
1 tablespoon minced fresh parsley
½ teaspoon ground cumin
Salt and freshly ground black pepper, to taste
Lemon wedges, for serving
Parsley sprigs, for garnish

MAIN DISHES

◎◎◎

Stews, Grills, and the Three-Rock Stove

On much of the African continent, the main dish *is* the meal. As often as not, that dish is a thick or soupy stew served over a mash of some sort. When stew isn't on the menu, tastes turn toward grilled meats like kebabs or grilled chicken. The prevalence of stewing and grilling is a direct result of the widespread rural use of a simple stove consisting of three rocks placed on the ground with a fire built between them.

◎◎◎

Fish and Seafood

SARDINES EN ESCABECH
Pickled Sardines *(Algeria)*

BOULETTES DE SARDINES
Fried Sardine Balls *(Algeria)*

POISSON BRAISÉ
Grilled Fish *(Côte d'Ivoire)*

CAMARÃO GRELHADO PIRI PIRI
Grilled Shrimp Piri Piri *(Mozambique)*

YASSA AU POISSON
Fish Yassa *(Senegal)*

CRABE BENINOISE
Benin-Style Baked Crab *(Benin)*

HUÎTRES AZI DESSI
Fried Oysters *(Togo)*

SAUCE AZI DESSI
Azi Dessi Sauce *(Togo)*

SAUCE CRABE
Crab Sauce *(Benin)*

SAUCE AIMÉE
Aimée's Crab Sauce *(Benin)*

FISH CAKES
(Nigeria)

SOUPIKANYA
Senegalese Gumbo *(Senegal)*

KALDOU
Casamance Fish Stew *(Senegal)*

THIEBOU DIENN SOUS VERRE
Senegalese Rice and Fish Stew *(Senegal)*

Chicken and Fowl

CHICKEN SOSATIES
Spiced Skewered Chicken *(South Africa)*

MUAMBA DE GALINHA
Chicken Muamba *(Angola)*

MELOUKHIA
North African Greens with Chicken *(Egypt)*

GALINHA A PIRI PIRI
Piri Piri Chicken *(Mozambique)*

FRANGO GRELHADO PIRI PIRI
Hot and Spicy Grilled Chicken *(Angola)*

YASSA AU POULET CLASSIQUE
Classic Chicken Yassa *(Senegal)*

YASSA AU POULET II
Chicken Yassa *(Senegal)*

KEDJENOU
Terra-Cotta Stewed Chicken *(Côte d'Ivoire)*

BASTILLA
Pigeon Pie *(Morocco)*

TAJINE DE POULET AU CITRON ET AUX OLIVES
Chicken Tajine with Lemons and Olives *(Morocco)*

SUYA
Chicken Skewers *(Nigeria)*

BASSI SALTE
Malian Millet Couscous *(Mali)*

PEITO DE GALINHOLA
Guinea Fowl Breasts *(South Africa)*

MOYO DE POULET FUMÉ
Smoked Chicken with Sauce *(Benin)*

Meats and Organ Meats

GIGOT D'AGNEAU AUX ÉPICES MAROCAINES
Leg of Lamb Encrusted with Moroccan Spices *(Morocco)*

BROCHETTES DE ROGNONS DE MOUTON
Brochettes of Lamb Kidneys *(Algeria)*

TAJINE D'AGNEAU AUX PRUNEAUX
Lamb Tajine with Prunes *(Morocco)*

SOSATIES
Grilled Lamb Kebabs *(South Africa)*

KOFTA KEBABS
Minced Lamb Kebabs *(Kenya)*

KESKOU FASSIA
Fez-Style Lamb Couscous *(Morocco)*

BROCHETTES D'AGNEAU
Lamb Kebabs *(North Africa)*

MAFÉ
Peanut Butter Stew *(Senegal)*

KHLIGH
Beef Shanks *(Morocco)*

MWAMBE
Mwambe Beef *(Congo)*

DAMBUN NAMA
Shredded Beef *(Nigeria)*

KITFO LEB LEB
Cooked Kitfo *(Ethiopia)*

SAUCE GRAIN
West African Beef and Okra Stew *(West Africa)*

ABENA'S PALAVER SAUCE
(Ghana)

M'CHERMIA
Liver with Vinegar *(Algeria)*

FRIED LIVER SUDANESE-STYLE
(Sudan)

MANCHUPA
Cape Verdean Stew *(Cape Verde Islands)*

ROMAZAVA
Malagache Mixed Meat Stew *(Madagascar)*

JAGACIDA
Cape Verdean Bean and Sausage Stew
(Cape Verde Islands)

Leftovers

BOBOTIE
South African Meat Pie *(South Africa)*

EGYPTIAN-STYLE STUFFED PEPPERS
(Egypt)

SUKUMA WIKI
Leftover Special *(Kenya)*

✳

The Fishermen of Yoff

At first, they're tiny specks on the horizon. Then, as your eyes adjust to the glare of the setting sun on the water, they grow, transforming themselves into pirogues, small fishing boats gaily decorated with the green, red, and gold colors of the Senegalese flag. Onward they come, unicorn-prowed bearers of the bounty of the sea. These are the small boats that carry the fishermen of Yoff out beyond the bar each morning to brave the djins and the spirits of the deep in search of the fish that come to table at noon as the day's *thiebou dienn.* Women in bird-of-paradise–colored billowing boubous await them at their homeports throughout Senegal. They watch in Yoff, near the airport. They pace the seashore in Soumbedioune, next to the tourist crafts market. They scan the horizon in Cayar. All are waiting for the first boat to reach shore.

The first fisherman is rewarded with the highest prices of the day, for his catch is the first to reach the tables and the shops. Those who come later may be rewarded equally if they have returned with a particularly prized denizen of the deep. Arms akimbo, the ebony-hued women stand and chatter among themselves, balancing their brightly decorated enameled bowls on hips thrust out in emphasis. When the boats arrive, they swoop down, scurrying over the sandy beaches like so many crabs, hurrying to get the choicest piece and the best price. It all takes about an hour, and then it's over. The beach returns to normal. The latecomers get the leftovers and the rest is left to the beggars and the seagulls. The fisherman of Yoff have braved the sea for yet another day.

FISH AND SEAFOOD

SARDINES EN ESCABECH
◉◉◉

PICKLED SARDINES (ALGERIA)

The word escabech *or* escabeche *comes from the Arabic word* cisbech, *which, in turn comes from the Persian* siquisbe, *which means pickled food. These dishes have a long history in North Africa and have made the Atlantic crossing to turn up as the escabeches and ceviches of the Latin World and the* escovitched *fish of Jamaica. Here sardines are used and the tart marinade is flavored with cumin and paprika.*

This is a dish that can be prepared in advance, and some feel that it improves in taste if the sardines are allowed to marinate for a day.

SERVES 4

Prepare the sardines by removing their heads, splitting them down the middle, removing the spine, eviscerating them, and seasoning them with salt and pepper. Roll them in the flour. Heat the oil in a heavy skillet or saucepan and cook the sardines, a few at a time, until they are golden, turning them once. Remove them to a serving platter, reserving the cooking oil. Lower the heat and add the garlic, paprika, cumin, and chile to the oil. Cook for 2 to 3 minutes, stirring constantly, then add the vinegar. Pour the warm sauce over the sardines and allow them to cool, as the escabech is eaten at room temperature.

NOTE: See Glossary (page 55) and Mail-Order Sources (page 74).

1 pound fresh sardines

Salt and freshly ground black pepper, to taste

¼ cup flour

2 tablespoons olive oil

3 cloves garlic

1 teaspoon paprika

1½ teaspoons ground cumin

2 minced fresh bird chiles (see Note)

1 tablespoon white wine vinegar

BOULETTES DE SARDINES
◎◎◎

FRIED SARDINE BALLS (ALGERIA)

Fresh sardines are the small fish of preference in much of the Mediterranean Basin. They are grilled and fried; they are made into fritters or transformed into fish balls. While boulettes appear on appetizer tables, these are also served as a light dinner or snack.

SERVES 4

1 pound fresh sardines
2 small cloves garlic, minced
1 tablespoon minced flat-leaf parsley
½ cup fresh bread crumbs
2 eggs
Salt and freshly ground black pepper, to taste
½ cup flour
Olive oil

Clean the sardines by removing the heads, splitting them down the middle, removing the spine, and eviscerating them. Mix the garlic, parsley, and bread crumbs together in a medium-sized bowl. Chop the sardines and add them to the mixture, using your hands to make sure that there are no small bones and that the ingredients are well mixed. Add 1 of the eggs and continue to mix until you have a thick dough. Form the dough into small balls about 1 inch in diameter. Beat the second egg in a small bowl. Heat ½ inch oil in a heavy skillet. Dredge the balls in the flour, dip them in the beaten egg, and fry them, a few at a time, in the oil until they are golden brown. Drain, season, and serve hot.

POISSON BRAISÉ
◉◉◉

GRILLED FISH (CÔTE D'IVOIRE)

Most of the streets of Cotonou, the capital of Benin, are sandy stretches of road bordered by tall palm trees and the garden walls of houses. In the evening, enterprising women set up small restaurants in front of their homes. Eating in one of these alfresco dining spots is a treat.

I remember my favorite. Sitting at a small table under the shade of a large mango tree was enchantment. Service began with the waitress bringing a basin of warm water and a towel so that we could wash our hands. The menu was simple, but when she said that poisson braisé *was available, I knew what I would have. The dish is not Beninoise, but rather a transplanted favorite from Côte d'Ivoire. It is simply grilled fish. It's the freshest fish in the market, however, and it usually comes to the table redolent of wood smoke and accompanied by a spicy tomato-based sauce. You may not be able to duplicate the atmosphere of an outdoor restaurant in Cotonou, but you can enjoy the taste of fresh grilled fish anywhere.*

This is a perfect dish for an outdoor barbecue. Leftover fish can be used to prepare Fish Cakes (page 223).

SERVES 4

Have your fishmonger eviscerate and scale the fish, keeping the head on. When ready to cook, preheat the broiler. Mix the oil and seasonings together and brush it on the fish. Place the fish on a greased rack, place it under the broiler, and cook it for 5 to 7 minutes on each side, brushing it frequently with the oil mixture. The fish should be slightly golden on the outside and slightly translucent near the bones. Serve immediately with white rice and Hot Sauce (page 152).

3 pounds whole sea bass
½ cup peanut oil
Powdered hot chile and salt, to taste

CAMARÃO GRELHADO PIRI PIRI
◎◉◎

GRILLED SHRIMP PILI PILI (MOZAMBIQUE)

Although Cameroon was named by the Portuguese for the shrimp that were once abundant there (Camarões means "shrimp" in Portuguese), this dish comes from Mozambique, which is also known for its big, beautiful shrimp. Here the shrimp are given a little extra zing with the addition of a bit of the hot chile that is known in many parts of western Africa as pili pili.

The shrimp need to be marinated for at least three hours before cooking. SERVES 4 TO 6

2 pounds uncooked jumbo shrimp

1 teaspoon minced hot bird chile, or to taste (see Note)

4 medium cloves garlic, coarsely chopped

2 tablespoons freshly squeezed lemon juice

⅔ cup peanut oil

Salt and freshly ground black pepper, to taste

Lemon quarters, for serving

Shell and devein the shrimp, leaving the tail shells intact. Wash them under cold water and pat them dry with absorbent paper. Place the chile, garlic, and lemon juice and ⅓ cup of the peanut oil in a bowl and whisk them until they are well mixed. Gradually drizzle in the remaining ⅓ cup of oil and add the salt and pepper. Place the shrimp in a separate large bowl and pour the oil mixture over them, making sure that they are well covered with it. Cover the bowl with absorbent paper and place it in the refrigerator for at least 3 hours to allow the shrimp to absorb the marinade. Stir the shrimp occasionally.

When ready to cook, preheat the broiler. Remove the shrimp from the marinade and place them under the broiler. Cook for about 2 minutes on each side, or until the shrimp are pink. Serve hot with white rice and the lemon quarters.

NOTE: See Glossary (page 55) and Mail-Order Sources (page 74).

Yassa au Poisson
◉◉◉

FISH YASSA (SENEGAL)

In order to stand up to this recipe's grilling and stewing, the fish selected must be whole or steaks (fillets will not work). Select a firm-fleshed white fish. (I would suggest something slightly sweet like a butterfish.) In this recipe, I have called for individual fish, but you can also use one large fish. Vary the cooking times accordingly. SERVES 6

Two hours before cooking, prepare a marinade of the lemon juice, salt, pepper, chile, and 3 tablespoons of the oil. Place the onion slices in the marinade, mixing them well to be sure they are all well coated. After 1½ hours, add the fish, making sure that they are well covered with the marinade, and let sit in the refrigerator for about 30 minutes.

When ready to cook, preheat the broiler at the highest setting. Remove the fish from the marinade, reserving the marinade and the onions, and broil the fish for 1 or 2 minutes on each side. Drain the onions from the marinade. Heat the remaining tablespoon of oil in a heavy deep skillet and sauté the onions over medium heat until they are tender and translucent. Add the reserved marinade and the water and cook the onions until the liquid is heated through. Add the fish, lower the heat, and continue to cook for 2 to 3 minutes, or until the fish is cooked through. Serve hot with white rice.

¼ cup freshly squeezed lemon juice
Salt and freshly ground black pepper, to taste
⅛ teaspoon minced habanero chile, or to taste
4 tablespoons peanut oil
4 large onions, thinly sliced
6 small (2½ to 3 pounds all together) butterfish, cleaned and with heads off
¼ cup water

CRABE BENINOISE

◉◉◉

BENIN-STYLE BAKED CRAB (BENIN)

This dish eaten in Benin is clearly a product of that country's colonial heritage; the bread crumbs and the baking are signs that this is a dish that has not been in the country's culinary repertoire long. The colonial culinary legacy is also a part of the cuisine of the continent, however, and this delicious dish deserves a place in the telling of that history. Think of it as Coquilles Saint-Jacques meets African crab without the sauce blanche.   SERVES 6

2 pounds fresh lump crabmeat

¾ cup minced scallion, including some
    of the green top

½ cup minced parsley

1 cup chopped tomato

2 eggs

2 cloves garlic, minced

1 stalk celery, minced

1 tablespoon Hot Sauce (page 152)

½ cup stale French bread crumbs

6 ramekins or crab shells

1 tablespoon butter

Preheat the oven to 350 degrees. Combine the crabmeat, scallion, parsley, tomato, eggs, garlic, celery, hot sauce, and ¼ cup of the bread crumbs in a medium-sized bowl and mix them thoroughly. Prepare 6 ramekins or well-washed crab shells for baking by coating them lightly with the butter. Divide the crabmeat mixture among the ramekins and top each one off with a dusting of the remaining bread crumbs. Place the ramekins in the oven and bake for 20 to 30 minutes, or until they are golden brown on top. Serve hot.

HUÎTRES AZI DESSI

◎◎◎

FRIED OYSTERS (TOGO)

Deep frying is a West African culinary technique that has found favor all over the African-Atlantic world. Here we go back to its roots to look at one of the Togolese ways with oysters. In this recipe the oysters, which are usually mangrove oysters, are dredged in a spicy mixture, deep-fried until they are crisp, and served with a hot sauce. Mangrove oysters are difficult to find (not to say impossible), so I have used the more readily available bluepoint oyster.

If you like to walk on the wild side of culinary life, you can use powdered habanero chile or even minced fresh chiles.

SERVES 6

Place the lemon juice in a medium-sized bowl. Shuck the oysters, detach them from their shells, and drop them into the lemon juice. Heat the oil for deep frying to 375 degrees in a heavy Dutch oven or a deep fryer. Drain the oysters and pat them dry on absorbent paper. Mix the flour and seasonings together in a paper bag. Add the oysters to the bag a few at a time, close the bag, and shake to make sure that they are well coated with the flour mixture. When the oysters are coated, remove them from the bag and fry them, a few at a time, for about 5 minutes, turning once. Drain on absorbent paper and serve immediately with their accompanying sauce.

1½ cups freshly squeezed lemon juice

24 large oysters

Peanut oil for deep frying

¾ cup flour

1 teaspoon cayenne pepper, or to taste

Salt and freshly ground black pepper, to taste

Sauce Azi Dessi (recipe follows)

SAUCE AZI DESSI

◎◎◎

AZI DESSI SAUCE (TOGO)

Fried oysters (page 219) and this sauce can be served separately, as they are in this version. The fried oysters can also be served in the sauce—in this case, the whole is served with fufu *(page 284) or with white rice.*

MAKES ABOUT 2 CUPS

1 pound tomatoes, peeled, seeded, and
    coarsely chopped

3 tablespoons red palm oil (see Note)

2 medium onions, chopped

⅛ teaspoon minced habanero chile, or to
    taste

2 cloves garlic, minced

½ cup dried smoked shrimp (see Note)

1 teaspoon ground ginger

2 tablespoons chunky peanut butter

Purée the tomatoes in a blender or food processor until you have a thick liquid. Pour the liquid into a heavy skillet, add the palm oil, and cook over low heat for 15 minutes, or until the mixture takes on a ketchup-like consistency. Add the onions, chile, and garlic and continue to cook, stirring occasionally, for 5 minutes. Place the dried smoked shrimp in the bowl of a food processor and pulverize them into a powder. Add the shrimp powder and the ginger to the tomato mixture and continue to cook, stirring often, for an additional 10 minutes. When ready to serve, add the peanut butter, stir to mix it in well, and serve hot.

NOTE: See Glossary for palm oil (page 66) and dried smoked shrimp (page 70) and Mail-Order Sources for both (page 74).

SAUCE CRABE
◎◎◎

CRAB SAUCE (BENIN)

This crab sauce, which is not a sauce at all but really one of the soupy stews that are so emblematic of African cooking, will make many think of the gumbo of the United States. In fact, these dishes are the ancestors of America's Creole gumbo. It is thought that the gumbo that is eaten in New Orleans, in Charleston, and even in Philadelphia gets its name from one of the Bantu words for okra: tchnigombo or kingombo. Even today in much of French-speaking Africa, when heading off to the market to purchase okra, all you have to remember is one word: gombo. SERVES 6 TO 8

Place the crabmeat, onions, tomatoes, chicken broth, and seasonings in a heavy stockpot. Cover and simmer over low heat for 20 minutes. Wash the okra. Top and tail it, discarding any blemished or hard pods, and cut it into ½-inch rounds. Add the okra and continue to cook for 5 minutes, or until the okra is fork-tender. Serve hot over white rice.

3½ pounds fresh lump crabmeat
2 medium onions, chopped
4 medium tomatoes, peeled, seeded, and
   coarsely chopped
1 quart chicken broth
Salt and cayenne pepper, to taste
1 pound okra

BIG FISH

SAUCE AIMÉE

◎◎◎

AIMÉE'S CRAB SAUCE (BENIN)

One afternoon, when my friend Aimée was visiting from Benin, she made one of her kamikaze shopping raids on my favorite neighborhood vegetable store. We were heading back to the apartment of her sister, whom she wanted to surprise with dinner. In short order, she'd purchased okra, tomatoes, and hot chile. As we were leaving, she spied some small fresh blue land crabs. When we returned to her sister Theodora's apartment, Aimée headed to the kitchen, and in less than an hour dinner was ready and on the table.

If you do not want a spicy sauce, remove the pricked chile midway through the cooking.

For a different taste, add a pinch of the West African Spice Mixture (page 149) to the sauce as it cooks. SERVES 4

1 pound fresh okra

2 large ripe tomatoes, peeled, seeded, and coarsely chopped

1 habanero chile, pricked with a fork (see Note)

¼ cup dried smoked shrimp, pulverized (see Note)

3 cups water

Salt and freshly ground black pepper, to taste

½ pound fresh lump crabmeat

8 large shrimp, shelled and deveined

Wash and top and tail the okra, discarding any blemished or hard pods. Place the okra in a large saucepan with the tomatoes, chile, pulverized shrimp, and water and bring it to a boil. Lower the heat and cook for 5 minutes. Add the seasonings, crabmeat, and shrimp and cook for an additional 5 to 7 minutes, or until the crabs are done. Remove the chile pepper when the desired heat is attained. Serve hot over white rice or a mash.

NOTE: See Glossary for chiles (page 55) and dried smoked shrimp (page 70) and Mail-Order Sources for both (page 74).

FISH CAKES

◎◎◎

(NIGERIA)

Leftovers are never an issue in the cooking of the African continent. If they haven't been eaten by members of the extended family or given to the needy in the neighborhood, they just take on another life and reappear on the plate at the next meal. This time leftover fish is mixed with true yam to make cakes that are then pan-fried to a golden brown. SERVES 4 TO 6

Mix the fish, the yam, I tablespoon of the oil, the butter, and the seasonings together in a medium bowl. Beat the egg and add it to the mixture, making sure that the ingredients are well distributed. Form the mixture into about 12 small, flat cakes with your hands. Heat the remaining 2 tablespoons oil in a heavy skillet and fry the cakes, a few at a time, for 3 minutes on each side over high heat, or until they are golden brown. Drain on absorbent paper and serve.

2 cups cooked fish, boned and flaked

2 cups mashed cooked yam

3 tablespoons peanut oil

1 tablespoon melted butter

Salt and freshly ground black pepper,
*   to taste*

½ teaspoon powdered hot red chile,
*   or to taste*

1 egg

Do not leave your host's

house throwing mud

in his well.

—ZULU PROVERB

SOUPIKANYA

◎◎◎

SENEGALESE GUMBO (SENEGAL)

This soup is more accurately called a stew—it is rich with the tastes of seafood and okra. Kanya means "okra" in Wolof, one of the languages of Senegal. The "soup" is finished with a float of red palm oil. The following is a basic recipe, but there are infinite variations that can be prepared with the addition of a few shrimp, a piece of shellfish, or more. The guedge and yete that are called for in the recipe are highly aromatic pieces of dried smoked mollusk and fish that are available in shops selling African ingredients. Soupikanya is slimy, and this is not a dish for those who do not care for the mucilaginous pod.

SERVES 6

1 quart water

Salt, to taste

Three 1-inch-thick firm white-fleshed fish steaks, like cod

1½ pounds small young okra

2 small eggplants, peeled and coarsely chopped

1 medium onion, peeled and grated

2 cloves garlic, minced

1 small piece guedge (see Note)

1 small piece yete (see Note)

2 tablespoons red palm oil (see Note)

Bring the water to a boil in a large saucepan, salt it, and add the fish steaks. Lower the heat to a simmer and cook the steaks for 8 to 10 minutes, or until they are cooked through but not overdone. Remove the fish steaks with a slotted spoon and reserve them and the cooking liquid.

Wash and top and tail the okra, discarding any blemished or hard pods. Crush the okra in a mortar and pestle until it is a thick paste and add it to the cooking liquid along with all the remaining ingredients except the palm oil. You may need to add more liquid to cover the vegetables. Bring to a second boil and simmer for 10 minutes, or until the okra and eggplant are cooked. Shred the cooked fish, removing any bones, and add it to the *soupikanya*. Add the palm oil and bring it to a third boil for a few seconds, then remove and serve hot with white rice.

NOTE: See the Glossary for guedge (page 61), *yete* (page 73), and palm oil (page 66), and see the Mail-Order Sources for all three (page 74).

KALDOU

◉◉◉

CASAMANCE FISH STEW (SENEGAL)

This fish stew is a light and simple dish that comes from the Casamance region in the southernmost part of Senegal. Kaldou is very similar to the blaff *of the Caribbean and like it is served with white rice.* SERVES 4

Clean and wash the fish and rub it down with 1 tablespoon of the lemon juice. Heat the oil in the bottom of a saucepan wide enough to hold the fish and cook the onion slices until they are golden. Add the water and the chile, which you will remove when the *kaldou* is seasoned to taste. Bring the mixture to a boil. Add the fish, reduce the heat, and cook, covered, for 10 minutes. Add the remaining lemon juice and continue to cook for 3 minutes. Serve hot with white rice.

2 pounds red snapper

½ cup freshly squeezed lemon juice

2 tablespoons peanut oil

2 large onions, sliced

1 quart water

1 habanero chile, pricked with a fork
   (see page 55)

THIEBOU DIENN SOUS VERRE

◎◎◎

SENEGALESE RICE AND FISH STEW (SENEGAL)

This savory rice and fish stew is the national dish of Senegal. It is an African classic and one that nobody who visits Senegal will miss. There are myriad ways of preparing thiebou dienn *and almost as many ways of spelling it. I stick to this spelling because this is how it was spelled when I first ate it in Dakar in the early 1970s.*

Like many of Africa's festive dishes, this is not a stew to prepare for a few guests. The multiple ingredients necessary for the truly elegant version that is called thiebou dienn sous verre, *as well as the time necessary to prepare it properly, mean that this is a dish to save for special entertaining.*

Thiebou dienn, *though, is frequently simplified and shows up on so many lunch tables that the joke goes that the Senegalese version of the Lord's Prayer should be amended to read, "Give us this day our daily* thieb." *This is only too true, for the Senegalese, like many of their neighbors of the former Grain Coast, are rice-eating folk. Rice appears on the table virtually every day and sometimes more than once a day. This habit of rice eating, as well as the know-how of rice cultivation, also crossed the Atlantic in the fetid holds of slave ships to transform the agriculture of the Low Country of South Carolina. The Africans who came from various regions brought with them their agricultural knowledge as well as their culinary expertise. The result is that the red rice of Charleston, South Carolina, bears a remarkable similarity to the red rice that is traditionally a component of* thiebou dienn.

SERVES 8 TO 10

4 tablespoons peanut oil

2 large onions, minced

3-inch piece smoked fish (guedge or yete if possible) (see Note)

1 6-ounce can tomato paste

9 cups slightly salted cold water

1 bunch parsley, trimmed

2 large cloves garlic

1 fresh bird chile (see Note)

2 scallions

3 pounds sea bass tail, cleaned and cut into steaks 1½ inches thick

Heat the oil in a large stockpot and brown the onion. Add the smoked fish, the tomato paste, and ¼ cup of the salted water. While the onion mixture is browning, prepare the stuffing for the sea bass steaks by placing the parsley, garlic, chile, and scallions in a food processor and pulsing until they form a thick paste. When the paste is ready, score the sea bass steaks and poke the stuffing into the slits.

Place the sea bass in the stockpot with the onion mixture, allow it to cook for 5 minutes, and add the remaining water. When the fish mixture comes to a boil, cover the pot, lower the heat, and add the vegetables in the order given, finishing off with the the pricked habanero chile, which you will remove (and reserve) when the *thiebou dienn* is spicy enough for you. Cook for 20 minutes. Remove the sea bass steaks, keeping them whole, and place them on a serving platter. Cover them with a bit of the cooking liquid, and keep them warm.

Continue cooking the *thiebou dienn* for an additional 15 minutes, then remove the vegetables and arrange them on a platter and keep them warm. Reserve 2 cups of the cooking liquid to make the sauces. Return the remaining liquid to a boil, add the rice, cover, and cook for 20 minutes, or until the liquid is absorbed and the rice is done.

While the rice is cooking, pulverize the habanero chile that you have reserved and add it to 1 cup of the reserved cooking liquid. Heat it, stirring occasionally, and place it in a sauceboat. Heat the remaining cup of reserved cooking liquid and place it in a separate sauceboat. This will give you a regular sauce and a fiery hot one.

When ready to serve, mound the rice on one platter and the fish and vegetables on another. Alternatively, you can place the rice in a large basin or deep dish and arrange the vegetables and fish on top and eat Senegalese-style with your hands (right hand only, please!) or with a large spoon.

NOTE: See Glossary for guedge (page 61), *yete* (page 73), chiles (page 55), calabaza (page 53), and broken rice (page 69) and Mail-Order Sources for all five (page 74).

½ pound calabaza, peeled and cut into
  1-inch dice (see Note)
½ pound sweet cassava, peeled and cut
  into 1-inch dice
5 small purple turnips, quartered
1 small green cabbage, cut into eighths
4 sweet potatoes, quartered
2 small eggplants, cut into 1-inch slices
5 carrots, scraped and cut into chunks
12 small okra pods, washed and
  topped and tailed (any hard pods
  discarded)
1 habanero chile, pricked with a fork
  (see page 55)
2 pounds broken rice (see Note)

CHICKEN AND FOWL

CHICKEN SOSATIES

◉◉◉

SPICED SKEWERED CHICKEN (SOUTH AFRICA)

The term sosaties *comes from the Malay words* sate, *meaning "spiced sauce," and* sesaste, *meaning "skewered meat." Early Cape spellings of the word range from* soesaties *to* sasaties *to* sassatees. *While the traditional* sosaties *are prepared from lamb, chicken is increasingly popular. Supermarkets in large cities even sell pre-marinated chicken pieces already on the skewer. The chicken needs to marinate for 24 hours before cooking.*   SERVES 4 TO 6

1½ pounds skinless, boneless chicken breast

2 tablespoons vegetable oil

4 onions, thinly sliced

1 tablespoon hot Madras curry powder

2 cloves garlic, minced

1 teaspoon coriander seeds

1 tablespoon light brown sugar

1 cup freshly squeezed lemon juice

Cut the chicken into ¾-inch cubes and place them in a deep nonreactive bowl. Heat the oil in a nonreactive saucepan and fry the onions until they are lightly browned. Add the remaining ingredients and cook for 2 minutes over low heat, stirring constantly to make sure that the sugar has dissolved. Allow the marinade to cool and pour it over the chicken. Cover the bowl with plastic wrap and refrigerate it for 24 hours.

When ready to grill the chicken pieces, remove them from the marinade, drain them, place them on skewers, and grill over hot coals or under the broiler for 10 minutes, turning once, or until the chicken is cooked through. Serve hot with Apricot Chutney (page 157), Lime Atjar (page 140), or Sweet and Sour Pears (page 156).

MUAMBA DE GALINHA

◉◉◉

CHICKEN MUAMBA (ANGOLA)

One of the classic dishes of Central Africa, this chicken stew flavored with palm oil is so popular it has given its name to an entire meal: a muambada *is a meal at which this dish is the centerpiece. There it is usually served with* eba or funge, *a cornmeal mash that has crossed the Atlantic and is known as* fungi *in the Caribbean.*

Some cooks thicken the sauce with a sprinkling of finely ground cornmeal.

SERVES 4

Wash the okra and pat it dry with paper towels. Top and tail it, discarding any blemished or hard pods. Set aside. Heat the oils in a heavy saucepan or Dutch oven. Add the chicken and brown it lightly on all sides. Add the remaining ingredients, except the okra and the calabaza. Bring to a boil over medium heat, lower the heat, and simmer, covered, for 30 minutes, or until the chicken is nearly cooked. Add the calabaza pieces and continue to cook for 10 minutes. Add the okra and cook for an additional 3 minutes. Remove the chile when the dish is seasoned to taste. Check the seasoning and serve hot.

NOTE: See Glossary (page 66) and Mail-Order Sources (page 74) for red palm oil.

20 small okra pods

1½ tablespoons olive oil

3½ tablespoons red palm oil (see Note)

1 chicken (3½ to 4 pounds), cut into serving pieces

3 onions, chopped

2 cloves garlic, minced

3 tomatoes, peeled, seeded, and coarsely chopped

1 bay leaf

1 tablespoon freshly squeezed lemon juice

1 habanero chile, pricked with a fork (see page 55)

½ pound calabaza, peeled and cut into ½-inch chunks (see page 53)

MELOUKHIA
◎◎◎

NORTH AFRICAN GREENS WITH CHICKEN (EGYPT)

Meloukhia is a leafy summer vegetable that is extremely popular in North Africa, where the leaves are available fresh, frozen, and dried. The leaves are used in a variety of soupy stews that capitalize on the slightly slippery taste of the leafy green. I'd tried it in Tunisia in a stew, but was underwhelmed by its taste until I sampled the mossy green stew prepared by my Egyptian friend Magda one evening. The simple dish was served so that the meloukhia *could be eaten in one of two ways, either as a sauce over chicken that had been boiled and stripped off the bone, or as a soup. It was delicious, and I was delighted to find that dried and frozen* meloukhia *are available in stores selling Arab products. The fresh kind is a little harder to come by but can be found occasionally. As with many transliterations from the Arabic, the green is spelled many ways, most notably* mulukhia *or* mulukhiya.

SERVES 4 TO 6

1 chicken (2½ pounds)
1 large onion, cut in half
1 bay leaf
2 cardamom pods
1 pound frozen meloukhia
    (see Note)
Salt to taste
10 cloves garlic
1 tablespoon ground coriander
2 teaspoons olive oil
1 tablespoon freshly squeezed lemon
    juice

Place the chicken in a heavy stockpot with water to cover. Tie the onion, bay leaf, and cardamom pods in a cheesecloth bag and add them to the pot. Bring to a boil, then lower the heat and cook, covered, for 40 minutes, or until the chicken is well cooked. Remove the chicken from the pot, reserving the broth. Skin the chicken and strip the meat from the bones. Shred the chicken meat and reserve it, keeping it warm. Remove the onion from the cheesecloth, mash it with a fork, add it back to the pot, and return the chicken broth to a boil. Add the *meloukhia*, season with salt, lower the heat, and cook for 3 to 5 minutes. *Be careful* not to overcook the *meloukhia.* The leaves should not sink to the bottom of the pot.

Crush the garlic in a mortar with salt to taste and the coriander. Heat the oil in a heavy skillet, add the garlic mixture, and fry it until it is golden brown. Add this garlic mixture (known as *ta'liya*) to the *meloukhia* in the stockpot, stirring well to make sure that it is mixed through. Continue to cook for an additional 2 minutes.

Add the lemon juice and serve hot with white rice and the shredded chicken on the side.

NOTE: See Glossary (page 63) and Mail-Order Sources
(page 74) for *meloukhia*.

━◆━

OSTRICH OMELETS

One of my earliest images of the food of the African continent is a Time-Life cookbook, which featured a
picture of an ostrich egg omelet. The large pan was filled to the brim with foamy egg and seemed to be de-
lighting all those present. I was amazed, decades later, when I finally made it to South Africa to find that
Margi Biggs, one of my several guides, was the daughter of ostrich farmers. I didn't get to try an ostrich
omelet during my stay, but I heard that still very much in style in this country that has yet to reel from cholesterol madness. As I was leaving for the plane, Margi gave me a well-wrapped package; in it were five
empty ostrich eggs. The massive eggs now sit on my mantel and remind me of the wonders of the continent where culinary delights like ostrich omelets await the adventurous.

━◆━

Galinha a Piri Piri

PIRI PIRI CHICKEN (MOZAMBIQUE)

Piri piri is a small fiery hot chile that is called gindungo *in Angola. It is similar to the bird or bird's-eye chile that is used in preparing Tabasco sauce. These chiles are available both fresh and dry, and can even be found in powdered form in some specialty shops. Use two or three for a mild version or add to your heart and your palate's delight. Some African cooks use as many as ten!*

The chicken must marinate for 12 hours before cooking.   SERVES 4 TO 6

6 cloves garlic, minced

2 bay leaves

½ teaspoon hot paprika

3 minced fresh bird chiles, or to taste
   (see Note)

2 cups fresh coconut milk (see Note)

2 chickens (3½ to 4 pounds each)

1 tablespoon freshly squeezed lemon
   juice

2 tablespoons butter

3 tablespoons olive oil

Mix the garlic, bay leaves, paprika, and chiles together in a large bowl to form a thick paste and slowly add the coconut milk, stirring to make sure that the ingredients are well mixed. Cut the chickens into serving-sized pieces and score the skin. Place the chicken in the marinade, cover with plastic wrap, and refrigerate for 12 hours, turning often to make sure that all the pieces are well coated.

When ready to cook, remove the chicken from the marinade, reserving the liquid. Add the lemon juice, butter, and olive oil to the marinade and bring it to a boil over medium heat. Reserve a little marinade in a separate bowl as a dipping sauce. Allow the mixture to cool slightly and use it to baste the chicken. Grill the chicken over medium coals or under the broiler, using the marinade mixture as a basting sauce. Serve hot, with the reserved marinade as a dipping sauce.

VARIATION: Substitute 3 pounds shelled, deveined prawns for the chicken.

NOTE: See Glossary for chiles (page 55) and coconut milk (page 56), and see Mail-Order Sources for chiles (page 74).

FRANGO GRELHADO PIRI PIRI

◎◎◎

HOT AND SPICY GRILLED CHICKEN (ANGOLA)

Pili pili *is the name given to hot chile in many parts of western and southern Africa. The word is pronounced and spelled many different ways and sometimes transcribed as* periperi, piri piri, *or even* peli peli, *but the thought and the zing of the taste are the same.* Pili pili *is the transcription of the word that is used to refer to the red hot chile frequently found in the marketplace. I have replaced the* piri piri *chile in this recipe with the even hotter habanero. I've used it sparingly, but the chile-heads among you can go for it. This dish is a simple but delicious way with broiled chicken.*   SERVES 4 TO 6

Preheat the broiler to its highest setting. Wash the chicken parts and pat them dry with absorbent paper. Arrange the chicken in a broiling pan. Mix the lemon juice, oil, and chile together in a small bowl and brush some of it over the chicken with a pastry brush. Place the chicken under the broiler and cook for about 7 to 10 minutes on each side. When done, remove and serve hot with white rice. This dish can also be prepared on an outdoor grill.

1 frying chicken (3½ pounds), cut into serving pieces
2 tablespoons fresh lemon juice
¼ cup peanut oil
¼ teaspoon finely minced habanero chile, or to taste (see page 55)

AN EGYPTIAN MEAL

YASSA AU POULET

Chicken yassa, from Senegal, has become one of my hallmark dishes. Not only do I serve it frequently in my home, even daring to serve it when I have Senegalese visitors, but I have also presented it on television on several occasions. One of the reasons that I am so attached to *poulet yassa* is that it is the first sub-Saharan African dish that "clicked" with my taste buds. I can remember the time I first tasted it, near the end of my first trip to Africa in the early 1970s. My mother and I were staying in the N'Gor area of Dakar in a large hotel left over from colonial vacationers. Down a long and somewhat dark street were a few local restaurants catering to tourists. We ventured off in search of some food other than the quite good restaurant fare and happened upon a small place. The tables were set with tie-dyed fabric, the lamp shades were made from woven baskets, and the seating was on small stools. When presented with the menu, I saw *poulet yassa*. I ordered it and it's been love ever since.

I have learned on many subsequent trips, and by eating *yassa* not only in Senegalese restaurants but also in many Senegalese homes, that the dish is traditional to the Casamance region of southern Senegal. While chicken *yassa* has become the best-known dish, there are many other types of *yassa*. There is lamb *yassa* and fish *yassa*, and even monkey *yassa!* Currently the trend is to heartier *yassa*, which may include such nontraditional additions as stuffed olives, carrot slices, and Dijon-style mustard. I still prefer the classic *yassa*, but select for yourself. *Yassa* is traditionally served with white rice.

YASSA AU POULET CLASSIQUE
◎◎◎

CLASSIC CHICKEN YASSA (SENEGAL)

For full flavor, the chicken needs to marinate overnight (or at least two hours) before being cooked.   SERVES 6

The night before, prepare a marinade by mixing the lemon juice, onions, salt, pepper, and 4 tablespoons of the peanut oil in a deep bowl. Prick the chile with the tines of a fork and add it to the marinade as well. When the dish has reached the desired degree of hotness, remove the chile and reserve (it can be minced and served separately to the chile heads). Place the chicken pieces in the marinade, cover with plastic wrap, and refrigerate overnight. (If you're pressed for time, you can marinate just 2 hours, but the flavor will not be as intense.)

When ready to cook, preheat the broiler. Remove the chicken pieces from the marinade, reserving the marinade and the onions. Place the pieces on the broiler rack and grill them briefly, until they are just lightly browned on both sides. Set aside. Drain the onions from the marinade. Heat the remaining tablespoon of oil in a deep skillet and sauté the onions over medium heat until they are tender and translucent. Add the remaining marinade and cook until the liquid is heated through. Add the chicken pieces and the water and stir to mix well. Lower the heat and simmer, covered, until the chicken pieces are cooked through, at least 30 minutes. Serve the *yassa* hot over white rice.

¼ cup freshly squeezed lemon juice

4 large onions, sliced

Salt and freshly ground black pepper, to taste

5 tablespoons peanut oil

1 habanero chile (see page 55)

1 frying chicken (2½ to 4½ pounds), cut into serving pieces

½ cup water

YASSA AU POULET II
◎◎◎

CHICKEN YASSA (SENEGAL)

This variation on the classic yassa *uses carrots and pimento-stuffed olives to create a rich chicken stew. It always comes up a winner.*

The chicken should marinate at least three hours before cooking.   SERVES 6

¼ cup freshly squeezed lemon juice

4 large onions, thinly sliced

Salt and freshly ground black pepper, to
    taste

⅛ teaspoon minced fresh habanero chile,
    or to taste (see page 55)

5 tablespoons peanut oil

1 frying chicken (2½ to 3½ pounds),
    cut into serving pieces

1 habanero chile, pricked with a fork

½ cup pimento-stuffed olives

4 carrots, scraped and thinly sliced

1 tablespoon Dijon-style mustard

½ cup water

In a large nonreactive bowl, prepare a marinade by mixing the lemon juice, onions, salt, pepper, minced chile, and 4 tablespoons of the peanut oil in a large bowl. Place the chicken pieces in the marinade, making sure that they are all well covered. Cover the bowl with plastic wrap and allow the chicken to marinate for at least 3 hours in the refrigerator.

Preheat the broiler. Remove the chicken pieces, reserving the marinade and onions, and place the chicken in a shallow pan. Broil the chicken until it is lightly browned on both sides. Remove the onions from the marinade. Heat the remaining tablespoon of oil in a flameproof 5-quart casserole or Dutch oven and cook the onions slowly until tender and translucent. Add the reserved marinade. When the liquid is thoroughly heated, add the chicken pieces, pricked chile, olives, carrots, mustard, and water. When the dish has reached the desired degree of hotness, remove the chile and reserve (it can be served separately to the chile heads). Stir to mix well, then bring the *yassa* slowly to a boil. Lower the heat and simmer, covered, for about 30 minutes, or until the chicken is cooked through. Serve hot over white rice.

KEDJENOU

◎◎◎

TERRA-COTTA STEWED CHICKEN (CÔTE D'IVOIRE)

If there is a dish that is emblematic of Côte d'Ivoire for many it is kedjenou. *Traditionally served with* attieké, *a fermented starch that is also traditional to the Côte d'Ivoire, the* kedjenou *is a slowly cooked dish that is easily adapted to western kitchens. Traditionally* kedjenou *is prepared in a canari, or terra-cotta pot, that is sealed and then placed in the ashes of an open fire. The top is sealed with a banana leaf and the pot is left to cook slowly until the stew develops a taste that has been described by some as sublime. This is a perfect way to tenderize the roadrunner chickens that are frequently found in traditional markets and it takes full advantage of their rich full flavor. Many traditional* kedjenous *are not prepared with chicken at all, but rather with guinea hen, which equally gains from this slow-cooking method. If you don't have a canari or an open fire, use a heavy Dutch oven or a flameproof terra-cotta cooker.* SERVES 4 TO 6

Place all the ingredients in a Dutch oven or flameproof terra-cotta cooker. Cover with a lid that is heavy and tightly fitting enough so that no steam escapes. Place the cooker over medium heat and cook until you hear the contents begin to simmer. (*Do not peek.* The lid must not be lifted at any time during the cooking process so that the *kedjenou* can cook in its own juices.) When you hear the simmer, lower the heat and cook for 45 minutes to 1 hour. While cooking, shake the pot gently every 5 minutes or so to keep the ingredients from sticking to the bottom. Remove the bay leaf. Serve hot with *fufu* balls (page 284) or over white rice.

1 roasting chicken (4½ to 5½ pounds), cut into serving pieces

4 medium onions, coarsely chopped

5 ripe tomatoes, peeled, seeded, and coarsely chopped

⅛ teaspoon minced habanero chile, or to taste (see page 55)

3 large cloves garlic, minced

1 tablespoon minced fresh ginger

¼ teaspoon ground ginger

1 bay leaf

Salt and freshly ground black pepper, to taste

BASTILLA

◎◎◎

PIGEON PIE (MOROCCO)

This classic pigeon pie is a festive Moroccan dish that is usually served at large banquets. Most of the recipes that I've seen for the dish have several pages of steps and are prepared in banquet-sized quantities. I live by myself, and unless I'm preparing for a large party, I am unlikely to have more than six folk at a time to dinner. This, then, is an adaptation of the classic recipe using Cornish hens, suitable for those who want bastilla done relatively rapidly and for few people. SERVES 4

2 Cornish game hens, including giblets

1 teaspoon sea salt

2 cloves garlic

3 tablespoons minced fresh parsley

1 small onion, minced

2 teaspoons ras al-hanout (see Note)

1½ tablespoons plus ¼ cup butter

2 cups water

½ cup blanched almonds

1½ tablespoons olive oil

3 eggs

15 to 20 sheets of filo

¼ cup confectioners' sugar

½ teaspoon cinnamon

Wash the hens and giblets. Place the salt, the garlic, and the parsley in the bowl of a mortar and pound until you have a paste. Rub the paste on the hens. Place them in a stockpot with the onion, the ras al-hanout, 1½ tablespoons of the butter, and the water. Bring to a boil, then lower the heat and cook, covered, for 35 to 45 minutes, or until the hens are cooked and tender.

While the hens are cooking, sauté the almonds in the olive oil until they are lightly browned. Place them in the bowl of a food processor and pulse until they are finely chopped. When the hens are cooked, reserve the cooking liquid and reduce it by boiling to 1 cup. Let the hens cool and pick the meat from the bones. When the cooking liquid has thickened, beat the eggs until light and drizzle them into the cooking liquid, stirring constantly, until you have a thick curd. The bastilla is now ready to be assembled.

Preheat the oven to 350 degrees. Grease a deep cake pan (I use a 2-inch-deep springform pan.) Melt the remaining ¼ cup butter in a small saucepan. Separate the filo sheets and line the pan with 4 of them so that they overhang the edges. Place another filo sheet in the bottom and coat them all well with the melted butter. Place a few of the hen pieces and giblets on top of the pastry and sprinkle it with a few chopped almonds. Add some of the curd, top it with 3 sheets of the filo, and coat the filo with melted butter. Continue in this manner with the hen pieces and curd until they have been used up. Add a final layer of filo and fold the overhanging layers in. Bind it shut with some of the melted butter and sprinkle the top with the remaining melted butter and almond pieces. Bake for 15 minutes, or until the bastilla is golden brown. When ready, remove and flip the bastilla onto a serving plate. Sprinkle the top with a mixture of the confectioners' sugar and cinnamon and serve hot.

NOTE: See Glossary (page 68) and Mail-Order Sources (page 74) for ras al-hanout.

LUNCH WITH THE MZEE IN MOMBASA

I have lived on islands for most of my life, going from Long Island to Manhattan Island to Martha's Vineyard. It was once inconceivable to me that there were people who had never seen the sea. In Kenya, many years ago, an old man (or *mzee*) challenged my insularity.

I'd met him at his small upland coffee plantation in the Mount Kenya area when his nephew, my tour guide, made an unexpected stop on an improvised tour. The old man greeted me warmly with steaming hot coffee and bananas picked from the tree in his front yard. As we talked, I mentioned that we were heading to Mombasa the following day and he asked if he could join us. When we arrived in Mombasa the next morning and took the ferry across the water, the light in his eyes was riveting. I asked the nephew why the old man was so excited. "He's never seen the sea," was the reply. I was amazed; the joy on his face made the trip a cherished memory.

I'd rather forget the uncomfortable ride of more than eight hours down and back in the same day, and I've long since dismissed the lunch of mediocre biryani in a dingy small hole-in-the-wall spot of dubious cleanliness. I'm still amazed that I survived eating blood sausage in an open market on a dare on the way down. But the unforgettable part of my trip to Mombasa was seeing the sea for the first time through the eyes of a *mzee*.

TAJINE DE POULET
AU CITRON ET AUX OLIVES

◎◎◎

CHICKEN TAJINE WITH LEMONS AND OLIVES (MOROCCO)

*Another memorable clay pot dish is the tajine of Morocco, named for the conical clay pots in which these dishes are tradition-
ally prepared. There are numerous tajines in the culinary repertoire of the Maghreb, ranging from the pie-like lamb-liver
tajine of Tunisia to the classic slow-cooked stews of Morocco. This variation uses the olives that grow throughout the region
and the wonderfully aromatic preserved lemons that are hallmarks of Moroccan cooking.*

*Traditionally served as one of the many dishes in a Moroccan meal, this tajine can also be a main dish when served with
white rice.*   SERVES 6

2 tablespoons olive oil

1 chicken (4 pounds), cut into serving
    pieces

1 medium onion, minced

2 cloves garlic, minced

1½ cups water

3 Preserved Lemons, (page 139), cut
    into quarters

½ pound pitted Moroccan-style green
    olives

Bay leaf

Salt and freshly ground black pepper,
    to taste

Heat the olive oil in a heavy Dutch oven and brown the chicken
pieces. Add the onion and garlic and cook, stirring occasionally,
until the onion is translucent. Add the water and the remaining
ingredients and bring to a boil over medium heat. Cook for 15
minutes, then lower the heat and continue to cook, covered, for
an additional 30 minutes, or until the chicken is fork-tender.
When ready to serve, remove the bay leaf and transfer the stew
to a serving dish. If you have cooked the dish in a tajine, simply
cover it and bring it to the table.

Suya
◎◎◎

CHICKEN SKEWERS (NIGERIA)

This is a favorite dish from northern Nigeria that can be prepared with beef, lamb, or chicken. The suya *seasoning can be made in large batches and will keep for a month or more in a tightly sealed jar.* SERVES 4

Preheat the broiler. Cut the chicken breasts into thin slices. Mix all the dry ingredients together and sprinkle the mixture on the chicken slices. Allow the chicken to marinate for 5 minutes. Thread the chicken onto skewers and brush with the oil. Cook on a grill or broil for 3 minutes on each side. Remove the *suya* from the skewers and serve hot with sliced onions and tomatoes.

1 pound skinless, boneless chicken breast
1 tablespoon powdered garlic
1 tablespoon ground ginger
1 tablespoon paprika
2 tablespoons cayenne pepper
1 tablespoon minced dried onion
2 tablespoons finely minced peanuts
2 tablespoons peanut oil

BASSI SALTE
◎◎◎

MALIAN MILLET COUSCOUS (MALI)

This couscous is a classic from the area that was formerly known as French Sudan. In Mali and Senegal it is served with a millet couscous. Some people think this couscous may actually be the predecessor of the more famous Moroccan one. No matter which one came first, this couscous is a delicious addition to the repertoire. If you are able to find millet couscous, you will have the more authentic version. If not, use regular couscous or even whole-wheat couscous for variety.

The habanero chile can be placed in a small separate bouquet garni of cheesecloth and removed when the bassi salte *is hot enough for your individual taste.* SERVES 6

Heat the oil in the bottom of a couscoussière or in a heavy Dutch oven and brown the chicken pieces, the leeks, and the onions. Stir occasionally to make sure that nothing sticks and overcooks. Add the vegetables in the order given, except the beans, and cook lightly to make sure that all the vegetables are lightly browned. Prepare a bouquet garni by tying the seasonings up in a piece of cheesecloth. Add it and the water to the mixture. Bring to a boil. Lower the heat, cover, and simmer for 1½ hours, or until the chicken is cooked through. Remove the bouquet garni. Add the beans and continue to cook for 2 to 3 minutes. Serve hot over couscous.

3 tablespoons peanut oil

1 stewing hen (4 pounds), cut into serving pieces

2 leeks, minced, including 1 inch of green part

3 onions, coarsely chopped

2 large sweet potatoes, peeled and cut into chunks

3 small turnips, peeled and cut into chunks

3 carrots, scraped and cut into thick slices

1 large zucchini, cut into ½-inch slices

1 pound calabaza, peeled and cut into 1-inch chunks (see page 53)

3 small eggplants, cut into 1-inch chunks

3 large tomatoes, peeled, seeded, and coarsely chopped

1 cucumber, cut into ½-inch slices

1 stalk celery, cut into thirds

3 branches fresh thyme

1 bay leaf

3 sprigs flat-leaf parlsey

1 habanero chile, pricked with a fork (see page 55)

7 cups water

1 cup canned Great Northern beans, drained

PEITO DE GALINHOLA
◎◎◎

GUINEA FOWL BREASTS (SOUTH AFRICA)

This bird with speckled plumage and a piercing call was known to the Ancient Egyptians. The Romans called it the Numidian, or Carthage, hen, after its region of origin. This appellation is still visible in the bird's scientific name, Numida meleagris. *It would later take its name from another part of Africa, Guinea. The lean meat of the guinea fowl is quite low in cholesterol. It is not readily available, but your butcher should be able to order some for you. In this recipe from the Portuguese in South Africa, the boneless breasts are marinated for 24 hours and then pan-fried.* SERVES 4 TO 6

6 guinea fowl cutlets

4 small cloves garlic, minced

2 teaspoons crumbled fresh thyme

1 teaspoon mild paprika

¼ teaspoon ground cumin

1 bay leaf

Salt, to taste

Minced fresh bird chile, to taste (see Note)

4 teaspoons plus 2 tablespoons olive oil

½ cup Portuguese white wine

2 tablespoons butter

Have the butcher remove the breasts from the guinea fowl and cut them into cutlets (one fowl should yield 6 cutlets). Place the cutlets in a deep bowl. Prepare a marinade from the garlic, thyme, paprika, cumin, bay leaf, salt, and chile, the 4 teaspoons olive oil, and the wine and pour it over the cutlets. Cover with plastic wrap and refrigerate for 24 hours.

When ready to serve, heat 1 tablespoon each of the olive oil and butter in a heavy skillet. Remove 3 of the cutlets from the marinade and pan-fry them in the oil and butter for 5 to 8 minutes on each side, or until the cutlets are cooked through. Repeat with the remaining oil and butter and the second 3 cutlets. Serve hot—and don't forget the accompanying *vinho verde.*

NOTE: See Glossary (page 55) and Mail-Order Sources (page 74) for bird chiles.

MOYO DE POULET FUMÉ
◎◎◎

SMOKED CHICKEN WITH SAUCE (BENIN)

I learned this dish from my West African sister and friend Suzanne, who is a fabulous cook. Although she's a dentist by profession and the mother of two, she always takes time to share her recipes with me. One of my favorites, this dish combines such West African staples as tomatoes and hot chiles with the taste of smoked chicken. The surprise of soy sauce is not traditional. It's just my lower-sodium way of replacing the seasoning cube of Maggi-brand bouillon that is ubiquitous in much of French West African cooking today.　　　　　SERVES 4 TO 6

Wash the chicken, pat it dry with paper towels, and cut it into serving pieces. Place the chicken and the remaining ingredients in a heavy saucepan or Dutch oven. Bring to a boil, then reduce the heat to low and simmer, uncovered, stirring occasionally, for 20 minutes, or until the flavors have mixed and the onions are tender. When the dish has reached the desired degree of hotness, remove the chiles and reserve (they can be served separately to the chile heads). Serve hot with white rice.

1 smoked chicken (3½ pounds), skinned

6 medium-sized ripe tomatoes, peeled, seeded, and coarsely chopped

2 medium onions, thinly sliced

1 tablespoon peanut oil

2 teaspoons reduced-sodium soy sauce

2 habanero chiles, pricked with a fork (see page 55)

●━●

FISH EYES AND FRIENDSHIP

My mother accompanied me on my first trip to the continent. Raised in the old school of eat-everything-that's-given-to-you, she was an invaluable traveling companion. Nowhere were her talents of taking a deep breath and swallowing rapidly more needed than in Abidjan, Côte d'Ivoire.

As some of the early tourists to the continent, we were invited to a diplomatic reception in the grand ballroom of the newly opened Hôtel Ivoire. We attended gladly, circulating and meeting people. One of our new friends invited us home to meet his family and have dinner. We accepted with alacrity, by now used to the expansive hospitality of the continent.

When we arrived, we had cocktails and then proceeded to table where a lavish Western spread was served. We ate our fill and were astounded when the hostess then proceeded to say, "We want you to taste some of our food as well, and so I've made *foutou* with *sauce claire.*" We dug in again, only to find that Mom's portion featured a fish head, considered to be a delicacy and accorded to her by virtue of her age. Well, trouper that she is, she dug in, navigated enough mouthfuls to honor the chef, and then attacked the fish eye with a masterful gulp. I simply watched in amazement. Even today, more than twenty-five years later, I only have to say *"sauce claire"* to Mom to start a giggle going. We've known the Abidjan family for a quarter of a century, but this is the first they'll know of just what rough going that first meal was and how glad we are that fish eyes didn't interfere with friendship.

●━●

MEATS AND ORGAN MEATS

GIGOT D'AGNEAU AUX ÉPICES MAROCAINES

◎◎◎

LEG OF LAMB ENCRUSTED WITH MOROCCAN SPICES (MOROCCO)

This is not a traditional Moroccan dish but one that I invented, in which the spices that scent the tajines and méchouis *of the region are used to flavor a leg of lamb.*

You can use any kind of wine you wish. If vin gris *is not available, I use whatever red wine I have around the house.*

SERVES 10

Pat the leg of lamb dry. With the sharp end of a paring knife, make about 10 to 15 1-inch slits all over the leg. Cut the garlic cloves into thin slivers and place a sliver of garlic into each of the slits. Rub the lamb with the wine, cover it with cheesecloth, and allow it to sit for 1 hour.

Preheat the oven to 450 degrees. Remove the cheesecloth from the leg. Mix the Moroccan Spice Mixture and the lemon pepper together and slather them on the lamb. Roast the meat for 15 minutes at 450 degrees, then lower the heat to 350 degrees and cook at 15 minutes per pound for medium rare and 20 minutes per pound for well done. Allow the roast to rest for 15 minutes, then slice against the grain and serve.

One 5-pound shank-end leg of lamb
2 cloves garlic
2 cups Moroccan vin gris
¼ cup Moroccan Spice Mixture
  (page 147)
1 tablespoon lemon pepper

BROCHETTES DE ROGNONS DE MOUTON
◎◎◎

BROCHETTES OF LAMB KIDNEY (ALGERIA)

The pied noir *(the French living in Algeria) have a fondness for innards. Their tables feature* meguena, *or brain pâté, liver sausages,* schkemba, *or tripe, and stuffed spleen—all delicious tastes that are way too "exotic" for all but die-hard gourmands. These brochettes of lamb kidney should be more palatable for the timid.*

Kidneys occasionally have a slight unpleasant odor of urine. Soaking them for one hour in water to which salt or vinegar has been added can eliminate this. The proportions of salt to water are one tablespoon to one quart.

SERVES 4 TO 6

12 lamb kidneys
Salt and freshly ground pepper, to taste
½ cup olive oil

Prepare the kidneys by removing the membrane surrounding them and cutting the kidneys in half. Remove all the internal fat and blood vessels and cut the kidneys into ¾-inch cubes. Season the cubes with salt and pepper and place them in a large bowl. Cover them with the olive oil, making sure that all the pieces are well coated. Let the kidney cubes marinate in the oil for 30 minutes, then slip them onto small skewers. Grill them on a barbecue or under the broiler for 8 to 10 minutes, turning them occasionally. Serve hot.

TAJINE D'AGNEAU AUX PRUNEAUX
◎◎◎

LAMB TAJINE WITH PRUNES (MOROCCO)

This tajine is reserved for special occasions like breaking the fast during Ramadan. It brings together the richness of lamb, the sweetness of prunes, and the tastes of cinnamon, saffron, and rosewater in a dense stew. SERVES 6 TO 8

Heat the butter and oil in a heavy saucepan. Add the onion, lamb, salt, pepper, cinnamon, and saffron. Cook for 5 minutes over medium heat, stirring so that the lamb is browned. Add the water and bring to a boil. Cover, lower the heat, and cook for 1 hour, or until the lamb is tender.

While the lamb is cooking, soak the prunes and raisins in water to cover for 20 minutes. Transfer them with the soaking water to a small saucepan, add the sugar and cinnamon, and simmer for 10 minutes.

When the meat is done, remove the cinnamon stick and add the prunes and raisins to the cooked lamb. Mound the dish in a tajine or on a serving platter, drizzle the rosewater on top, and sprinkle with the sesame seeds and toasted almonds. Serve hot.

NOTE: See Glossary for almonds (page 49), rosewater (page 69), and sesame seeds (page 70), and see Mail-Order Sources (page 74) for all three.

1 tablespoon butter
1 tablespoon olive oil
1 small onion, minced
2½ pounds boneless lamb shoulder, cut into 1-inch cubes
Salt and freshly ground black pepper, to taste
½ teaspoon ground cinnamon
¼ teaspoon saffron
1 cup water
1 pound pitted prunes
½ cup dark raisins
3 tablespoons sugar
1 3-inch piece cinnamon stick
1 tablespoon rosewater (see Note)
⅓ cup toasted sesame seeds (see Note)
½ cup toasted almonds (see Note)

SOSATIES

◎◎◎

GRILLED LAMB KEBABS (SOUTH AFRICA)

Sosaties *are a prime offering at any South African* braai, *or barbecue, worthy of note. Traditional recipes call for a marinating process that lasts for three to four days before the meat is finally grilled and yields results that are tender and tasty. This recipe calls for two to three days of marination. Lamb is the traditional meat used, but chicken, fish, and even prawns find themselves skewered and presented unto the great South African god of barbecue.*

MAKES ABOUT 30 SOSATIES

4½ pounds boneless leg of lamb

1 tablespoon butter

2 large onions, thinly sliced

1½ cups water

1½ cups cider vinegar

½ cup apricot jam

10 dried apricot halves, snipped into small pieces

½ teaspoon mild curry powder

½ teaspoon turmeric

1 bay leaf

4 teaspoons sugar

Salt and freshly ground black pepper, to taste

Cut the lamb into ¾-inch cubes and place them in a deep nonreactive dish. Heat the butter in a deep nonreactive saucepan until foaming. Add the onions and cook them until they begin to brown. Add the water and cook for an additional 2 minutes, or until the onions are tender. Add the remaining ingredients and bring to a boil over medium heat. Cook for 3 minutes, then remove the marinade from the heat, allow it to cool, and pour it over the lamb. Cover with plastic wrap and refrigerate for 2 to 3 days. When ready to grill, drain the lamb, reserving the liquid, and thread the lamb pieces onto small skewers. Grill over hot coals or under the broiler for 15 minutes, or until the lamb is done to taste. Serve hot accompanied by a chutney such as the one on page 157 or Sweet and Sour Pears (page 156).

KOFTA KEBABS

◎◎◎

MINCED LAMB KEBABS (KENYA)

One of eastern Africa's legacies from the period of British colonialism is a large population of people from India. They have, in many cases, brought their culinary traditions with them, and the streets of cities like Mombasa in Kenya are pungent with the aroma of curries cooking and the smoky perfume of kebabs being grilled over wood braziers. These kebabs are prepared from minced lamb and have some of the tastes of the Middle East and of Mughal India. They are delicious when accompanied by rice or even when made smaller and served on skewers as cocktail party food.

If you are preparing these for a cocktail party, you may wish to shape them in smaller cylinders and thread them on bamboo skewers. In that case, soak the bamboo skewers in water beforehand so that they will not catch fire when they are under the broiler.

SERVES 4

Preheat the broiler. Mix all the ingredients together in a medium bowl, making sure that the spices are evenly distributed throughout the ground lamb. With your hands, form 2-inch cylinders of the minced lamb mixture and thread them onto metal skewers. Place the skewers on a broiler rack and cook for 5 minutes on each side, or until the lamb is cooked through. Serve hot with white rice.

1 pound minced lamb

1 large onion, minced

2 cloves garlic, minced

1 teaspoon minced fresh cilantro

Pinch of minced habanero chile, or to taste (see page 55)

2 teaspoons hot Madras-style curry powder

¼ teaspoon ground cinnamon

⅛ teaspoon ground cloves

KESKOU FASSIA

◉◉◉

FEZ-STYLE LAMB COUSCOUS (MOROCCO)

Fez, the walled city in the middle of Morocco, seems to have been transported from Biblical times. The streets of the Medina of Fez el Bali and Fez el Djedid are magical for those who love the past, with their twisting alleyways and souks where the stands are still set out according to the ancient guild system. For those fortunate enough to eat in Fez, it is clear the food of this city is some of the most sophisticated in Morocco. I consider couscous as it is served in Fez to be one of the Moroccan classics. It's time-consuming, but the result is worth it. I've cut out a few of the steps in the interest of saving time. SERVES 6

MÉCHOUI (SPIT-ROASTED LAMB)

Cut the lamb into 1-inch pieces. Place the olive oil, saffron, ginger, coriander, salt, and pepper in the bottom of a couscoussière with the cold water and whisk them until they are well mixed. Add the lamb pieces and bring them to a boil for 2 minutes over high heat. Lower the heat. Add the hot water, parsley, cilantro, and onions and cook for 45 minutes, or until the lamb is tender. Place the vegetables on top of the cooking meat. Cover and cook, beginning with the harder vegetables like the carrots and turnips, then gradually add the softer: eggplant, calabaza, and zucchini, so that they will all be done at the same time. While the meat and vegetables are cooking, prepare the couscous according to the directions on page 275.

When ready to serve, heat the serving platter, mound the couscous in the middle, and serve the meat and vegetables in a bowl.

3 pounds lamb shoulder
1 tablespoon olive oil
¼ teaspoon saffron
½ teaspoon minced fresh ginger
½ teaspoon ground coriander
Salt, to taste
½ teaspoon freshly ground black pepper
3 cups cold water
6 cups hot water
4 sprigs flat-leaf parsley
4 sprigs fresh cilantro
3 medium onions, minced
1 pound carrots, scraped and cut into 1-inch chunks
1 pound small white turnips, peeled and cut into 1-inch chunks
½ pound small eggplants, cut into 1-inch chunks
1 pound calabaza, peeled and cut into 1-inch chunks (see page 53)
1 pound zucchini, cut into 1-inch chunks
Couscous (page 275)

BROCHETTES D'AGNEAU
◎◎◎

LAMB KEBABS (NORTH AFRICA)

Lamb kebabs are a way of life in many parts of northern Africa. They appear on the menus at fancy restaurants, are served as snacks in small cafés, and can even be found as street food at vendor stalls in large marketplaces. The spicing depends on the talent of the cook and market availability. This recipe is just a suggestion. Personalize it by using your own favorite North African spices. You may find that you want a bit more cumin, a hint of hot chile, or no cumin at all. Taste, try, and decide.

This works well on the outdoor grill in the summer. Cut the lamb into smaller pieces for perfect snacks or hors d'oeuvre nibbles.

The lamb needs to marinate for two to three hours before grilling.   SERVES 4 TO 6

1½ pounds boneless leg of lamb
1 tablespoon paprika
½ teaspoon ground cumin
1 teaspoon freshly ground black pepper
1 sprig flat-leaf parsley, minced
2 tablespoons olive oil

Prepare the lamb by cutting it into 1-inch chunks. Mix the remaining ingredients together in a bowl, place the lamb chunks in it, and allow them to marinate for 2 to 3 hours. When ready to cook, preheat the broiler. Remove the lamb chunks from the marinade, reserving it. Thread the lamb on skewers and place them on a rack under the broiler. Grill them for 5 to 7 minutes on each side, turning once, or until they have reached desired doneness. Baste them frequently with the reserved marinade, making sure all the marinade used on the lamb is well cooked. Serve hot.

MAFÉ
◎◎◎

PEANUT BUTTER STEW (SENEGAL)

Mafé is a Senegalese classic. It is also an entrant into the peanut stew sweepstakes that could be held for dishes from all over the continent. Here the meat of choice is lamb, but mafé *could also be prepared from beef or chicken. Traditionally the stew is served with white rice.*
SERVES 4 TO 6

Heat the oil in a heavy saucepan, add the onion, and cook over medium heat until it is translucent. Add the meat and continue to cook, stirring occasionally, until it is lightly browned on all sides.

In a small bowl, mix the peanut butter with the cold water and pour it over the meat. Dilute the tomato paste with the hot water, pour the liquid over the stew, and stir well to make sure all the ingredients are well mixed. Add the remaining ingredients, lower the heat, cover, and cook, stirring occasionally, for I hour, or until the meat is tender. Remove the thyme sprigs and bay leaves. Serve hot over white rice.

2 tablespoons peanut oil

1 large onion, minced

2 pounds lamb stew meat, cut into 1½-inch pieces

½ cup creamy peanut butter

1½ cups cold water

⅓ cup tomato paste

2 cups hot water

4 large carrots, scraped and cut into 1-inch pieces

3 sprigs fresh thyme

2 bay leaves

Salt and freshly ground black pepper, to taste

KHLIGH

◎◎◎

BEEF SHANKS (MOROCCO)

I once had occasion to speak to a group of Moroccan Jews about the wonders of their cuisine. In studying their foodways, I was taken by the way they have adapted the tastes of a country to the dietary traditions of a religion. Morocco's cumin and paprika, saffron and cinnamon all turn up in their dishes, but with twists that are unique to the Sephardic cuisine. Although simpler in its seasonings than many dishes, lovingly slow-cooked khligh *is just such a dish. It is so popular that some families even have it at breakfast with fried eggs.*　　　SERVES 6

2 pounds beef shank, cut into 4-inch pieces

5 tablespoons olive oil

1½ quarts water

2 tablespoons minced flat-leaf parsley

Salt, to taste

Place all the ingredients in a heavy Dutch oven and bring them to a boil. Lower the heat, cover, and simmer for 3 hours, until the liquids become a thick sauce and the meat is falling-off-the-bone tender. Serve hot with a green salad, fresh crusty bread, and mint tea (page 340).

MWAMBE

◎◎◎

MWAMBE BEEF (CONGO)

This dish is a classic from Central Africa. Though this version is made with beef, mwambe *can be prepared with beef, lamb, fish, or the ubiquitous chicken.*

Rub the beef pieces with the lemon juice and salt. Heat the oil in a heavy stockpot or Dutch oven, add the beef and the onions, and cook until the onions are translucent and the beef is lightly browned. Add the remaining ingredients, lower the heat, cover, and cook for 1½ hours, or until the beef is fork-tender. Serve hot with white rice.

3 pounds stewing beef, cut into 1-inch pieces

1 tablespoon freshly squeezed lemon juice

½ teaspoon salt

2 tablespoons peanut oil

2 large onions, chopped

⅛ teaspoon minced habanero chile, or to taste (see page 55)

7 medium-sized ripe tomatoes, peeled, seeded, and coarsely chopped

4 cups water

DAMBUN NAMA

◎◎◎

SHREDDED BEEF (NIGERIA)

This crispy shredded beef is served as a snack or is sprinkled on top of salads in parts of Nigeria. The ginger gives it a spicy, almost Asian, taste.
SERVES 4

1 pound lean beef round steak
¼ cup water
Peanut oil for deep frying
1 teaspoon cayenne pepper
1 teaspoon ground ginger
Salt, to taste

Cut the beef into 3-inch pieces, place it in a 3-quart saucepan with the water, and cook it, covered, over low heat for 20 minutes, or until well cooked. Heat the oil for deep frying to 375 degrees in a heavy Dutch oven or deep fryer. Remove the meat, place it in a mortar, and pound it until it is shredded. Deep-fry the shredded meat in the oil a bit at a time until all the meat is cooked. Mix the dry ingredients together and sprinkle them over the beef to season it. Serve hot.

KITFO LEB LEB

◎◎◎

COOKED KITFO (ETHIOPIA)

Unlike many of their African cousins, Ethiopians are lovers of meat. To them that means red meat and quite frequently raw meat. Kitfo leb leb, an Ethiopian classic, is that nation's equivalent of steak tartare. In this recipe, the ingredients are the same, only the meat is slightly cooked. You could use the seasonings for a well-done hamburger if you wish, but you'll have something else again.

Clearly, this is not a recipe for those who are concerned about the E. coli bacteria and the quality of their beef, but if you know your butcher and you usually eat your steak rare or raw in defiance of the USDA dietary guidelines, you might want to try this.

SERVES 4

Place the beef on a chopping board and mince it with a knife until you have a hamburger-like consistency. Place all the spices in a heavy skillet and toast them over medium heat for 3 minutes or so, stirring constantly to make sure they do not burn. Grind them all together in a mortar or a spice mill. Add the toasted spices and the onion to the ground-beef mixture. Heat the *nit'ir qibe* in another heavy skillet over low heat for 5 minutes. Add the spiced ground beef to the pan and cook over medium heat until slightly rare. Serve hot.

NOTE: See Glossary for chiles (page 55) and grains of paradise (page 60) and see Mail-Order Sources for both (page 74).

2 pounds filet mignon
2 teaspoons minced fresh hot red serrano chiles
Pinch of ground cloves
Pinch of ground cardamom
¾ tablespoon grains of paradise (see Note)
¼ teaspoon freshly ground black pepper
Salt, to taste
½ cup minced red onion
¾ cup Nit'ir Qibe (page 135)

SAUCE GRAIN

◎◎◎

WEST AFRICAN BEEF AND OKRA STEW (WEST AFRICA)

The African taste for the slippery is nowhere more evident than in this traditional sauce. Here the okra is cut into rounds to allow it to thicken the sauce. The sauce is further thickened with the addition of powdered melon seeds.

I find that I like the taste of this sauce better if I've added a bit of hot chile while it is cooking. SERVES 6

1 tablespoon peanut oil

1 large onion, minced

2 pounds stewing beef, cut into 1-inch cubes

5½ cups water

½ pound young okra pods

½ cup egusi seed powder (see Note)

Salt and freshly ground black pepper, to taste

Heat the oil in a large saucepan and brown the onion. Add the beef and cook it until it is browned. Add 5 cups of the water, cover, and simmer for 45 minutes. Wash and top and tail the okra, discarding any blemished or hard pods. Add the okra and continue to cook for an additional 15 minutes. Mix the melon seed powder with the remaining ½ cup of water and slowly pour it into the sauce while stirring. Season to taste, cover, and continue to cook for 7 to 10 minutes. Serve hot with boiled yam (page 279).

NOTE: See Glossary (page 59) and Mail-Order Sources (page 74) for *egusi*.

ABENA'S PALAVER SAUCE
◉◉◉

(GHANA)

Abena Busia, the Ghanaian writer, and I have never met face to face, but one evening I received a telephone call from her about a video that I'd made about the migrations of African foods. I agreed to send her a copy and extorted a recipe from her as "payment." After much confusion, Abena finally received the video and I got a variation of the following recipe for palaver sauce with notes that were longer than the recipe.

Palaver stew can be prepared from any meat, fowl, or dried fish. It is not, however, made with fresh fish. Traditionally, the sauce is made with bitter leaf (page 52). But if that is difficult to find, Abena suggests using a mixture of the more readily available dandelion greens and spinach.

Those who are leery of using a cup of palm oil can use another vegetable oil or a mixture of palm and vegetable oil, but they'll miss the whole point of the palm oil's rich taste. SERVES 6 TO 8

Season the beef with salt and place it in a large saucepan with just enough water to cover. Bring to a boil, then lower the heat and allow it to cook, covered, for 1 hour, adding more water if necessary, while preparing the remaining ingredients. Heat the palm oil in a deep, heavy saucepan and sauté the onion until it is translucent. Add the chile, tomatoes, and ground *egusi* and simmer for 5 minutes. Add the chopped spinach and dandelion greens and the simmered beef with all its pan juices. Add the shrimp and salt and pepper to taste and continue to cook over low heat for 30 minutes, or until the beef is tender. Serve with Plain White Rice (page 290) or Boiled Yams (page 279)

NOTE: See Glossary for *egusi* (page 59) and dried smoked shrimp (page 70) and see Mail-Order Sources for both (page 74).

3 pounds stewing beef, cut into 1-inch cubes

Salt, to taste

1 cup palm oil

1 large onion, coarsely chopped

Minced fresh chile, to taste (see page 55)

1 pound tomatoes, peeled, seeded, and coarsely chopped

1 cup egusi powder (see Note)

2 pounds fresh spinach, washed and finely chopped

1 pound fresh dandelion greens, washed and finely chopped

½ cup dried smoked shrimp, ground (see Note)

Freshly ground black pepper, to taste

M'CHERMIA

◉◉◉

LIVER WITH VINEGAR (ALGERIA)

Throughout the continent there is a love of innards. They turn up in the tiny rolls of goat chitterlings in kpete *of Benin, in the sausages served at a South African* braai *(barbecue), and in this spicy calf's liver from Algeria that is simple to prepare and served with white rice as dinner.*

The liver can also be speared on toothpicks as khemia, *an appetizer nibble.*

SERVES 4

1 tablespoon olive oil

1 clove garlic, minced

½ teaspoon cayenne pepper

Salt and freshly ground black pepper, to taste

½ cup water

1 pound calf's liver, cut into ½-inch cubes

1 tablespoon red wine vinegar

Heat the olive oil in a heavy skillet, add the spices, and cook them over low heat for 10 minutes, stirring occasionally. Add the water and continue to cook until half the water has evaporated. Add the liver and continue to cook for an additional 20 minutes. Remove the skillet from the heat and add the vinegar, stirring to mix it in. Return the skillet to the heat and continue to cook for 5 minutes. Serve hot with white rice.

Fried Liver Sudanese-Style

◎◎◎

(SUDAN)

A gift from my friend, this Sudanese recipe for sautéed liver uses not only tomato paste but cinnamon too. SERVES 4

Heat the oil in a saucepan and sauté the garlic until it is lightly browned. Add the salt, cinnamon, and tomato paste and cook for 2 minutes, stirring well. Add the liver and the water and continue to cook until the liver is cooked to taste. Serve hot with white rice.

2 tablespoons olive oil

2 cloves garlic, minced

Salt, to taste

¼ teaspoon ground cinnamon

2 teaspoons tomato paste

1 pound calf's liver, cut into ½-inch cubes

2 tablespoons water

DINNER WITH THE VIRGIN

Of all the dinners that I've had on the African continent, one of the most unusual was one several years ago at a friend's home in Cotonou, Benin. The guest of honor was the Virgin Mary. It seems that the particular church that my friend attended had a policy whereby the statue of the Virgin left the sanctuary to spend an evening at the home of one of the parishioners. While it was there, the family invited the rest of the congregation as well as friends and family members to have dinner with the Virgin.

The dinner was a lavish spread—we'd shopped and prepared food for multitudes. The house was decorated with fresh flowers, and the guest of honor arrived on time to be situated in a corner of the living room surrounded by masses of white tapers plunged into sand in brightly colored enamel basins. Hail Marys were said and the feasting began. I cannot recall the dishes that were prepared that day, but I'll never forget the faith and fervor of my fellow dinner guests. The next time I return to Cotonou and pass the church, I will enter and light a candle to the Virgin. After all, we've had dinner together.

MANCHUPA

◎◎◎

CAPE VERDEAN STEW (CAPE VERDE ISLANDS)

I first tasted manchupa *on an early trip to Dakar, Senegal, where friends of friends served it. I remember being fascinated by the mix of meats and by the beans, onions, and vegetables. In those pre-Brazil days, this was a pretty exotic dish; I remember it was called* katchupa. *Today, I recognize it as having some connections to the feijoada of Brazil.*

Although I have only made brief stops in the Cape Verde Islands, usually on plane routings, I never forgot the katchupa. *As I was finishing this book on Martha's Vineyard, I met Carleen Cordwell, a New World Cape Verdean from New Bedford. We hit it off right away and she was thrilled when I asked her for a recipe for* katchupa. *"We call it* manchupa," *she told me, "but the name varies from island to island." She vowed to find me the best recipe and several days later I received a fax with the notation that it was from Loretta Silva, whose folks hark from Brava Island. The map that followed showed it to be the southernmost of the Cape Verde Islands.*

Cape Verdeans love entertaining in true African-style large gatherings, and the recipe was for 40 to 45 people. This mixed-meat feast, like its Brazilian counterpart feijoada, is quite simply not a dish that can be prepared in small quantity. It's a traditional Saturday dish and prepared in quantity so that everyone who arrives can have some. So follow suit. When you're ready to invite all the gang over and truly treat them to something wonderful, prepare a large cauldron of manchupa. *Add large quantities of* vinho verde *and blast Cesaria Evora singing the Cape Verdean blues, or search out some music by Os Tubaroes or Finacon.*

SERVES 40 TO 45

4 pounds pig's feet, split, cleaned, and quartered

1½ pounds corned spareribs, cut into 2-inch pieces

2 tablespoons vegetable oil

¼ pound salt pork, cut into cubes

3 medium-sized onions, coarsely chopped

3 bay leaves

8 quarts water

Prepare the pig's feet and the corned spareribs by placing them in a large saucepan with water to cover, bringing them to a boil, and cooking for 3 to 5 minutes. Drain, rinse, and reserve.

Heat the oil in an 18-quart stockpot, add the salt pork, and cook until most of the fat is rendered. Add the onion and the bay leaves and cook until the onion becomes translucent. Add the water, bring it to a boil, and add the samp. Allow the water to return to boiling, then simmer, covered, for 30 minutes. Add the beans and continue to cook for an additional 30 minutes. Add the pig's feet, corned and fresh spareribs, ham hocks, chile, and garlic and continue to cook for 1 hour, checking periodically to make sure that the *manchupa* does not burn or stick. As the juices thicken, add hot water for the cooking liquid that has been displaced. Cover and continue to cook over low heat for 2½ hours, checking occasionally for sticking and to make sure that the meat and samp are thoroughly cooked. The *manchupa* remains covered during the entire cooking process, except when it is being stirred. Turn the pot from time to time so that it heats evenly. Remove the chile when the desired degree of hotness is reached.

When ready, add the kale and the paprika, salt, and pepper. Continue to cook for 5 minutes, then add the calabaza. When the dish has reached the desired degree of hotness, remove the chile and reserve (it can be served separately to the chile heads). When the calabaza is done, the *manchupa* is ready. Serve hot.

2 pounds dried samp (white hominy corn), washed and picked over (see page 173)

½ pound dried baby lima beans, washed and picked over

½ pound dried yellow-eyed beans, washed and picked over

1½ pounds fresh spareribs, cut into 2-inch pieces

2 ham hocks (1½ pounds each)

1 habanero chile, pricked with a fork (see page 55)

2 bunches fresh kale, cleaned, blanched, and chopped

¼ cup paprika

2 cloves garlic, minced

Salt and freshly ground black pepper, to taste

3 pounds calabaza, peeled and cut into 1-inch cubes (see page 53)

ROMAZAVA
◎◎◎

MALAGACHE MIXED MEAT STEW (MADAGASCAR)

This is the national dish of Madagascar. The trick here is to cook all the different types of meat so that they are perfectly done at the same time. This is accomplished by adding them at different points of the process. SERVES 6 TO 8

1 tablespoon peanut oil

1 pound stewing beef, cut into 1-inch chunks

1 pound fresh pork shoulder, cut into 1-inch chunks

3 whole chicken breasts, split and cut into serving-sized pieces

6 large ripe tomatoes, peeled, seeded, and coarsely chopped

2 medium-sized onions, coarsely chopped

7 cloves garlic, minced

2-inch piece of fresh ginger, scraped and cut into thin julienne

1 pound fresh spinach leaves, washed and shredded

Salt and freshly ground black pepper, to taste

Heat the oil in a heavy saucepan or stockpot and sear the beef without browning it. Add water to cover, bring to a boil, lower the heat, and simmer, covered, for 30 minutes. Add the pork and continue to cook for an additional 30 minutes. Add the chicken pieces and continue to cook for another 10 minutes. Add the tomatoes and continue cooking until they are incorporated into the sauce. Add the onion, garlic, and ginger and continue to cook for about 10 minutes, or until they are cooked but still slightly chewy. Finally, add the spinach, season with salt and pepper, and stir until the leaves are wilted and just cooked. Serve hot with white rice.

JAGACIDA

◉◉◉

CAPE VERDEAN BEAN AND SAUSAGE STEW
(CAPE VERDE ISLANDS)

Not everyone is going to be preparing manchupa *on a daily or even weekly basis. When my Cape Verdean friends want a bean hit, they'll fix up a quick version of* jagacida, *affectionately known as jag. It can even be prepared with canned beans, as in this version that was given to me by Jeanne Costa, another of the New Bedford bunch.*

The trick with jag *is to get the right consistency. A Cape Verdean trick suggests placing a teaspoon in the middle of the pot. If it falls easily, there's too much water; if it stands too firm, there's not enough. Use your own judgment.* SERVES 4

Heat the olive oil in a heavy saucepan and sauté the onion and the chouriço for about 2 minutes. Add the garlic and paprika and continue to cook for 3 minutes, or until the onion is translucent and the sausage is cooked. Add the water, salt, pepper, and bay leaves. Cover and bring to a boil. Add the beans and rice and stir to make sure that all the ingredients are well mixed. Cover and simmer over low heat for about 35 minutes. Remove the bay leaves. Serve hot.

2 tablespoons olive oil
1 small onion, minced
½ cup minced chouriço or linguiça (Portuguese sausage)
2 teaspoons minced garlic
¼ cup paprika
2 cups water
Salt and freshly ground black pepper, to taste
2 bay leaves
One 16-ounce can butter beans
1 cup long-grain rice (preferably Uncle Ben's)

LEFTOVERS

BOBOTIE

◎◎◎

SOUTH AFRICAN MEAT PIE (SOUTH AFRICA)

This South African classic is prepared with chopped lamb or beef and was probably an innovative way of dealing with left-overs. Hildagonda Duckitt's 1917 cookbook gives a recipe that was her mother's; it's remarkably similar to the ones in use today. Hildagonda spells the dish bobotee *and suggests that it may have an Indian origin rather than the Cape Malay ancestry more commonly given the dish.*

If you wish to serve the bobotie *the old-fashioned way, spoon it into individual ramekins and bake. Place a lemon slice at the top of each ramekin.*

SERVES 6 TO 8

2 slices dense white bread, such as
   Pepperidge Farm

1 cup milk

2 medium-sized onions, minced

1 clove garlic, minced

1 tablespoon butter

2 pounds minced cooked lamb

2 tablespoons mild curry powder

1 tablespoon sugar

Salt, to taste

2 tablespoons tamarind liquid
   (see Note)

3 tablespoons slivered blanched almonds

2 eggs

3 lemon leaves

3 bay leaves

Preheat the oven to 375 degrees. Soak the bread in ¼ cup of the milk for 20 minutes and squeeze it dry. While the bread is soaking, sauté the onions and garlic in the butter in a skillet until they are lightly browned. In a large bowl, mix together the meat, soaked bread, curry powder, sugar, salt, tamarind liquid, and almonds. Add 1 egg to the mixture and stir to make sure that all the ingredients are well combined. Spoon the *bobotie* into a well-greased deep-dish pie pan and place the lemon and bay leaves throughout the mixture. Place in the oven and bake for 30 minutes. Drain off the fat, then whisk the remaining egg with the remaining ¾ cup of milk, pour it over the top, and continue to cook until the *bobotie* is set but not dry. Traditionally *bobotie* is served with rice and chutney and any other curry accompaniments you may wish.

NOTE: Tamarind liquid can be prepared by soaking 2 ounces of tamarind pulp—available in Asian, Indian, and West Indian markets, or through mail order (page 74)— in 1 cup of boiling water for 25 minutes, then straining it.

EGYPTIAN=STYLE STUFFED PEPPERS

◎◎◎

(EGYPT)

Stuffed vegetable containers seem to be one of the Mediterranean world's favorite ways of dealing with leftover meats. Cases include peppers, bell peppers, and zucchini. This Egyptian recipe can be used for beef or lamb.   SERVES 4

Preheat the oven to 350 degrees. Wash the bell peppers, cut them in half lengthwise, core them, and remove the seeds. Place the meat, parsley, garlic, and onion together in a bowl and mix them together well. Shred the saffron and add it to the mixture, then season with salt and pepper to taste. Add the eggs and mix well to make sure that all the ingredients are blended. Grease an ovenproof dish with the oil. Fill the red bell pepper halves with the meat mixture and place them in the greased dish. Add the water to the dish, place in the oven, and cook for 40 minutes. Serve hot with white rice.

4 large red bell peppers
1 pound leftover roast beef, minced
1 sprig parsley, minced
4 cloves garlic, minced
1 medium onion, minced
Pinch of saffron
Salt and freshly ground black pepper,
*   to taste*
2 eggs
1 tablespoon olive oil
⅓ cup water

Before one cooks one

must have the meat.

—MAURITANIAN PROVERB

SUKUMA WIKI

◎◎◎

LEFTOVER SPECIAL (KENYA)

The name of this dish means "push the week" in Swahili. It frequently turns up on tables in one of its infinite varieties just before payday. The recipe given here is simply a starting point. Do what the Kenyan cooks do—improvise with whatever you have in your refrigerator. You may even discover that you like the taste so much you'll make it even when you don't have leftovers.

SERVES 6 TO 8

2 tablespoons canola oil

1 large onion, chopped

4 large ripe tomatoes, peeled, seeded, and coarsely chopped

1 medium green bell pepper, cored, seeded, and chopped

4 cups diced leftover roast beef

Pinch of minced habanero chile, or to taste (see page 55)

1 pound fresh spinach, well cleaned and coarsely chopped

Salt and freshly ground black pepper, to taste

Heat the oil in a large, heavy skillet and sauté the onion until it is translucent. Add the tomatoes, green pepper, beef, and chile and cook for 5 to 7 minutes, or until the ingredients are heated through. Add the spinach to the skillet and season with salt and pepper to taste. Lower the heat, cover, and cook for 5 minutes, then uncover and continue to cook for an additional 5 minutes. Serve hot with rice.

STARCHES

◎◎◎

Couscous and Cassava Meal

From north to south, the African continent uses a variety of starches to balance its meals and fill its plates. In the North, the couscous of the Maghreb takes pride of place, but it is accompanied by flat breads that hark back to the breads of pharaonic Egypt. In the East and West, starchy mashes serve as a base for many meals. Rice plays a special role in areas like southern Senegal and in parts of Liberia and Sierra Leone. In the South, mealie pap dominates the traditional diet, while those with a more European outlook eat the starches of that continent.

◎◎◎

COUSCOUS
(North Africa)

MHAMMES BET-TSOUM
Spicy Couscous *(Tunisia)*

SOHLEB
Millet Porridge *(Tunisia)*

DROO
Millet Porridge with Nuts and Dried Fruit *(Tunisia)*

BOILED YAMS
(Nigeria)

DUNDU
Yoruba Fried Yams *(Nigeria)*

OKA OR AMALA
Cooked Yam Flour *(Yoruba)*

IYAN
Yoruba Yam Porridge *(Nigeria)*

PURE DE INHAME
Mashed Yam *(Cape Verde Islands)*

FUFU
Pounded Yam *(West Africa)*

EBA
Cassava Porridge *(Benin)*

NTOMO KRAKO
Sweet Potato Fritters *(Ghana)*

TUO
Turned Cornmeal *(Niger)*

STEAMED RICE
(All Africa)

PLAIN WHITE RICE
(All Africa)

YELLOW RICE
(South Africa)

POMMES DE TERRE AUX FEUILLES DE MENTHE
Potatoes with Mint Leaves and Garlic *(Algeria)*

POTATO PANCAKES
(Zimbabwe)

FAROFIA ANGOLANA
Angolan Farofa *(Angola)*

✳

A Couscous Factory in Sfax, Tunisia

Couscous is a staple in North Africa; there are over 300 recipes for it in the Tunisian repertoire alone. It is becoming increasingly common in the United States, with couscous salads and spice- and herb-infused couscous turning up everywhere from fancy gastronomic palaces to local salad bars. It's surprising, then, that most Americans don't realize that couscous is pasta and not a grain. This fact was brought home to me when two busfuls of assorted foodies were deposited on the doorstep of the DIARI couscous factory in Sfax, Tunisia, several years back. The welcome was warm, a true Maghrebian *marhaba* (welcome), with the directors of the factory and their wives circulating among the crowd looking for kindred souls and French speakers. We were guided through the factory to watch the process. Enormous galvanized steel containers noisily whirred, rotated, and extruded, creating millions of tiny pellets of couscous in staggering quantities.

When we returned from the visit, a display had been set up featuring heaping platters of couscous prepared in some of the many ways that are traditional to Tunisia. There were spice-laden savory dishes rich with the tastes of cinnamon and cumin, and ethereally light desserts sweetened with dates and perfumed with orange-flower water. They were delicious and occupied most of the crowd. I was intrigued by the scene that took place in the back, where for the benefit of those on the tour, women in traditional dress prepared the couscous in the old manner, painstakingly rolling each tiny pellet of pasta on a tray; their hands flew like lightning. They worked rapidly and chatted among themselves as their hands moved in the same gestures their foremothers had used for centuries. They didn't prepare a fraction of the amount extruded by the machines, but somehow, their production was the one that made an impression on me. It spoke to the creativity of the African cook and reminded me of the labor-intensive processes that are a part of much of the cooking of the continent. Whenever I open a package of couscous, even if it's machine-made, I always think of the twinkling eyes and chattering voices of the women of the Tunisian couscous factory and of the culinary community that they had created for themselves, transforming flour and water into a bowl of sustaining food.

Couscous

◎◎◎

(NORTH AFRICA)

Couscous is the quintessential North African starch. It is not a grain but a pasta, traditionally made by rolling it into small pellets of differing size and drying it in the sun. Today, couscous is made in factories. But artisanal couscous is still made in many places and is much prized by connoisseurs. There are many brands of couscous. Some can be prepared by simply adding water. The taste of these brands as opposed to that of a true steamed couscous is indescribable. Learn how to prepare this simple North African staple; it requires very little special equipment. Later you may find that you want a couscoussière, but you can make do with a sieve, some cheesecloth or a clean dish towel, and a saucepan that will fit under the sieve.

Pour the couscous into a large plate. Rub your hands with 1 tablespoon of the olive oil and rub the couscous through your hands so that each pellet is covered with the oil. Drizzle on 2 cups of the water, continuing to roll the couscous, separating the grains to aerate them and remove any clumps. Allow the couscous to rest for 15 minutes, then repeat the process with the remaining tablespoon of olive oil. After the couscous has rested for the second time, place it in a sieve on top of a saucepan, or in the top part of a couscoussière. Wrap the join with a clean dish towel and steam the couscous, uncovered, for 10 to 15 minutes. Usually the couscous is cooked atop the bubbling stew that will be served over it. This impregnates the couscous with its flavors. If there is no stew, fill the saucepan with water and cook the couscous. When it is cooked, spread the couscous on a platter and allow it to cool. Sprinkle it with the remaining 1 cup of water and fluff the pellets with a fork. Replace the couscous in the sieve and steam for an additional 10 minutes.

When ready to serve, melt the butter with the thyme, skim off the milk solids, and pour the butter over the couscous. Add the raisins, fluff with a fork, and serve mounded on a heated platter.

2 pounds couscous
2 tablespoons olive oil
3 cups water
1 tablespoon butter
2 branches fresh thyme
½ cup dark raisins, plumped

When a woman is hungry,
she says, "Roast something
for the children that
they may eat."
—Ashanti proverb, Ghana

MHAMMES BET-TSOUM
◉◉◉

SPICY COUSCOUS (TUNISIA)

For many of us who think of hard-wheat pasta as an Italian invention, it comes as a shock to realize that northern Africa also boasts a large variety of hard-wheat pastas. Mhammes is a large-grain couscous that is especially popular in Tunisia. Here it is prepared with red bell peppers and chiles. The dish, like many throughout the African continent, is one that can be adapted to the taste of the cook and the guests. Use mild bell peppers and chiles, hot ones, or a mixture of both.

SERVES 6

¼ cup olive oil

6 cloves garlic, minced

6 medium-sized red bell peppers, cored, seeded, and cut into thin strips

1 teaspoon caraway seeds

1 teaspoon paprika or powdered hot chile to taste

Salt and freshly ground black pepper, to taste

2 quarts water

½ pound mhammes, or large-grain couscous (see Note)

Heat the oil in a large, heavy saucepan. Add the garlic, bell peppers, seasonings, and water and bring the mixture to a boil over medium heat. When it begins to bubble, add the *mhammes.* Allow the *mhammes bet-tsoum* to cook until the liquid is completely absorbed. Serve hot.

NOTE: *Mhammes* is available by mail order (see page 74).

SOHLEB

◎◎◎

MILLET PORRIDGE (TUNISIA)

Sohleb is traditionally served on cold winter nights or during the nights of Ramadan. It's easy to prepare and can be made less sweet if you like. Some versions use cinnamon and finely pounded dried rose petals instead of ginger.   SERVES 6

Place the flour and sugar in a medium-sized saucepan and slowly pour in the water, stirring to make sure that there are no lumps. Place over medium heat and cook for about 5 minutes, or until the porridge thickens, while continuing to stir. Stir in the orange-flower water. Remove from the heat and pour into a decorative bowl or individual custard cups. Allow it to cool to room temperature. Serve with a dusting of ginger.

2 cups millet flour
1½ cups confectioners' sugar, or to taste
1 quart water
2 tablespoons orange-flower water (see Note)
1 teaspoon ground ginger

NOTE: See the Glossary (page 66) and the Mail-Order Sources (page 74) for orange-flower water.

PREPARING MILLET PORRIDGE

DROO

◎◎◎

MILLET PORRIDGE WITH NUTS AND DRIED FRUIT
(TUNISIA)

This is another of the Ramadan porridges that are so much a part of the holiday celebrations. Here the porridge is enriched with a mixture of minced nuts and dried fruits.   SERVES 8

2 cups millet flour

1 tablespoon water

½ cup hazelnuts

½ cup almonds

½ cup sesame seeds

¼ cup milk

1½ cups confectioners' sugar, or
*   to taste*

2 tablespoons finely ground cornmeal

⅓ cup minced pistachio nuts

Place the millet flour in a mixing bowl with the water and knead it into a ball of dough. Place the dough ball in a saucepan with water to barely cover it and bring it slowly to a boil over medium heat. When it begins to bubble, remove the dough ball, reserving the water. Allow the water to cool to room temperature. Remove any brown outer covering from the nuts (see Note), place them and the sesame seeds in the bowl of a mortar, and pound them until they are well minced. Place the nut mixture in a heavy skillet and toast it over low heat until it is lightly browned. Thin the nut mixture slightly with the milk and reserve it.

When ready to serve, dissolve the millet dough in the reserved cooking water and add it to the nut mixture. Strain the millet and nut mixture through a wide-mesh strainer to remove any lumps, then sweeten to taste with the confectioners' sugar. Add the cornmeal. Place the *droo* in a saucepan and bring it to a boil over medium heat. Add water as needed. When the *droo* begins to bubble, remove it from the heat and serve in small glasses. Garnish with a dusting of minced pistachio nuts.

NOTE: To skin the hazelnuts, toast them in a 350-degree oven and rub them in a clean dish towel. For the almonds, drop them into a pot of boiling water for 30 seconds; drain and pinch the skins off.

BOILED YAMS

◎◎◎

(NIGERIA)

If you have read any of my other cookbooks, you already know that true yams are botanically different from what many of us erroneously call yams in the United States. The true yam is one of Africa's oldest foods. There are many different types, which in Nigeria are named for their different types, sizes, and shapes. Yellow yams seem to be good for all purposes, while white yams are best for pounding when a mortar is called for. New yams and old yams are, according to many Nigerians, not as tasty as those in the middle of their cycle. Yams turn up in a variety of dishes, ranging from boiled yam to complex yam fritters and even yam flour. In this basic dish, which might be served up at any meal, the yams are simply boiled.

SERVES 6

Wash the yams thoroughly, peel them, and cut them into serving-sized pieces. Place the yams in a medium-sized nonreactive saucepan with salted water to cover and allow them stand for 5 minutes. Bring the water to a boil over medium heat. When the water is boiling, cover, lower the heat, and simmer until the yams can be pierced with a fork. This will depend on the size and shape of the yams, but will usually take about 35 minutes or so. When ready, drain the yams and arrange them on a serving platter. Yams are traditionally served with the best possible grade of red palm oil.

1½ pounds yellow yams

DUNDU

◎◎◎

YORUBA FRIED YAMS (NIGERIA)

These fried yams are traditional in the Yoruba cooking of southwestern Nigeria. They are perfect with meals and can replace French fries. Remember that the yams called for in the recipe are not *the orange Louisiana or North Carolina yams (those are really sweet potatoes). You can find true yams in shops in West Indian or Hispanic neighborhoods.*

You may want to elminate or reduce the amount of palm oil. See page 66.   SERVES 6

1½ pounds white yams
Red palm oil for deep frying
¼ teaspoon red pepper flakes, or to taste
4 large onions, quartered
Salt and freshly ground pepper, to taste

Peel the yams, cut them into slices, and place them in a bowl with salted water to cover for 5 minutes. Heat the oil for deep frying in a heavy Dutch oven or deep fryer to 375 degrees. When the oil is hot, drain the yam slices and dry well. Add the yam slices a few at a time and fry until they are lightly browned on each side. Remove with a slotted spoon and drain on absorbent paper. Continue until all the yam slices are fried. When done, transfer them to a serving platter and keep warm. Place the remaining ingredients in the bowl of a food processor and grind them to a thick paste. Carefully remove 2 tablespoons of the hot oil into a heavy skillet and reheat. When the oil is hot, add the onion mixture and cook for 5 minutes, or until heated through. Serve the onion paste over the fried yam slices.

Oka or Amala

◎◎◎

COOKED YAM FLOUR (YORUBA)

This dish is called oka *in some parts of Yoruba and* amala *in others. In some parts of Nigeria,* eba *(cooked* gari, *page 285) is also called* oka. *Whatever it's called, this traditional Yoruba dish is a hearty starchy porridge. When called* amala, *it is usually prepared as a ritual dish and served to the* orisa *(venerated spirit) Shango, the legendary Alafin of Oyo. While New World* orisa *worshipers prepare their* amala *with cornmeal, traditional* amala *is made from yam flour, which is called* elubo *in Yoruba. The* amala *or* oka *is used as a starch base for any of the many Yoruba soupy stews. It's not a dish with a lot of eye appeal, but taste it, you might just like it.*   SERVES 6

Sift the yam flour to remove any lumps or impurities. Bring the water to boil in a medium-sized saucepan. Sprinkle a bit of the yam flour on the water while stirring constantly, adding more and more until you have added all the flour. The cooking should take 3 to 4 minutes all together. When done, the *oka* should pull away from the sides of the saucepan. If the mixture is too thick, add more water; if too thin, add more yam flour. When perfect, it should be the right consistency for eating with your fingers. Allow it to cool slightly before serving. The *oka* can be served straight from the saucepan onto separate plates, or can be shaped for serving, simply by putting a little cold water on your hands and forming it into a mound.

4 cups yam flour
6 cups water

IYAN

◎◎◎

YORUBA YAM PORRIDGE (NIGERIA)

This is a pounded-yam dish that has crossed the ocean. In the Candomblé houses of Bahia, Brazil, where the descendants of enslaved Yoruba people maintain their African traditions (sometimes with more fervor than in the motherland), iyan has given its name to one of the orisa, or venerated spirits: Olxaguian. He is the avatar of Oxala who is known for his love of the pounded-yam porridge known as iyan. Thus the culinary circle from east to west is unbroken. Traditionally, iyan is prepared in a mortar and pestle, which is not as difficult as it sounds. The wary, though, can use a food processor with a strong motor.   SERVES 6

1½ pounds white yams

Wash the yams well, peel them, and cut them into small pieces. Place the yams in a medium-sized saucepan with salted water to cover. Slowly bring the yams to a boil and cook until fork-tender, about 35 to 40 minutes. When cooked, drain the yam pieces and put them a few at a time into a food processor and process using the chopping blade. You may have to add a bit of hot water to get it started. As you gradually add the yam bits, add hot water as needed to loosen the paste slightly when it gets too thick. When the yam is a thick paste, spoon it from the bowl of the food processor into a serving dish and serve warm with any West African stew, such as Sauce Grain (page 260).

PURE DE INHAME
◉◉◉

MASHED YAM (CAPE VERDE ISLANDS)

This is a case of colonial invention, with yams being used to replace the white potatoes that this dish would have included in Portugal. The result is a culinary mixing of north and south that would be at home with an African meal or an interesting addition to any meal.

SERVES 4 TO 6

Put the cooked yam pieces through a food mill to purée them. Gradually add the beaten egg, the butter, and the salt, mixing well to make sure that all the ingredients are blended. Spoon the mashed yam into an ovenproof casserole, paint the top with the beaten egg yolk, and place it in the oven for 15 minutes, or until golden brown. Top with a few gratings of nutmeg. Serve hot.

5 cups yam pieces, boiled until soft

1 egg, beaten

1 tablespoon butter, at room temperature

Salt, to taste

1 egg yolk, beaten

Nutmeg for dusting

Fufu

◎◎◎

POUNDED YAM (WEST AFRICA)

This is the classic accompaniment for many West African stews. Preparing it requires a large mortar and a fair amount of elbow grease, but the results are tastier that those of the Cream of Wheat and mashed potato flake substitutes that turn up in some cookbooks.   SERVES 6

6 cups Boiled Yams (page 279)
½ cup hot water

Place the yam pieces in the bowl of a large mortar or in a large heavy mixing bowl one at a time and pound them briskly with a pestle or potato masher. Gradually add the other pieces while continuing to pound. Moisten the mixture by adding a few tablespoons of the water at a time, but the *fufu* should not become too loose. When all of the yam is pounded and the *fufu* sticks together in one ball, roll the *fufu* into balls about 2 inches in diameter. You will end up with about a dozen balls. Place them in a serving bowl to be served with the sauce or stew that you have selected.

PREPARING *FUFU*

EBA

◎◎◎

CASSAVA PORRIDGE (BENIN)

This dish is pure starch, not a side for dieters. The oil is an embellishment in the traditional recipe and the chicken stock is my own addition for flavor. Traditionally the dish is prepared with one part gari, or cassava meal, to two parts water. Variations of this are served throughout the continent. It is called funge in Angola.   SERVES 4 TO 6

Place the oil, water, and chicken stock in a heavy saucepan, mix together, and bring to a boil. Slowly drizzle in the *gari*, stirring constantly, and continue to cook and stir for 3 to 4 minutes, or until the *eba* has a firm consistency. Like other Nigerian starches, the *eba* can be served with stews or soups. It is eaten with the fingers. Serve hot.

NOTE: *Gari* is available in health-food stores or through the Mail-Order Sources (page 74).

2 tablespoons red palm oil (see page 66)

2 cups water

1 cup chicken stock

1½ cups gari (see Note)

NTOMO KRAKO

◎◎◎

SWEET POTATO FRITTERS (GHANA)

While the sweet potato is a New World vegetable and not indigenous to the African continent, there are several African recipes that make wonderful use of it. This one, in which the sweet potatoes are dipped in batter, breaded, and then deep-fried, is a delicious albeit relatively modern dish.   SERVES 4 TO 6

4 large sweet potatoes
1 tablespoon flour
1½ tablespoons peanut oil, plus more
   for deep frying
Salt, to taste
2 tablespoons milk
2 eggs
Dried bread crumbs

Wash the sweet potatoes, cut them into chunks, and place them in a large saucepan with water to cover. Bring them to a boil over medium heat and cook for 20 minutes, or until fork-tender. When they are done, peel them and place them in a bowl. Mash them with a potato masher while slowly adding the flour, 1½ tablespoons of the oil, the salt, and the milk. Add the milk gradually because you do not want a runny mixture. Stop when the potato paste is of a consistency where it can be formed into small cakes. To form the cakes, take a tablespoonful of the mixture at a time and press it into a 1-inch fritter.

Heat the oil for deep frying to 375 degrees in a heavy Dutch oven or deep fryer. Beat the eggs in a small bowl. Place the bread crumbs in a saucer. When the oil is hot, dip the sweet potato cakes a few at a time into the egg, then dredge them in the bread crumbs and fry them in the oil, turning once, for about 5 minutes, or until they are golden brown on both sides. Serve hot. Traditionally, in Ghana, these are served with a meat or fish stew, but you might want to serve them as appetizers or as a vegetable accompaniment to just about anything instead.

TUO

◎◎◎

TURNED CORNMEAL (NIGER)

Cornmeal porridge is another of Africa's dishes where West meets East. The New World's corn turns up in the coocoos *and* fungis *and* amalas *of the Caribbean as well as the corn pones and coush coush of the American South. This dish is simply the Nigerien (that's Nigerien from Niger, not Nigerian from Nigeria) way with what is known in Bermuda as "turned cornmeal." It goes by the name of* sadzai *in Zimbabwe,* bogobe *in Botswana,* nsima *in Zambia, and* ugali *in Kenya. As with all cornmeal porridges, the trick is to keep stirring, no matter how stiff it gets; that's how you keep the lumps out. Some even say stir in one direction only.*   SERVES 4 TO 6

Place 2 cups of the water and the salt in a medium-sized saucepan and bring to a boil over medium heat. Meanwhile, mix the cornmeal with the remaining 1 cup water into a paste. Slowly pour the paste into the boiling water, stirring constantly. Lower the heat and cook the *tuo*, stirring constantly, for 10 minutes, or until the mixture is a thick mush that pulls away from the side of the pan. Serve with the butter and a sprinkling of red pepper flakes.

3 cups cold water
Pinch of salt
1¼ cups yellow cornmeal
1 tablespoon butter
1 teaspoon red pepper flakes, or to taste

GRINDING CORN

STEAMED RICE
◎◎◎

(ALL AFRICA)

Another variation for rice is one in which the rice is simply cooked like pasta in a large pot of water. When it is almost done, it is drained and placed in a colander and fluffed and steamed over a small amount of water.   SERVES 4 TO 6

2 cups uncooked rice
2 quarts plus 2 tablespoons water
1 tablespoon butter
Salt, to taste

Place the rice and the 2 quarts water in a large stockpot and bring to a boil. Cook for 15 minutes over high heat. Drain the rice and place it in a sieve. Put the sieve atop the rice pot, lower the heat, add the 2 tablespoons of water to the pot, and allow the rice to steam dry. Season with butter and salt, fluff with a fork, and serve hot.

RICE AND RESISTANCE

Senegalese filmmaker Ousmane Sembene's film *Emitai* portrays the life of the rice growers of the Casamance region of Senegal during the war. In it, the viewer is taken into the rice fields and watches as the grain, which is considered sacred by the people of the region, is planted and harvested. I've always felt that this film, with its theme of the corruption of pastoral society by the forces of war and modernization, is a microcosm of what's happening to much of the traditional food and the traditional foodways of the continent.

North, south, east, and west, growing numbers of people are looking to Europe and America for dietary guidance rather than under their own noses. Roadrunner chickens are being replaced by plump cellophane-wrapped *poulets morgues* (morgue chickens), as they are called. Fresh fruit juices and infusions are replaced by the sugars and empty calories of soft drinks, and meat is taking over the plate as a sign of affluence.

Emitai and moments from varying films on the continents—as well as recent works by African dieticians, nutritionists, and scholars—remind me that we are what we eat, and if we change what we eat, we may change who we are. May this never happen to Africa: a continent of wide and diverse cuisines.

PLAIN WHITE RICE

◎◎◎

(ALL AFRICA)

While mashes and couscous varieties are popular throughout the continent, one of the dishes that also turn up on tables from north to south is rice. Rice has been cultivated on the African continent for millennia. The continent even boasts its own variant of rice, Oryza glaberima, *which is grown in the area from southern Senegal to Sierra Leone and Liberia. Rice turns up in numerous dishes, and many Americans who have spent time in Senegal joke that the Lord's Prayer should be amended there to read, "Give us this day our daily* thieb." (Thieb *is the Wolof word for "rice"). In Senegal, many use* riz cassé, *or broken rice, but different occasions call for different types of rice. Basmati rice is the rice of preference in the Swahili areas of East Africa and in southern Africa, where the Indian influence is more keenly felt. There is no right or wrong way to cook rice. In fact, there are as many different methods for cooking rice as there are African grandmothers; therefore I'm using the recipe that my mother uses, which seems to work with almost every kind of rice.* SERVES 4

3½ cups water
1½ cups uncooked rice
1 teaspoon salt
1 tablespoon butter

Bring the water to a boil in a medium-sized saucepan. Stir in the remaining ingredients, cover, and simmer over low heat for 20 minutes. Remove the rice from the heat and allow it to stand for 5 minutes, or until all the water has been absorbed. Fluff with a fork and serve hot.

YELLOW RICE

◎◎◎

(SOUTH AFRICA)

This is a simple version of the rice pilafs that grace tables throughout eastern and southern Africa. It is easy to prepare and makes a busy weeknight dinner a little special.
SERVES 4

Pick over the rice and wash it. Bring the water to a boil in a large saucepan over medium heat and add the rice and the remaining ingredients except the raisins. Cover and simmer for 20 minutes, or until it is cooked through. When ready, drain the rice in a sieve. Add the raisins and stir them through with a fork. Steam the rice over a pan of water for 5 to 7 minutes, or until the rice is light and fluffy and the raisins are plump. Serve hot.

1 cup rice

1 quart water

2 tablespoons sugar

1 tablespoon butter

1 teaspoon salt

½ teaspoon turmeric

¼ cup golden raisins

POMMES DE TERRE AUX FEUILLES DE MENTHE

◎◎◎

POTATOES WITH MINT LEAVES AND GARLIC (ALGERIA)

The recent history of Algeria mixes the European or French with the African, Arab, and Berber. Here we see this same mixture on the plate, where the infrequently used European potato combines with the traditional seasonings of garlic and mint leaves.   SERVES 4 TO 6

2 tablespoons olive oil

1 clove garlic, minced

Salt, to taste

Black pepper, to taste

2 pounds Yukon Gold potatoes or any boiling potatoes, peeled and thinly sliced

3 tablespoons water

¼ cup fresh mint leaves

Heat the oil in a heavy cast-iron skillet. Add the garlic, salt, and peppercorns and cook until the garlic is light brown. Add the potatoes to the garlic with the water and most of the mint. Cook, covered, over medium heat, stirring occasionally, for 30 minutes, or until the potatoes are done. Serve hot, garnished with the remaining mint leaves.

POTATO PANCAKES

◎◎◎

(ZIMBABWE)

Potato pancakes may seem an unlikely offering in an African cookbook, but they are part of the colonial legacy of the food of the continent. Cookbooks written by housewives longing for the staples of home are noted for showing all sorts of inventive uses for African ingredients. Potato pancakes, which could have been prepared in Hertfordshire as well as in Harare, are an example of this tradition.

SERVES 4

Peel the potatoes and place them in cold water to cover for several hours. When ready, drain the potatoes and pat them dry on absorbent paper. Grate them into a bowl using a food processor or hand grater. Beat the eggs and add them to the grated potato. Stir in the flour, salt, pepper, and baking powder. Form the pancakes by making flat cakes with your hands. You should have enough for about 12 pancakes. Heat the butter in a heavy skillet and fry the potato pancakes over medium heat a few at a time for 3 to 5 minutes on each side, or until they are golden brown. Serve hot.

6 large potatoes

2 medium eggs

1½ tablespoons flour

Salt and freshly ground black pepper, to taste

⅛ teaspoon baking powder

3 tablespoons butter

Farofia Angolana
◎◎◎

ANGOLAN FAROFA (ANGOLA)

A perusal of any cookbook from Portuguese Africa reveals a startling number of dishes that are ancestors of those that turn up on tables in Brazil. A fish moqueca from Angola shows up, but has none of the palm oil richness that is imperative in its Bahian namesake. A calalu, from São Tomé and Principe, is similar to its Brazilian cousin, caruru, which is served for the twin saints of Cosme and Damião. And this farofia angolana could turn up on any table in Rio or Bahia.

MAKES 2 CUPS

2 cups cassava meal (see page 54)
1 tablespoon olive oil
1 teaspoon red palm oil
1 medium-sized onion, minced
Salt and freshly ground black pepper,
    to taste
1 teaspoon red wine vinegar

Pick over the cassava meal to remove any impurities. Heat the oils in a heavy skillet and brown the onion. Slowly add the cassava meal, stirring, and cook so that it is lightly toasted. Add the seasonings and vinegar and serve warm to accompany fried or grilled fish or meat.

DESSERTS

⊚⊚⊚

Makroud and Mangoes

Desserts are not part of the traditional African diet outside the northern and southern regions of the continent. In the other areas of the country, a piece of fruit—a ripe mango, a slice or two of pineapple, and the like—are the substitute for the sweets. Recent developments, though, have brought European traditions of sweets to the whole continent, and the result is desserts where the exotic bounty of the land meets up with the culinary wizardry of the twentieth century to create such delights as soursop creams, pineapple fritters, and avocado with honey.

⊚⊚⊚

MANGOES
(West Africa)

MANGO CREAM
(Cameroon)

PINEAPPLE BOATS
(Côte d'Ivoire)

BEIGNETS DE BANANES
Banana Fritters *(West Africa)*

BEIGNETS D'ANANAS
Pineapple Fritters *(Côte d'Ivoire)*

BEIGNETS DE MANGUES
Mango Fritters

PUMPKIN FRITTERS
(South Africa)

COLONIAL FRUIT SALAD
(Ghana)

TIERE SOW
Millet Couscous with Buttermilk *(Senegal)*

TIAKRI
Steamed Millet Couscous *(Senegal)*

GOSSI
Milk Rice *(Senegal)*

SOW
Buttermilk *(Senegal)*

CRÈME DE COROSSOL
Soursop Cream *(Senegal)*

SUCRE VANILLE
Vanilla Sugar *(French-Speaking Africa)*

ABACATES COM MEL
Avocados with Honey *(Cape Verde Islands)*

BANANA ENROLADA
Fried Bananas *(Cape Verde Islands)*

DOCE DE MANDIOCA
Cassava Sweet *(Mozambique)*

DATES
(North Africa)

DATES FOURÉES
Stuffed Dates *(Algeria)*

ROASTED ALMONDS
(Morocco)

SALADE D'ORANGES
Orange Salad *(Algeria)*

TEKOUA
Sugared Sesame Balls *(North Africa)*

MUKASSARAAT
Mixed Nuts *(Egypt)*

MAKROUD
Tunisian Date Cookies *(Tunisia)*

✳

A *Pâtisserie* in Kairouan, Tunisia

The culinary caravan in Tunisia included many stops—olive groves, couscous factories, archaeological sites, and marketplaces. The visit to the *pâtisserie* was unscheduled and informal. Roaming from the group, my friend Priscilla Martel and I made our way out of the mosque and back to the center of town. We had walked and entered into the walled section of the city when off to the left, my friend, a pastry chef with an interest in North African sweets, sprang to attention and started to walk faster. She'd discovered a pastry shop. We entered and were confronted with three walls of counters, all crowded with an astonishing assortment of cookies and sweets. Some had a familiar look, like the *makroud,* which I think of as Tunisian fig newtons; others were violent green, the color of the prophet, which brings good luck, and there was every color combination in between.

As we talked to the owner and explained my friend's interest, he perked up and began to explain the names of the confections. The sweets of Morocco, Egypt, and Turkey were all represented in the small shop. There were the gazelle horns that I knew from Morocco, as well as some delicate short-bread cookies and stuffed dates. The eastern Mediterranean contributed a selection of crunchy threads of nut-filled pastry covered with sticky sugar syrups and honey. There were even small brown cylinders that were called slave fingers, and we all giggled as I held up one of my fingers and measured them for size.

Later on in the trip, my friend spent the afternoon at the home of a traditional pastry cook. When she returned to the hotel, clutching a box of the pastries that they'd prepared, she generously allowed me to taste one, and even I, the most resolute non–dessert eater in the world, was taken. They were dense, rich, and alive with the flavors of almond paste and rosewater. I even had a second one.

MANGOES

◎◎◎

(WEST AFRICA)

When it's mango season in western Africa, no meal is complete without a beautiful woven basket full of them passed about as dessert after meals. Children filch them from neighbors' trees, and entire areas of markets are perfumed with their heady fragrance. There are many different types of mangoes in western Africa, each with its particular local name. The work of writers like Nigeria's Wole Soyinka and Senegal's Nafissatou Diallo abound with descriptions of the childhood joy of sucking on a tree-ripened mango. Most of us who live in the more northern climates do not know the true joy of a tree-ripened mango. Until very recently, we didn't know mangoes at all. Now, however, they are usually readily available in supermarkets. I said in my Caribbean-region cookbook, Sky Juice and Flying Fish, *that the best way to eat a ripe mango is naked and in the bathtub. I stand by that, but for those who can't do that, this is a more socially acceptable alternative.* SERVES 1

1 ripe, succulent mango

With a sharp knife, slice the mango lengthwise along each side of the pit. This will give you two small sections and the middle section with the pit. Make a crosswise pattern of cuts on the flesh side of one mango section. Then press on the skin side of the mango to flip the mango piece inside out. The mango will fan out, leaving little cubes of mango attached to the skin. Repeat the same procedure with the other slice. The middle section . . . well, there's nothing to do with the middle section but suck the mango pulp off the pit and *enjoy!*

MANGO CREAM

◎◎◎

(CAMEROON)

Where Europeans have journeyed throughout the continent, there are numerous dishes that marry European ingredients and culinary techniques to African ones. Here is one such hybrid dish.   SERVES 6

Peel the mangoes and cut them into pieces. Place the mango pieces in a medium-sized saucepan with water to cover and cook them over low heat for 10 minutes, or until very tender. When cooked, put the mango through a food mill until you have a thick pulp. Place the pulp in a small bowl, cover it with plastic wrap, and chill it for 1 hour. Meanwhile, whip the cream with an electric mixer or wire whisk, slowly sprinkling in the sugar. When the mango pulp is chilled, slowly fold in the sweetened cream, stirring only enough to make sure that the ingredients are well mixed. Pour the mango cream into individual sherbet glasses, sprinkle each serving with some of the toasted coconut, garnish with mint, and serve.

4 large mangoes
1 cup heavy whipping cream
3 tablespoons confectioners' sugar
2 tablespoons freshly toasted Coconut Crisps (page 100)
Fresh mint, for garnish

PINEAPPLE BOATS

◎◎◎

(CÔTE D'IVOIRE)

The pineapples of Côte d'Ivoire are some of the sweetest in the world. Unlike mangoes, pineapples present minimal problems. In much of western Africa, pineapples come to the table as slices. In parts of the Côte d'Ivoire, however, where tourism has brought Western aesthetics to African plates, pineapples are made into pineapple boats. The pineapple slices can be served in the boats, or the pineapple can become part of anything from a fruit salad to a crabmeat appetizer (page 99), which is then served in the pineapple boats.

SERVES 4

1 large ripe pineapple

With a very sharp knife, slice the pineapple lengthwise into 4 equal quarters, cutting through the green leaves. Cut the thick core from each of the quarters with a sharp paring knife. Slice the pineapple meat from the skin to form the pineapple boat. The pineapple can then be cut into 1-inch pieces and rearranged back in the pineapple boat or cut into chunks to become a part of whatever salad you wish.

⬤◗◆◗•◗◆◗•◗◆◗•◗◆⬤

We are the first to offer

basil and the scent of apples

perfumes our hands.

—MOROCCAN PROVERB ON

POLITENESS

⬤◗◆◗•◗◆◗•◗◆◗•◗◆⬤

BEIGNETS DE BANANES

◎◎◎

BANANA FRITTERS (WEST AFRICA)

Fritters are simply a part of life in western Africa. They turn up as Nigeria's akara, *as Senegal's* pastel, *and as here, as* beignets de bananes. *Frying in deep oil is one of western Africa's gifts to the continent's cuisine. Fruit fritters are a perfect and, yes, traditional end to any meal.*

The batter needs to sit for a day in the fridge before cooking.   SERVES 8

Place the flour, sugar, and salt in a medium-sized bowl. Separate the eggs. Make a well in the ingredients and place the egg yolks in the well. Mix, adding the water and, gradually, the milk. Beat the egg whites to stiff peaks and gently fold them into the mixture. Add the lemon zest and the nutmeg, stirring to mix them in. Cover the bowl with a damp clean dish towel and place it in the refrigerator for a day.

When ready to prepare the fritters, heat the oil to 375 degrees in a heavy Dutch oven or deep fryer. Peel the bananas and cut them crosswise into 1-inch pieces. With tongs, dip the pieces into the batter and fry them until they are golden brown on each side. Remove the fritters with a slotted spoon and let them drain on absorbent paper. Place them on a serving plate and sprinkle them with confectioners' sugar by placing the sugar into a small sieve and shaking it over the fritters. Serve warm.

¾ cup sifted flour

2 tablespoons sugar

Pinch of salt

2 eggs

2 tablespoons water

2 tablespoons milk

⅛ teaspoon grated lemon zest

Dash of nutmeg

Peanut oil for deep frying

4 large, firm, ripe bananas

3 tablespoons confectioners' sugar

VARIATIONS:

Beignets d'Ananas

◉◉◉

PINEAPPLE FRITTERS (CÔTE D'IVOIRE)

Substitute 2 pineapples, cut into 1-inch chunks. Add a pinch of powdered cinnamon to the batter and to the confectioners' sugar that goes over the finished fritters.

Beignets de Mangues

◉◉◉

MANGO FRITTERS

I cannot claim that this is a traditional recipe, but it is delicious nonetheless; the surprise of the mango inside the fritter is one that will make your mouth sing. Eight mangoes, cut into 1-inch chunks, should serve eight people. You'll need more, though, if they're hungry.

PUMPKIN FRITTERS
◎◎◎

(SOUTH AFRICA)

Here, fritters take on a South African flavor, spiced with cinnamon and lemon.

Place the mashed pumpkin, egg, and milk in a medium-sized bowl. Slowly stir in the remaining dry ingredients, making sure that there are no lumps. (If the mixture is too stiff, add a little bit more milk.) Heat the oil for deep frying in a heavy Dutch oven or a deep fryer to 375 degrees. When the oil is hot, drop in the fritters a tablespoonful at a time. Cook for 2 minutes, or until lightly browned, on each side, turning once. Allow them to drain on absorbent paper and then sprinkle with a dusting of the mixed sugar and cinnamon. Serve warm.

1 cup mashed cooked pumpkin

1 egg

2 tablespoons milk

½ cup sifted flour

1 teaspoon baking powder

1 tablespoon sugar

Pinch of salt

½ teaspoon ground cinnamon

⅛ teaspoon grated lemon zest

Grating of nutmeg

Vegetable oil for deep frying

2 tablespoons sugar, for sprinkling

*1 tablespoon ground cinnamon, for
    sprinkling*

COLONIAL FRUIT SALAD
◎◎◎

(GHANA)

This fruit salad is an obvious colonial inheritance, but it does make a simple and refreshing dessert that harmonizes with many of the more traditional African dishes. It is unusual in that some of the fruit is poached and allowed to cool before being mixed into the salad.

SERVES 6

1 pineapple, peeled, cored, and sliced
    into rounds
1 medium-sized papaya, peeled, seeded,
    and cut into chunks
1 large ripe banana, peeled and sliced
    into 1-inch rounds
2 large ripe oranges, peeled and
    segmented, membrane removed
1 cup milk
3 tablespoons light brown sugar
    (optional)

Place the pineapple slices in a medium-sized saucepan with water to cover and cook for 5 minutes, then drain and set aside. Place the papaya chunks in a saucepan with water to cover and cook for 2 to 3 minutes, then drain and set aside. When the pineapple and papaya are cool, layer all the fruit in a glass salad bowl, alternating fruit and color until all the fruit has been used. Add the milk and serve at room temperature. You may sprinkle the top with the brown sugar.

TIERE SOW
◎◎◎

MILLET COUSCOUS WITH BUTTERMILK (SENEGAL)

The tiere, *or millet couscous, of Senegal and Mali, which turns up on the dinner table as* bassi salte *(page 242), also puts in an appearance at the end of the meal. As dessert, it is chilled and served with sweetened buttermilk, which is called* sow. *The recipe is simple, but the dessert is stick-to-the-ribs filling, and the buttermilk makes it cooling and refreshing.*

SERVES 6

Sweeten the buttermilk with the sugar to taste. Spoon the cooked millet couscous into a serving bowl or into individual dishes and cover it with the sweetened buttermilk. Mix well and serve at room temperature.

3 cups buttermilk, chilled
Sugar, to taste
3 cups cooked millet couscous (page 308) or regular couscous (page 275)

FRUIT SELLER

TIAKRI

◎◎◎

STEAMED MILLET COUSCOUS (SENEGAL)

These steamed lentil-sized balls of millet flour are a traditional special-occasion food in Senegal. I had my first taste of **tiakri** *at the baptism of a girlfriend's nephew. The tangy taste of the buttermilk and the almost Wheatena-like flavor of the small pellets of millet reminded me of my childhood.*

SERVES 6

1 pound millet flour (see Note)
¼ cup water
1 quart buttermilk
¾ cup Vanilla Sugar (page 313)
Confectioners' sugar to taste

Place the millet flour in a medium-sized bowl and dampen it slightly with the water. Form small lentil-sized balls from the dampened flour by rubbing them around in your hands. Think kindergarten and making beads. (You may need more or less water depending on the texture of your millet flour, so add the water gradually.) When the balls are made, place them in the top part of a couscoussière or a steamer and steam until they are cooked through, about 20 minutes. When ready, remove and allow the *tiakri* to cool to room temperature. While the millet balls are cooling, add the sugars to the buttermilk and stir well to make sure that it is well mixed. When the millet balls have cooled, place them in a serving bowl, pour the sweetened buttermilk over them, and serve.

NOTE: For millet in general, see Glossary (page 63). Millet flour is available in health-food stores and through mail order (page 74).

GOSSI

◎◎◎

MILK RICE (SENEGAL)

The southern section of Senegal, the Casamance, is a rice-growing region, and the Peurl or Fulani people of the northern sections are known for their love of milk. While I have not been able to determine whether this dish of rice and milk harks from the Casamance region, it is a dessert that is favored throughout the country by young and old. It is one of the links in the long chain that stretches from the gossi *of Senegal through the* arroz de viuva *or milk rice of northeastern Brazil, to the rice desserts of the Caribbean, right into the rice puddings and milk rices of the American South.* SERVES 6 TO 8

Wash the rice and drain it. Bring the water to a boil in a large saucepan. Add the rice to the boiling water and allow it to cook for 5 minutes. Meanwhile, in a separate saucepan, bring the milk to a boil over medium heat. When the milk is boiling, remove the rice from the stove, drain it, and slowly drop it into the boiling milk. Lower the heat and add the salt, vanilla bean, and sugar. Cover and allow the rice to continue to cook over low heat for 15 to 20 minutes. Add more milk if necessary, while the rice is cooking, stirring to make sure that it is absorbed. The milk rice can be served warm, at room temperature, or cold.

2 cups short-grain white rice
6 cups water
4¼ cups milk
Pinch of salt
½ vanilla bean
6 tablespoons sugar, or to taste

Sow
◎◎◎

BUTTERMILK (SENEGAL)

Anyone who has spent time in Senegal may have seen one of the numerous sow vendors. These women, who are usually Fulani, can be seen in the streets of the medina and other quarters where the inhabitants are more traditional. They carry twin calabashes that are joined with a stick as a yoke and gracefully make their way through the dusty streets ensuring that sow lovers can have their treat. The sow is served either natural or sweetened, and it may turn up at virtually any time during the day. It is consumed as a treat and is even fed to young children as a food supplement after they have stopped nursing. Sow is so popular that it is now available in packages in large urban supermarkets. It is easy to prepare. Traditionally the ingredients are mixed together with a long wooden spoon called a rokhou, *but you can use any wooden spoon that you have. (Be careful how you pronounce this one—it's "so" as in "So, what's up?," not "sow" as in female pig. That has another meaning in Wolof, a Senegalese language.)*

MAKES 1 QUART

1 quart buttermilk
¼ cup sugar
2 tablespoons Vanilla Sugar
    (page 313)
⅛ teaspoon freshly grated nutmeg, or
    to taste

Place the buttermilk in a crock or pitcher. Add the sugar and vanilla sugar and stir well with a long wooden spoon. Cover the crock with a clean dish towel or with plastic wrap and set it aside overnight. (While it is not traditional, you may wish to let the sow rest in the refrigerator.) When ready to serve, sprinkle the top with a few gratings of fresh nutmeg.

DARKASSOU

CASHEW FRUIT (SENEGAL)

This pear-shaped reddish-orange fruit is no stranger to those who live in tropical climates, though it doesn't turn up regularly in American kitchens. This may be an African dessert that you'll have to wait for until you reach the continent. As the availability of exotic food is increasing, however, this slightly astringent yet delicious fruit may soon become a part of our culinary repertoire. The cashew fruit is the fruit from which the lone cashew nut hangs in solitary question-mark-like splendor. To see that there is only one nut per fruit is to know why cashews are so expensive. Cashew fruit are also found in Brazil and in parts of the Caribbean, where they turn up as juice and even in compotes. In Senegal, the slightly tart fruit is eaten raw.

CRÈME DE COROSSOL

◉◉◉

SOURSOP CREAM (SENEGAL)

The spiny light-green soursop can sometimes be found in African or Caribbean markets or in specialty greengrocers'. Western African cooks enjoy the aromatic fruit, with its creamy consistency and slightly sharp taste, in recipes from traditional juices and milks to sorbets. In this recipe the old meets the new, and the soursop is transformed into a thick cream. For more information on the soursop, see the Glossary (page 71).

SERVES 8

2 pounds soursops (see page 71)
½ cup water
¼ cup sugar, or to taste
1 cup heavy whipping cream
Lemon peel curls, for garnish
Coconut Crisps (page 100),
   for garnish

Peel the soursops and remove the seeds. Put the flesh into the bowl of a food processor with the water and sugar and pulse until you have a thick paste. In a separate bowl, beat the heavy cream with a whisk or an electric beater until it forms thick peaks. Slowly fold the soursop paste into the heavy cream, making sure that they are well mixed. When finished, cover with plastic wrap and refrigerate for at least 1½ hours. When ready to serve, spoon the cream into small bowls or footed sherbet dishes, garnish each with a lemon curl, and serve with coconut crisps.

SUCRE VANILLE
◎◎◎

VANILLA SUGAR (FRENCH-SPEAKING AFRICA)

This ingredient is commonly used in many of the French-speaking countries of western Africa. While normally I am an advocate of natural sugar, the taste of the cane will interfere with the delicacy of the vanilla in this recipe, so please use refined sugar here. The vanilla sugar needs to sit for three weeks before use. MAKES 4 CUPS

Place the sugar and vanilla beans in a glass jar with a screw or seal top, making sure that the beans are surrounded by the sugar. Close the jar and leave it for 3 weeks, shaking it from time to time. Then open and use to add sweetness with a hint of vanilla. The vanilla will have perfumed the sugar. Occasionally, the beans are so aromatic and full of vanilla oil that the sugar becomes somewhat gummy. Not to worry. Simply break it up and use it. It will be all the more flavorful.

4 cups granulated white sugar
2 vanilla beans

ABACATES COM MEL

◎◎◎

AVOCADOS WITH HONEY (CAPE VERDE ISLANDS)

This dessert recipe from the Cape Verde Islands is unusual in that it uses the avocado in a sweet dessert. It's an acquired taste to be sure, but one that isn't too hard to learn. The combination of avocados and sweet flavors may be Portuguese in origin; the only other recipe that I know of where avocados are used for dessert is a Brazilian one for avocado cream prepared with sugar. Traditionally, the honey used is cane honey; I've replaced it with bee's honey. Choose the type that you prefer or settle for the type that you can find.   SERVES 4

2 large avocados
Honey, to taste

Cut each avocado in half lengthwise and remove the pit. Scoop the flesh from the avocado, leaving the 2 shell halves intact. Place the avocado meat in a bowl and sweeten it with honey to taste. Replace the sweetened avocado in the shells, cover them with plastic wrap, and chill them. Serve them cold on a bed of lettuce or on a bed of avocado leaves, if you can find them.

BANANA ENROLADA
◎◎◎

FRIED BANANAS (CAPE VERDE ISLANDS)

The batter for these fried bananas is unusual. It is prepared with corn flour and has the added kick of a bit of white rum.

SERVES 4

Heat the oil for deep frying to 375 degrees in a Dutch oven or deep fryer. Mix the corn flour and sugar together in a bowl. Add the butter, egg, salt, rum, and milk, stirring constantly until you have a thick batter. Peel the bananas, cut them into quarters, and sprinkle them with a mixture of half of the cinnamon and half of the sugar. Roll the banana quarters in the batter and dip them slowly in the hot oil a few at a time. Fry them for 2 to 3 minutes on each side, turning once, or until they are golden brown. Drain on absorbent paper and dust with the cinnamon mixed with the brown sugar. Serve warm.

Olive oil for deep frying
1 cup corn flour
¼ cup sugar
1 tablespoon butter
1 egg
¼ teaspoon salt
2 tablespoons white rum
2 tablespoons milk
4 firm ripe bananas
1 teaspoon ground cinnamon
2 tablespoons dark brown sugar

DOCE DE MANDIOCA
◉◉◉

CASSAVA SWEET (MOZAMBIQUE)

This dish of Portuguese descent is traditionally served in a footed compote bowl; it would be equally at home gracing a dessert buffet in Brazil. The recipe uses the sweet cassava, available in tropical markets.   SERVES 6 TO 8

1 pound sweet cassava

1 coconut

1¾ cups sugar

2 teaspoons cinnamon, for dusting

Peel the cassava and cut it into bite-sized pieces. Open the coconut and prepare thick coconut milk according to the directions on page 56. Place the coconut milk in a saucepan, add the cassava pieces, and cook over low heat, drizzling in the sugar and stirring until the cassava has cooked and the mixture has thickened. Continue to cook for 3 minutes, then allow the mixture to cool. Spoon it into a compote bowl. Dust with cinnamon and serve at room temperature.

DATES
◎◎◎

(NORTH AFRICA)

Dates are a way of life in much of North Africa, and are nibbled throughout the day from Cairo to Casablanca. They come in a staggering number of varieties. For a special dessert, arrange an assortment of dates on a tray, accompanied by raw and roasted almonds (page 318) and a variety of citrus fruits, like tiny clementines and tart mandarins.

DATES FOURÉES
◎◎◎

STUFFED DATES (ALGERIA)

While dates are eaten either whole or pitted, folk often fancy them up a bit. They may appear on dessert tables stuffed with almond paste, like these dates from the pied noir *of Algeria.*　　MAKES 2 DOZEN DATES

2 dozen medjool dates (see pages 58–59)

⅔ cup marzipan

1 or 2 drops green food coloring

Select 2 dozen of the fattest, firmest medjool dates you can find. Slit them down one side and remove the pit. Mix the marzipan with the food coloring in a small bowl; the color should be a dark, not a pastel, green. Stuff each date with the marzipan, allowing some to show through the slit. Arrange the dates on a platter and serve.

ROASTED ALMONDS

◎◎◎

(MOROCCO)

Almonds turn up as street nibbles throughout Morocco. It is not unusual to drive down the Atlas Mountains into the city of Marrakesh and find small boys on the side of the road offering bags of almonds for sale. In this simple dish, which can be a snack or a dessert, the almonds are drizzled with olive oil, toasted to a deep brown, and served with a dusting of sugar.

SERVES 8

2 tablespoons extra-virgin olive oil
1 pound shelled, blanched almonds
Confectioners' sugar, to taste

Heat half the oil in a heavy skillet and brown half the almonds, turning them occasionally with a wooden spoon, until they are well toasted. When they have reached the desired color (some like them light; I prefer them a deep mahogany brown), drain them on paper towels and repeat with the second batch. Sprinkle with sugar to taste and serve warm.

HARVESTING BANANAS

SALADE D'ORANGES
◎◎◎

ORANGE SALAD (ALGERIA)

The citrus fruit of North Africa is wondrous. I remember a trip to Morocco where I was greeted at each hotel with a basket of small tart clementines—my favorite fruit—they were amazing, and I am always thrilled to hear the natives of Tangiers referred to as Tangerines. North African oranges, while slightly less exotic, are no less delicious. They come to the table all day long, from breakfast's tart frothy freshly squeezed orange juice right through the orange salad that ends the evening meal and re-freshes the palate.   SERVES 6 TO 8

Peel the oranges, slice them into thin circles, and remove all the seeds with the tip of a paring knife. Arrange the orange slices on a large platter or in a shallow glass bowl. Sprinkle the orange-flower water over the slices. Mix the cinnamon and sugar together and sprinkle it over the oranges. The salad is ready to serve, though I find it tastier if it is covered with plastic wrap and chilled for 30 minutes before serving.

12 Valencia oranges
2 tablespoons orange-flower water
* (see Note)*
1 teaspoon ground cinnamon
3 tablespoons confectioners' sugar

NOTE: See the Glossary (page 66) and the Mail-Order Sources (page 74) for orange-flower water.

TEKOUA

◎◎◎

SUGARED SESAME BALLS (NORTH AFRICA)

The use of sesame seeds is particularly interesting in this dish, which has its origins in sub-Saharan Africa. Here, the seeds are pounded and mixed with confectioners' sugar to form small balls.   SERVES 6

2 cups sesame seeds
1 cup confectioners' sugar

FOR THE GLAZE:
¼ cup confectioners' sugar
¼ cup water

Pick over the sesame seeds to remove any impurities. Toast the seeds in a heavy skillet over low heat until they are golden brown. When ready, place the toasted sesame seeds in the bowl of a mortar and pound them, adding the confectioners' sugar a bit at a time until the mixture is a thick paste. To make the glaze, mix the glaze ingredients together in a small bowl. Then, taking a small amount of the sesame mixture in your hands, roll the paste into small balls. Finish the balls by rolling them in the sugar glaze.

MUKASSARAAT
◎◎◎

MIXED NUTS (EGYPT)

These sugared nuts are a popular addition to desserts and drinks. The mixture is traditionally composed of two or more of the following: almonds, hazelnuts, pecans, and peanuts. MAKES 1 CUP

Prepare the nuts by rubbing the skins off. (If using almonds, prepare them by blanching them and roasting them as suggested on page 318.) Place the nuts in the bowl of a food processor with the sugar and pulse until you have a coarse mixture. (Do not overprocess or you'll wind up with nut butter instead of crumbs.) Moisten the mixture slightly with a few dashes of rosewater, and then the nuts are ready to serve as a topping for pastry or drinks or to sprinkle onto dishes as a topping.

⅔ cup unsalted mixed roasted nuts
⅓ cup sugar
Rosewater (see Note)

NOTE: See the Glossary (page 69) and the Mail-Order Sources (page 74) for rosewater.

MAKROUD
◎◎◎

TUNISIAN DATE COOKIES (TUNISIA)

My pâtissière friend Priscilla Martel came up with a recipe for makroud *that would do a pastry shop in Kairouan proud. It's complex, but the end result is well worth the effort.*

These pastries are best when prepared with a fruity olive oil, preferably Greek or, if you find it, Tunisian.

Once assembled, the pastries need to be refrigerated for 1 to 24 hours before cooking.

MAKES ABOUT 3 DOZEN

FOR THE DOUGH:

5 cups semolina flour (about 1¼ pounds)

½ teaspoon salt

Pinch of saffron

½ teaspoon baking soda

1 cup hot water

1 cup fruity olive oil

FOR THE FILLING:

8 ounces pitted dates

One 3-inch strip orange zest, coarsely chopped

⅓ cup fruity olive oil

Pinch of ground cloves

¼ teaspoon cinnamon

⅛ teaspoon freshly ground black pepper

⅓ cup hot water

FOR FRYING:

3 cups vegetable or peanut oil

To prepare the dough, place the semolina flour in a large skillet and toast it over medium heat for 3 to 4 minutes, stirring constantly, until it is well warmed and fragrant. Do not let the flour brown. Place the flour in a large bowl and add the salt and saffron. Make a well in the center of the mixture. Dissolve the baking soda in the hot water, add with the oil to the flour mix, and quickly mix it in with your fingertips. Continue mixing until the dough goes from crumbly to a firm ball. Add more oil if the dough is too dry. When the dough has formed a ball, remove it from the bowl and knead it for 3 to 4 minutes, until pliable. Cover it with plastic wrap and allow it to rest for 30 minutes before rolling.

While the dough is resting, prepare the filling. Cut the dates in half and place them in the bowl of a food processor. Add the orange zest and chop for 1 minute, or until the dates are finely chopped and begin to turn into a coarse paste. Add the olive oil and spices and continue to process for half a minute. Add the hot water and continue to process for another minute, or until the mixture becomes a smooth paste. Scrape the paste onto a greased baking sheet and divide it into 4 sections. Roll each section into a cylinder about ¾ inch in diameter and 10 inches long and set them all aside.

To assemble, divide the dough into 4 pieces. Working with one piece at a time, roll the dough into a fat log with your hands. Flatten it, then use a rolling pin to roll it into a long rectangle about ½ inch thick and about 4 by 10 inches. Arrange one strip of date paste along one of the long sides of the rolled dough, about ½ inch from the edge. Using a dough scraper or knife, lift the long edges of the dough and fold in to cover the paste. Using your fingertips, seal the edges of the dough and roll it lightly to make a firm cylinder. Then flatten the dough slightly.

Using the back of a paring knife, incise decorative lines on the dough and cut it on the diagonal into 2-inch-long pieces. Place the cut pieces on a greased tray and set aside as you repeat the process with the remaining dough and paste. Once the pastries have been formed, cover them with plastic wrap and refrigerate them for between 1 and 24 hours before deep-frying them.

To fry, place the oil in a small deep saucepan to a depth of 3 inches. Heat the oil to 350 degrees over medium heat. While the oil is heating, prepare the dipping syrup by placing the sugar and water in a small saucepan and bringing them to a boil over high heat. Reduce the heat and allow the mixture to simmer for about 5 minutes, or until the sugar has completely dissolved. Add the honey and stir well. Remove the syrup from the heat and add the orange-flower water.

When the oil has reached the desired temperature, lower 4 or 5 pieces of pastry into the oil with a slotted spoon. Cook for about 45 seconds on each side, or until they are evenly browned to a light golden color. Drain the pastries on paper towels and place them in the syrup while they are still warm, turning them to make sure that they are evenly coated. Remove them with a slotted spoon and place them on a serving platter while continuing to cook the remaining pastries.

To store *makroud*, place them in a shallow container, drizzle them with the remaining sugar syrup, and cover with plastic wrap. They will keep for 4 to 5 days at room temperature and

FOR THE DIPPING SYRUP:

1 cup sugar

1 cup water

½ cup honey

2 tablespoons orange-flower water
  (see Note)

longer if refrigerated. Remember, though, that as they sit they will lose some of their crispness.

NOTE: See the Glossary (page 66) and the Mail-Order Sources (page 74) for orange-flower water.

ALGERIAN TAFFY SELLER

BEVERAGES

◎◎◎

Mint Tea, Palm Wine, and Cool, Cool Water

The beverages of the African continent are as diverse as its foods. Vineyards in the more temperate areas to the north and south make wine that has its own African imprint. Among the popularly priced wines, the *vin gris* of Morocco and Tunisia are considered the perfect accompaniments to the foods of those areas by some, while the pinotages of South Africa are gaining popularity.

Throughout much of northern Africa, there is a tradition of hot and cold beverages that goes back many centuries. Coffee and tea are the most popular and the best known, but drinks also include infusions of herbs and spices and cooling fruit juice concoctions. Vendors can even be seen walking through the streets of Cairo and the alleyways of Marrakesh with Byzantine-looking dispensers, offering their liquid wares for consumption. In Egypt, these beverages are known as *mashroobaat*.

The continent boasts numerous beers, many of them named "Flag" in the former French colonies. There are also palm wine and the numerous thirst-quenching beverages, such as those flavored with lemon and ginger, that are hawked through the streets and markets of towns

from Cameroon to Cairo. Then there's mint tea and cardamom coffee, which originated on the continent. Cool, cool water, whether plain or perfumed with aromatic herbs, is still, for most, the beverage of choice on this continent that boasts both the Sahara and the Kalahari deserts.

◎◎◎

MAGDA'S KARKADEH
Roselle Beverage *(Egypt)*

'IRFA
Cinnamon Beverage *(Egypt)*

BABEURRE
Algerian Buttermilk *(Algeria)*

'AMAR AL-DIN
Apricot Drink *(Egypt)*

'IR 'SUS
Licorice Beverage *(Egypt)*

QAHAWAH BEL HABAHAN
Cardamom Coffee *(Egypt)*

EAU PARFUMÉE
Scented Water *(Morocco)*

JUS D'ORANGE MAROCAINE
Moroccan-Style Orange Juice *(Morocco)*

VIN À L'ORANGE
Orange Wine *(Algeria)*

LAIT PARFUMÉ
Minted Milk *(Algeria)*

SHANDY GAFF
(Zambia)

THÉ NAA NAA MAROCAINE
Moroccan Mint Tea *(Morocco)*

THÉ SÉNÉGALAISE
Senegal-Style Mint Tea *(Senegal)*

RAMADAN SHERBET
(South Africa)

MASALA FOR TEA
Tea Spice *(Kenya)*

MANGO JUICE
(South Africa)

NDIAR
Buttermilk *(Senegal)*

PINEAPPLE SHERBET
(South Africa)

DAKHAR
Tamarind Juice *(Senegal)*

COROSSOL
Soursop Milk *(Benin)*

DOUTE
Kinkéliba Tea *(Senegal)*

GINGEMBRE
Ginger Water *(Côte d'Ivoire)*

LICOR DE CAFÉ
Coffee Liqueur *(Cape Verde Islands)*

VAN DER HUM
Tangerine Liqueur *(South Africa)*

CITRONNELLE
Lemongrass Tea *(Côte d'Ivoire)*

SUGAR SYRUP

✳

The Gift of Bien Donné

Bien Donné harks back to the richness of the South African land that inspired the Dutch to colonize the area as a provisioning point for their ships rounding the Cape of Good Hope. The French Huguenots who arrived in the area around today's Capetown in the late seventeenth century went to work farming to provision the ships that called at the port in their circumnavigation of the continent. Later, the Huguenots turned their hands to growing wine grapes and producing wine—including the *vin de constance* that was Napoleon's favorite drink in exile. When the phylloxera epidemic hit in the mid-nineteenth century, many of the farms were converted to other uses. Some, like Bien Donné, re-

A SOUTH AFRICAN DAIRY

mained farms. Bien Donné eventually became a research farm experimenting with varieties of fruits and vegetables that are suitable for growth in the many microclimates that make up the area around the Cape. Today, a part of Bien Donné is open to the public and specializes in showcasing the bounty of the Cape region. One of the ways that they show off the taste of the area's fruits is with their own fruit wines and juice tastings. On the day I visited, they were celebrating the apricot. A glass of sweet-tart apricot juice greeted me on my arrival, followed by a taste of apricot sorbet topped with a local potable called *witblitz*, which literally translates as white lightning. *Witblitz* is more formally known as *manpoer*, but the taste of the *eau de vie*—like liqueur and its potency make the first appellation more appropriate. Apricots are not all that is grown at Bien Donné. They produce persimmons, peaches, nectarines, plums, apples, pears, and some berries. They also have an herb garden where they grow herbs to prepare their own teas, including *heuning bos* (honeybush tea) and *rooibos* (redbush tea), natural non-caffeinated teas that are part of the bounty of the Cape. I snipped and sniffed leaves of peppermint geranium, rose geranium, lemon balm, and lemon thyme and learned how to brew them into cooling iced teas, and I listened to the farm's plans for making their own fruit wines, like the *vin d'orange* that I also sampled.

I left with an appreciation of the richness of the land and the rewards of farming as well as a bag full of preserves, tea, and, of course, *witblitz*.

MAGDA'S KARKADEH
◉◉◉

ROSELLE BEVERAGE (EGYPT)

Magda is a wonderful Egyptian I met through friends. Tall and slender, with a profile that comes straight from the pyramid tomb paintings, she is an actress in the making. At our first meeting she taught me a surprise lesson about Egyptian hospitality by inviting us all to her brother's home for dinner the following week. When we arrived, she'd prepared a wonderful meal that was washed down with refreshing glasses of this typically Egyptian drink, which is also sometimes spelled carcade. *In the Caribbean, it is a traditional Christmas drink. There, it is prepared with a variety of spices for a beverage that is frequently mixed with rum. In Senegal and in Egypt, the drink, which is rich in vitamin C and is in fact one of the ingredients that make Red Zinger tea red, is served plain with only a bit of sugar added to cut the astringency of the tea. It is exactly like Senegalese* bissap rouge *and quite similar to the Caribbean holiday drink sorrel.*　　MAKES 2 QUARTS

Place the roselle pods in a nonreactive saucepan with enough of the water to cover and allow them to soak for 2 hours. When ready, place the saucepan over medium heat and bring to a boil. Allow the roselle to infuse for 5 minutes, then strain into a large container. Return the roselle to the saucepan, add more water, and again bring it to a boil. Continue this process until you have used all the water (or until the liquid poured off is a faint rose pink). Sweeten the mixture to taste, then chill and serve with or without ice.

1 cup roselle pods (see Note)
2 quarts water
Sugar or Sugar Syrup (page 354),
　to taste

NOTE: See Glossary (page 69) and Mail-Order Sources (page 74) for roselle pods. They can also be found at health-food stores, where they would be called sorrel or roselle.

'IRFA
◎◎◎

CINNAMON BEVERAGE (EGYPT)

The Egyptian love of spices is well documented. Cairo was one of the hubs of the spice trade in the seventeenth and eighteenth centuries and served as a transit point for many spices. Black and white pepper arrived from Sri Lanka, long pepper came from Java and Sumatra, cloves and nutmeg from the Moluccas, cardamom from India's Malabar Coast, ginger from India, and the cinnamon that is the basis of this beverage from Sri Lanka, India, and China. Perhaps this recipe arrived with the spice. Whatever its provenance, it has been taken to Egyptian hearts. MAKES 1 CUP

2 sticks cinnamon
2 teaspoons sugar, or sugar or Sugar
   Syrup (page 354) to taste
1 cup cold water
Mixed Nuts, for sprinkling
   (page 321)

Place the cinnamon and sugar in a small saucepan with the cold water and bring to a boil, stirring occasionally. Lower the heat and allow the mixture to simmer for 10 minutes, or until it is brownish. Remove the cinnamon sticks and pour the *'irfa* into a cup. Serve with mixed nuts sprinkled into the cup.

BABEURRE
◎◎◎

ALGERIAN BUTTERMILK (ALGERIA)

A taste for sour milk seems to prevail throughout much of northern and western Africa. This drink traditionally accompanies couscous au beurre, *plain buttered couscous (page 275), but it can also be savored by itself.* MAKES 2 QUARTS

2 quarts fresh milk
½ cup plain yogurt

Pour the milk and yogurt into an earthenware pitcher and stir them well. Cover the pitcher with a cloth and place it in a warm spot to allow the milk to curdle. This will take a few days, depending on the milk. When the milk has curdled, refrigerate it. When ready to serve, beat the *babeurre* briskly for 5 minutes, then serve chilled.

'AMAR AL-DIN
◎◎◎

APRICOT DRINK (EGYPT)

Arabs brought apricots to the Mediterranean region from China. While the Latin name for the fruit, Prunus armeniaca, *comes from the mistaken thought that the fruit originated in Armenia, the apricot gets its English name from the Arabic of Islamic Spain, where it was called al-barquq, which means "precocious" because the trees bloomed early in the spring. This version of the beverage calls for sheets of apricot paste, called apricot leather, which are found in many shops. They are simply sheets of apricot pulp mixed with a bit of olive oil and sugar and dried to leather-like consistency to preserve them.*

MAKES ABOUT 1 QUART

Tear the apricot sheet into small pieces and place them in a medium-sized nonreactive bowl. Add the cold water and soak until the apricot dissolves. Strain through a fine sieve and sweeten to taste. Serve cold, garnished with sprigs of mint.

NOTE: Apricot paste can be found at Middle Eastern stores.

1 5-inch-square sheet of apricot paste (see Note)
1 quart cold water
Sugar or Sugar Syrup (page 354), to taste
Mint sprigs, for garnish

'IR 'SUS

◎◎◎

LICORICE BEVERAGE (EGYPT)

This strong-tasting drink is prepared from powdered licorice root. Street vendors in Cairo sometimes simplify the process by preparing syrup of licorice, but this recipe is one of the more traditional ways of preparing the beverage.

SERVES 4 TO 6

2 to 3 heaping tablespoons licorice powder (see page 62)
2 teaspoons plus ½ gallon cold water

Place the licorice powder in a deep bowl. Sprinkle with 2 teaspoons of the water. With the back of a spoon, rub the mixture until it becomes a thick dark-brown paste. You may wish to do this with your fingers. If you do, use rubber gloves, as the licorice will stain your hands. Let the paste rest for 15 minutes, then place it in a square of cheesecloth, tie the ends together to make a pouch, and place the pouch in a wide-neck container with the remaining ½ gallon of cold water. Place the container in the refrigerator and allow the drink to infuse for at least an hour, or until ready to serve. (The water will turn a deep brown.) When ready, discard the pouch, and serve chilled over ice.

QAHAWAH BEL HABAHAN

◎◎◎

CARDAMOM COFFEE (EGYPT)

Coffee arrived in Egypt during the rule of the Ottoman Turks. It appeared at the beginning of the sixteenth century and was immediately taken to heart and stomach. By 1650, Cairo had 650 cafés. Today there are about 5,000 of them, including the famous El-Fishawi Café, or Café of Mirrors, that was to turn-of-the-century Cairo what the Café des Deux Magots and the Café de Flore were to Parisian artists and writers in the 1950s. It is currently one of the favored roosts of Nobel Prize–winning writer Naguib Mafouz, who probably sips a coffee similar to this one.

You can substitute ¼ teaspoon of grated nutmeg for the cardamom.   SERVES 2 OR 3

Place all the ingredients in a small saucepan or *kanaka* and stir to mix them together. Cook the coffee over medium heat for about 10 minutes, or until it begins to boil and the grounds sink. (The coffee should never be allowed to come to a full boil.) Serve immediately, pouring some of the coffee froth into each demitasse cup and the rest of the coffee over it.

1 cup cold water

1 cardamom pod, crushed

*1 teaspoon sugar, or sugar or Sugar
    Syrup (page 354) to taste*

*1 tablespoon finely ground, very dark
    roasted coffee*

EAU PARFUMÉE

◉◉◉

SCENTED WATER (MOROCCO)

The use of aromatic resins and gums in cooking is widespread in the elegant cooking of northern Africa, and has moved downward to the other Muslim parts of the continent as well. For this recipe, you will need a small brazier, or incense burner, with a quick-lighting kind of charcoal pellets that are used to burn incense.   MAKES 1 QUART

1 teaspoon gum arabic (see Note)
1 quart water
1 teaspoon orange-flower water
  (see Note)

Place the charcoal pellet in the incense burner and light it according to the package directions. When the charcoal has burned to a gray ash, sprinkle the gum arabic on the charcoal and allow it to burn. When it begins to smoke and perfume the room, cover the burner with an earthenware vessel and collect the smoke and the fragrance for 5 to 7 minutes. Add the water and the orange-flower water to the vessel, cover it, and chill. Serve cool.

NOTE: Gum arabic is available in Middle Eastern stores. For orange-flower water, see Glossary (page 66). Both are available through mail order (page 74).

JUS D'ORANGE MAROCAINE
◎◎◎

MOROCCAN-STYLE ORANGE JUICE (MOROCCO)

The citrus fruits of Morocco seem to have a special taste. Perhaps it's because they have a long history in northern Africa, where the Arabs introduced them. (The orange plant actually originated in China.) We get our word orange *from the Arabic* narandj, *which comes from the Sanskrit* nagarunga. *Not only are the fruits used extensively in cooking, the flowers of the bitter orange tree are distilled into orange-flower water, or* zhar, *which is added to everything from salads to something as simple as freshly squeezed orange juice.*

SERVES 1

Using a reamer or a juicer, squeeze the juice from the oranges and place it in a tall decorative glass. Add orange-flower water to taste. Garnish with a sprig of fresh mint and serve at room temperature.

3 large ripe juice oranges
2 dashes orange-flower water, or
*   to taste (see Note)*
1 sprig fresh spearmint, for garnish

NOTE: See the Glossary (page 66) and Mail-Order Sources (page 74) for orange-flower water.

Vin à l'Orange

ORANGE WINE (ALGERIA)

This is not really a wine at all, but a heady concoction made from red or white wine, rum, sugar, and oranges. Colette speaks about it as being one of the favorite beverages in Oran, Algeria, the birthplace of Albert Camus. This drink is much consumed in the south of France in the summertime and is a perfect beverage for anywhere and anytime that the climate approximates that of the Mediterranean.

This drink must sit for three weeks before consumption.

MAKES 1 QUART

4 large juice oranges

¾ cup sugar, or sugar or Sugar Syrup (page 354) to taste

¼ cup dark rum

4 cups red or white wine

Grate the orange zest and peel the oranges. Place the zest and the skinned oranges in a large crock with the remaining ingredients. Cover the crock loosely and allow it to sit for 3 weeks, stirring frequently. When ready, pour the orange wine into scalded wine bottles and cork tightly. Store in a cool, dark place until ready to drink. Serve chilled.

O tapster of soured

wine from the sheath

of the withered palm . . .

Draw wine for me in

the little flask that makes

a man stagger and sway.

—FROM A SWAHILI

DRINKING POEM

LAIT PARFUMÉ
◎◎◎

MINTED MILK (ALGERIA)

Even milk benefits from the infusion of an extra flavor. In this case it takes on a traditional North African hint of mint. You can substitute fresh marjoram or another aromatic herb for the mint in this recipe.   MAKES 1 QUART

Place the milk in a medium-sized saucepan and bring it slowly to a boil. Add 6 to 8 sprigs of the mint, lower the heat, and continue to cook for 15 minutes. Remove the milk and pour it into an earthenware pitcher. Cover the pitcher with plastic wrap and refrigerate. Serve chilled, garnished with a sprig of mint.

1 quart fresh milk
6 to 8 sprigs fresh spearmint, plus more for garnish

SHANDY GAFF
◎◎◎

(ZAMBIA)

The popularity of this thirst-quenching drink has spread throughout English-speaking Africa. I had my first taste of shandy in Lusaka, Zambia, in the 1970s. Since then, I've enjoyed the cooling beer and ginger beer mix in places as far afield as Capetown, South Africa, and Kumasi, Ghana, and even in the English-speaking Caribbean. It's a perfect beverage when you want the taste, but not the potency, of a cold beer.

You can personalize the shandy with a dash of a liqueur like Grand Marnier.   MAKES 2 QUARTS

Mix the beer and the ginger beer together in a large pitcher or crock. Add several ice cubes and allow the mixture to chill. Serve cold over ice in stemmed water glasses.

1 quart pilsner beer
1 quart ginger beer

THÉ NAA NAA MAROCAINE

◎◎◎

MOROCCAN MINT TEA (MOROCCO)

Mint tea in Morocco is said to cool one off in the heat of the day. It is traditionally served after the meal to aid digestion but is sipped all day long by shopkeepers in the medina of Fez. It is said that this mint tea appeals to all the senses. The eyes are gladdened by the amber hue of the tea; the nose twitches with the smell of the mint; the hand is warmed by the heat of the tea; and the mouth savors the taste. The ears? Well, when tea is traditionally served, the server pours a stream of tea into the glass from a teapot held aloft and the ears are delighted by the sound. Mint tea is traditionally served in small glasses that are held with the tips of one's fingers.

While spearmint is traditional, many Moroccans mix other herbs with the mint in preparing their tea. You may wish to try lemon verbena or even a dash of orange-flower water.

SERVES 6 TO 8

6 to 8 cups water

4 teaspoons Chinese gunpowder green tea

6 to 8 sprigs fresh spearmint

Sugar cubes, to taste

Heat the water to boiling in a kettle. Place the tea in a medium-sized teapot and pour the boiling water over it. Allow the tea to steep for a minute; add the mint and sugar. Allow the tea to steep for another minute or so, then pour a glass of tea and return it to the pot (to mix the sugar). Serve the tea very hot in small glasses. Tradition allows for slurping.

THÉ SÉNÉGALAISE
◎◎◎

SENEGAL-STYLE MINT TEA (SENEGAL)

This tea, which Senegal claims as its own, is clearly a variation on the mint tea of Morocco (page 340). In Senegal, however, the rules are changed slightly. The first tea is steeped along with the sugar. Women do not sample this first tea because it is very strong and bitter. It is thought to be bad for their health. (I, of course, had to try it. It's just strong!) The second and subsequent teas are lighter and more like their Moroccan counterparts. The second time, water is simply added to the same leaves, which are then boiled again. While Moroccans serve only three services of tea, with the third being considered the perfect point, the Senegalese seem to have no set number of servings. They like their tea sweet, and the tiny delicate glasses of tea are a perfect way to end a meal. MAKES 6 GLASSES

Heat a teapot with boiling water, then discard the water. Place the tea in the heated teapot. Wash the tea by pouring a bit of boiling water over it, pouring the water off into a glass, and discarding it. Place the mint sprigs and the sugar in the teapot and cover them with 6 glasses of boiling water. Pour out a glass of this tea by holding the pot as high over the glass as possible. This is to mix the sugar and the tea. Pour the tea back into the pot and repeat this procedure two more times until the tea, sugar, and mint are all mixed. Serve the six glasses in the same way, pouring the tea from as high as possible. The Moroccans say that this adds the pleasure of sound to those of sight, taste, smell, and touch. Serve the tea.

The second tea is prepared by adding 6 glasses of boiling water and a tiny bit more tea to the pot. The mint and sugar are added again. Mix the sugar as for the first tea, by pouring the tea into a glass and returning it to the teapot. Serve.

The third tea is prepared exactly as for the second tea. Diners take only one small glass at each serving. The rounds of tea may continue after the third one.

FOR THE FIRST TEA:
5 teaspoons Chinese gunpowder green tea
3 sprigs fresh mint, washed
8 sugar cubes, or the equivalent in loaf sugar
6 glasses boiling water

FOR THE SECOND AND SUBSEQUENT TEAS:
6 glasses boiling water
2 teaspoons Chinese gunpowder green tea, or to taste
2 springs fresh mint
5 sugar cubes, or the equivalent in loaf sugar, or to taste

RAMADAN SHERBET

◎◎◎

(SOUTH AFRICA)

The rose is totemic for many Muslims. Tradition suggests that it was the favorite flower of the Prophet Mohammed. It is certainly for this reason that this pink, rose-scented drink is a favorite at Ramadan. This is a recipe that is prepared by South Africa's Indian population, who also prepare a rose syrup called gulaab.

The sugar and water need to dissolve for four hours before preparation of the sherbet.   MAKES 1 QUART

4½ cups sugar

1 quart water

2 teaspoons red food coloring

2 tablespoons rosewater (see Note)

1 teaspoon ground cardamom

Place the sugar and water in a saucepan and allow it to sit for 4 hours to dissolve completely. Bring the saucepan to a boil over high heat, then simmer over medium heat for 30 minutes. Add the remaining ingredients and continue to simmer for 5 minutes. Allow the liquid to cool. Refrigerate. Serve ice cold, diluted with water to taste.

NOTE: See the Glossary (page 69) and the Mail-Order Sources (page 74) for rosewater.

MASALA FOR TEA
◎◎◎

TEA SPICE (KENYA)

One of my cherished purchases from a long-ago trip to Kenya is a brass spice box that I found in an antiques shop in Mombasa. Its tight cover opens to reveal small brass cups designed to hold the precious spices that Kenya's Indian population use to season their food. I remember finding a spice shop in the maze of streets and trying to match the spices on the shelves to the smells that were still alive in the newly purchased antique box. One that had eluded me thus far was a mixture known as masala for tea, or tea spice. Traditionally this mixture is prepared at home, and the recipes change from house to house. This is one that is similar to the original one that I found in Mombasa.

If you cannot find jaggery, you can substitute brown rock candy. If this is too much work for you, tea spice can be purchased in Indian foods stores or by mail (page 74).

MAKES 10½ OUNCES

Place all the ingredients in a heavy cast-iron skillet and toast them over medium heat for 5 minutes, or until they give off a strong aroma. Place them in a spice grinder and pulverize into a fine powder. Allow the powder to cool and pack it into an airtight bottle. When ready to prepare your tea, add a few sprinklings of tea masala to each pot as the tea steeps.

NOTE: See the Glossary (pages 71 and 54) and the Mail-Order Sources (page 74) for Tellicherry pepper and brown cardamom.

4 ounces jaggery

2 ounces dried gingerroot

1 ounce cinnamon sticks

1 ounce whole cloves

½ ounce green cardamom seeds removed from their husks

1 ounce Tellicherry peppercorns (see Note)

1 ounce brown cardamom seeds, removed from their husks (optional) (see Note)

MANGO JUICE
◎◎◎

(SOUTH AFRICA)

When it's mango season in South Africa, it's a sure thing that many Indian families will be enjoying the following variation on mango juice.

If you don't like creamy things, use orange juice instead of milk and omit the condensed milk.　　　SERVES 4

6 ripe mangoes
½ cup milk
¼ cup sweetened condensed milk,
　or to taste

Peel the mangoes, slice off the meat, and place it in a blender. Add half the milk and enough condensed milk to sweeten. Blend on high speed until you have a creamy liquid. Add the rest of the milk and serve chilled over ice in tall glasses.

NDIAR
◎◎◎

BUTTERMILK (SENEGAL)

In Senegal, I rediscovered buttermilk, which I only knew from my Southern father's love for it. The Senegalese would seem to love buttermilk as much as my father. It turns up as tiakri (page 308) and also as sow (page 307). The buttermilk that the Senegalese use traditionally is actually closer to the thicker clabber, but if you cannot find clabber, buttermilk is quite a good substitute.　　　MAKES 1½ QUARTS

1 quart buttermilk
1 pint water
¼ cup sugar, or to taste
Dash of orange-flower water, or to
　taste (see Note)

Place all ingredients in a large jar or pitcher, stir to mix well, and place in the refrigerator overnight. Serve chilled.

NOTE: See the Glossary (page 66) and the Mail-Order Sources (page 74) for orange-flower water.

PINEAPPLE SHERBET

◎◎◎

(SOUTH AFRICA)

This sherbet is more like the sharbats *of India, iced drinks designed to cool the Mughal princes.*   SERVES 4 TO 6

Peel and core the pineapple, place the fruit in a blender, and pulse until you have a thick pulp. Place the pulp in a large pitcher, add the remaining ingredients, and stir to make sure that it is well mixed. Allow the sherbet to chill and serve over ice in tall glasses.

1 medium-sized ripe pineapple
2 quarts water
Juice of 4 lemons
Sugar, to taste

COOL, COOL WATER

DAKHAR

◎◎◎

TAMARIND JUICE (SENEGAL)

This tamarind juice is a refreshing beverage prepared from the seeds of the tamarind pod. The slightly astringent juice is cool and refreshing, but should be taken in moderate portions, as it has prodigious laxative qualities (as I found out one day when I used it to "drown" the taste of something I didn't like).

MAKES ¹/₂ GALLON

4-inch block tamarind pulp (see Note)
½ gallon water
Sugar Syrup (page 354) (optional)

Place the tamarind pulp in a medium bowl and add 2 cups of the water. With your hands, massage the pulp to extract the juice. Pour the juice into a half-gallon bottle through cheesecloth. Add the remaining 6 cups water and shake to mix well. Place the bottle in the refrigerator overnight to chill. Serve cool. You may want to dilute the juice to reduce the bitterness or even add a bit of sugar syrup.

NOTE: Tamarind pulp is available at Asian, Indian, and West Indian stores and through mail order (page 74).

COROSSOL

◎◎◎

SOURSOP MILK (BENIN)

The soursop fruit is a member of the Annona genus. It has a prickly outer skin and white flesh that is dotted with smooth black seeds. The fruit is highly fragrant and wonderful, even when slightly overripe. I remember a basketful of them perfuming the car as my friend Theodora and I drove home from the market one day. When I asked what she planned to do with them, she replied simply, "Juice them." The juice was delightful—milky, cool, and refreshing, with a slightly tart undertone.

You can also prepare this in a blender. It's a little less authentic but it tastes just as good.   MAKES 1 QUART

Peel the soursops, seed them, and place the pulp in a medium bowl. Mash the pulp with the back of a soupspoon, taking care to break up the fibers. Place the soursop pulp in a large jar or pitcher, add the milk and sugar, and refrigerate overnight. Serve chilled.

2 large soursops (see page 71)
1 quart milk
Vanilla Sugar (page 313), to taste

PALM WINE

(ALL AFRICA)

Palm wine is the beverage of choice throughout much of western Africa. The "wine" is obtained by tapping the sap of a palm. The beverage, which is called *tionkom* by the Diola of Senegal, is clear and refreshing when freshly tapped. After standing for a few days, however, it becomes cloudy and sparkling and gains significantly in alcoholic properties. It also has the kick of the proverbial country mule and becomes western Africa's form of white lightning.

Among the Yoruba of southwestern Nigeria, palm wine is reputed to be the cause of the drunkenness of Obatala, the god of creation. He was drinking palm wine while he was forming the first humans. As his work continued, the wine became increasingly potent and he eventually became drunk and no longer paid attention to his task. Humans were created with no fingers and no feet. Deformity entered the world. When he saw what he had done, he wept. For this reason, adherents of the cult of Obatala do not drink palm wine, and in many countries do not drink at all. Freshly tapped palm wine is impossible to obtain in this country. Perhaps you can obtain a bottle of Benin's *sodabi*, a highly fermented palm wine–based white liquor, from a friend visiting that country. If so, go sparingly. If not, try to find some Brazilian *cachaca* or Haitian *clairin*, which are similar though made from cane and not from palm. Then, of course, there's the U.S. South's own corn liquor or South Africa's *witblitz*.

DOUTE

◉◉◉

KINKÉLIBA TEA (SENEGAL)

Kinkéliba, *which grows wild in many areas between Senegal and Benin, is a natural diuretic and is reputed to have a calming effect. It is drunk as a tea so much in Senegal that the government has packaged it and consumers no longer have to purchase the fresh or dried leaves in the marketplace. It is one of the herb teas that is always available in restaurants. Kinkéliba, in fact, is so widely used that it is thought of as being a general panacea for everything from coughs to malaria.*

Like may of the infusions or tisanes of Africa, kinkéliba *has as many variations as there are consumers. While the* kinkéliba *is steeping, some folk add a squeeze of lemon juice, others add a few fresh mint sprigs, and still others will slip in a few blades of citronnelle. Some who like their* kinkélibas *particularly aromatic will use a combination of lemon and citronnelle.*

MAKES 1 QUART

Bring the water to a boil in a medium saucepan. Add the *kinkéliba* leaves, lower the heat, and simmer for 10 minutes. Remove from the heat and allow it to steep for 5 minutes. Strain the *kinkéliba* into a teapot through cheesecloth. Serve hot and sweeten to taste.

1 *quart water*
½ *cup dried* kinkéliba *leaves*
   (see Note)
Sugar, to taste

NOTE: *Kinkéliba* is available at health-food stores or through mail order (page 74).

GINGEMBRE

◎◎◎

GINGER WATER (CÔTE D'IVOIRE)

Ginger appears frequently in several beverages from West Africa. When prepared traditionally, the ginger is scraped, pounded in a mortar, and used to perfume the water. Here, instead of a mortar, I've used a food processor.

MAKES 1 QUART

2 thumb-sized pieces fresh ginger,
    scraped

1 quart water

½ cup confectioners' sugar, or to taste

⅛ teaspoon orange-flower water, or to
    taste (see Note)

1 tablespoon freshly squeezed lemon
    juice (optional)

Place the ginger in the bowl of a food processor and pulse until it is a pulp. (You may have to add a bit of water to start it.) Place the ginger in a square piece of cheesecloth and tie all four ends together to make a large sachet. Place the sachet in a large jar or wide-mouth pitcher with the water, sugar, and orange-flower water and allow it to infuse for an hour. When ready, re-move the sachet of ginger and refrigerate the ginger water. Serve chilled. Some people add lemon juice to the beverage before serving.

NOTE: See the Glossary (page 66) and the Mail-Order Sources (page 74) for orange-flower water.

LICOR DE CAFÉ
◎◎◎

COFFEE LIQUEUR (CAPE VERDE ISLANDS)

Coffee is native to Ethiopia and therefore African in origin. In this recipe it meets up with the sugarcane that is grown on the Cape Verde Islands in the form of cane brandy. Here I have traded the sugarcane brandy for white rum, which is more readily available. If you can find Brazilian cachaça, it will do the trick nicely. Splurge and use Ethiopian coffee and you'll have something very nice indeed.

This liqueur requires a three-week aging process before consumption.

MAKES ABOUT 6 CUPS

Place a pound of coffee beans in the rum and allow them to infuse for 8 days. Place the sugar in a small saucepan and cover with the water. Bring to a boil, and cook until you have a thin syrup. Allow the syrup to chill and add it to the coffee mixture. Mix them together well, then pour the liqueur off into small decorative bottles. Add a few coffee beans to each bottle and allow the liqueur to age 3 weeks or longer before serving in tiny cordial glasses as an after-dinner drink.

1 pound roasted coffee beans, plus additional coffee beans
1 liter white rum
1 pound sugar
2 cups water

Van der Hum
◉◉◉

TANGERINE LIQUEUR (SOUTH AFRICA)

Naartjie *are the wonderful tangerines from South Africa that are the basis for this popular liqueur. While Van der Hum is available commercially, many traditionalists prefer to prepare their own, and there are numerous recipes. This one captures all the flavors that I love.*

The liqueur needs two or three weeks' sitting time before use.   MAKES 1 ½ QUARTS

1 quart brandy

2 heaping tablespoons fresh tangerine peels

1 tablespoon fresh Seville orange peel

½ cup dark Jamaican rum

7 whole cloves

½-inch piece whole nutmeg

¼ cup orange-flower water (see Note)

1½ cups Sugar Syrup (page 354)

Pour the brandy into a large crock. Place the peels, rum, cloves, nutmeg, and orange-flower water in a mortar and bruise them by hitting the mixture a few times with the pestle or a small mallet. Add the spice mixture to the crock. Cover it and put it in a cool, dark place. Let it stand for 2 to 3 weeks, shaking it every day to mix the flavors. To decant the liqueur, add the sugar syrup, verify the flavorings, and strain the Van der Hum into decorative bottles. Serve in tiny cordial glasses as an after-dinner drink.

NOTE: See Glossary (page 66) and Mail-Order Sources (page 74) for orange-flower water.

CITRONNELLE

◎◎◎

LEMONGRASS TEA (CÔTE D'IVOIRE)

While many of us are now familiar with lemongrass from the cooking of Southeast Asia, we don't think of it as a tea. In fact, herbalists around the world use lemongrass or citronella to treat stomachaches and fevers. Anyone who has ever had an outdoor barbecue will recall the fragrance of the citronella candles of summer, for the herb is also noted as an insect deterrent. In Côte d'Ivoire, it is used as a digestive tea in the manner of a French tisane. In neighboring Ghana, where British colonial tradition ruled, it is consumed with milk and sugar. SERVES 1

Bring the water to a boil in a teakettle or saucepan. Place the lemongrass in a small 2-cup teapot. Pour the boiling water over the lemongrass and allow it to steep for 5 minutes. Serve hot as an after-dinner tisane with sugar to taste.

2 cups water
3 or 4 blades peeled lemongrass
Sugar or Sugar Syrup (page 354), to taste

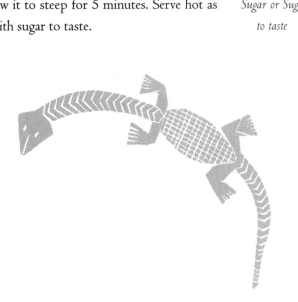

SUGAR SYRUP

◎◎◎

This is a kitchen basic for use in the bar or when preparing any cool drink that may need liquid sweetener that will dissolve more readily. The sugar syrup, also sometimes called a simple syrup, can be flavored with the rind of citrus fruit or with a vanilla bean for a different taste.

MAKES ABOUT 2 CUPS

4 cups sugar

2 cups water

Place the sugar and the water in a nonreactive saucepan, bring to a boil, and boil for 5 minutes. Allow the syrup to cool, then pour into a bottle, close it, and keep the syrup refrigerated until needed.

PLANTER WITH COCOA TREE

MENUS

◉◉◉

MOROCCAN DIFFA
Salades Variées
Tajine de Poulet au Citron et aux Olives
Keskou Fassia
Bastilla
Salade d'Oranges

A Moroccan *diffa* is a feast. While you probably will not invest in a *caïds* tent or the plush rugs that appear at some of these feasts in Morocco, you may wish to treat your guests to small hassocks and brightly colored woven rugs on the floor. Invest in a colored glass lantern or two and ask your guests to wear caftans or djellabas and slippers or *babouches*. Decorate the room with brass trays piled high with tangerines, clementines, dates of all types, and small Moroccan bowls of almonds. Invest in a CD or tape by Jil Jilala and enjoy.

SOUTH AFRICAN BRAAIWEIS
Sosaties

Chicken Sosaties

Plain White Rice

Wortel Sambal

Komkomer Sambal

This is a summer party that is best held outdoors with a barbecue grill and lots of food. Lay in a good stock of pinotage or some other South African wines. Listen to South African classics like Miriam Makeba and Hugh Masekela and play music from the townships like Ladysmith Black Mambazo and the dance music of Johnny Clegg & Savuka.

CAPE MALAY CURRY SUPPER
Curried Vegetables

Smoor Tomatoes and Onions

Yellow Rice

Lime Atjar

Bobotie

Set the table in traditional European style, but be sure to provide large napkins and encourage your guests to eat with their right hands in true Cape Malay style. Serve fruit punches and fruit juices and listen, if you can find it, to music from Capetown's District Six, the traditional Cape Malay neighborhood.

SENEGALESE LUNCHEON
Thiebou Dienn

Thé Sénégalaise

Mangoes

Spread a beautiful European tablecloth on the clean floor or carpet and arrange large enamel serving bowls on the floor. Present each guest with a 2½-yard piece of bright African fabric called a *pagne* to use as a wrap or as a large napkin. Eat with your hands. Music should be Senegalese classics like Youssou N'Dour and the Star Band or Baaba Mal or Salif Keita.

BAPTISM IN DAKAR
Tiakri

Tiere Sow

Western cookies and French pastries

Heap a table with delicacies as guests come and hear the praises of the new child and celebrate its birth. Music should be by traditional praise singers like Khar M'Baye Madiaaga or Ami Koita.

MAQUIS MADNESS
Poisson Braisé

Avocat Vinaigrette

Plain White Rice

Beignets de Mangues

Maquis are small clandestine restaurants that have sprung up all over Abidjan, where folk out for an inexpensive good time have great food for a pittance. Set up your own *maquis* with small tables decorated with brightly printed African batik "wax" designs and candles or lanterns. Serve food from Chinese enameled bowls onto wooden or enameled plates. Add to the atmosphere with music by Aïcha Koné and Nyanka Bell.

TABASKI IN DAKAR
Gigot d'Agneau aux Épices Marocaines
Plain White Rice
Cooked Carrot Salad
Moctar's Chile

Put on your ceremonial Senegalese best and enjoy a traditional-style lamb meal. Rhythm the meal with the sounds of Touré Kunda.

FOREST FOOD
Camarão Grelhado Piri Piri
Plain White Rice
Doce de Mandioca

Celebrate the forest lands of central Africa with a meal of the shrimp that gave Cameroon its name and the *pili pili* sauce that has become famous throughout the continent. Set the table with a Portuguese-style lace tablecloth and be sure to have lots of *vinho verde* around to put out the fires. Play music from Angola, Mozambique, and the central and southern parts of the continent.

PIED NOIR ALGERIAN COCKTAILS
Brik aux Champignons
M'chermia
Fèves Sèches Frites
Beignets de Sardines
Vin à l'Orange
North African wine

Serve the *khemia* (hors d'oeuvres) that make up this menu in French dishes from the 1940s and 1950s. Turn the lights down and pretend you're in a smoky café in Algiers or Casablanca. The music should be a *pied noir* mix of French music of the period, with Piaf predominating.

SOUKOUSS SUPPER
Mwambe
Plain White Rice
Pineapple Fritters

Spread the feast in enameled bowls on a tablecloth of bright fabric. Then turn up the CD player to high and blast the music of Tabu Ley, Mbilia Bel, Papa Wemba, and Tshala Muana. If you're not boogying by the end of the evening, the party has not been a success.

DINNER WITH THE PHARAOHS
Ful Medames
Flat bread
Karkadeh
Qahawah bel Habahan

You don't have to dress in thin cotton and wear cones of perfumed tallow on your head, but perhaps you might want to decorate the table with pyramids and photographs of Egyptian temples. Listen to the music of Ali Hassan Kuban or Mohamed Mounir, musicians who hark from the Nubian region of southern Egypt.

NIGHT ON THE NILE
Dukkah with Flat Bread
Meloukhia
Karkadeh
Plain White Rice
Mixed salad with Salgit Khall Bi-l-Toon
Store-bought Egyptian pastries

Set a tablecloth on a low table and decorate it with brass dishes and candles. Play music by Oum Kalsoum and pretend you're sitting watching the pyramids by moonlight.

NORTH AFRICAN SALAD SAMPLER
Slata Fel Fel
Cooked Carrot Salad
Salade de Concombre à la Menthe
Orange and Radish Salad
Pita bread

Decorate the room in Moroccan style as for the Moroccan Diffa (page 355), but play traditional Andalusian music that has echoes of Spanish Sevillianas such as Ustad Massano Tazi's *Classique Andalouse de Fès.*

ETHIOPIAN FEAST
Kitfo Leb Leb
Zelbo Gomen
Bamia Alich'a
Ethiopian Coffee

Set the table with Ethiopian baskets or trays filled with injera prepared from buckwheat pancake mix to cheat. Serve the food atop the injera in Ethiopian fashion, break off pieces, scoop up the food, and eat. Remind your guests to wash their hands first. Perhaps even provide them with a basin of warm water for the task. Serve Tej, Ethiopia's honey wine, or Ethiopian beer. For absolute authenticity don't forget music by Aster Aweke or old-timers like Mahmoud Ahmed.

LOOKING EAST—AN ISLE OF SPICE SAMPLER
Romazava
Plain White Rice
Colonial Fruit Salad

Although the menu is from Madagascar, think of the Seychelles when decorating the table. Not sure what that means? Think French Creole style, complete with bright Madras prints, woven baskets, and calabashes. Surprise your guests with Malagasy music like Tarika Sammy or Mama Sana. Or the Justin Vali Trio that played at Woodstock '94.

MARKET NIBBLES
Akara

Aloco

Maïs Grillé

Dodo=Ikire

Coconut Crisps

Suya

Celebrate the nibbles of the continent with a cocktail party that features snacks from all over. Decorate the table with bright fabric. Heap the snacks and nibbles in enameled bowls or in calabashes and blare out music from the great marketing areas of the continent, like Nigeria's King Sunny Ade and Fela Anikulapo Kuti.

TIMBUKTU TREATS
Bassi Salte

Couscous

Mangoes

Music by Malian griot Oumou Sangare should punctuate the meal. Serve it on indigo-dyed cloth in baskets and incised calabashes. Eat on the floor and savor the glory that was the greatness of Timbuktu. Ask your guests to wear *boubous* or Malian dress.

TEA IN THE HAREM
Thé Naa Naa Marocaine

Makroud

Salade d'Oranges

Create the background for this fete with women's music from North Africa like Algerian *rai* singer Cheikha Remitti. Then segue into belly-dancing contests using the pulsing drums that provide the background music for Oum Kalsoum. Check your neighborhood and see if you can find a henna or mehendi designer. Ask your guests to break out the caftans and djellabas, then kick back and enjoy the women's solidarity that tea in a harem provides.

CAPE VERDEAN FEAST
Manchupa
Abacates com Mel
Vinho Verde

Find forty or so friends and try a great Cape Verdean feast with Manchupa as the main event. Wash it down with vast amounts of *vinho verde* and top it off with the unusual *abacates com mel.* Through it all, savor the music of barefoot Cape Verdean diva Cesaria Evora.

SOME SOURCES
ON AFRICAN FOODS

The world of culinary studies is a growing one and works about the food of the continent of Africa are little known. I have therefore included a listing of some of the works that I have consulted. There are cookbooks as well as histories of the continent. This is only the tip of the iceberg.

Abdennour, Samia. *Egyptian Cooking: A Practical Guide.* Cairo: The American University in Cairo Press, 1996.

Achaya, K. T. *Indian Food: A Historical Companion.* Delhi: Oxford University Press, 1994.

Adadevoh, Anthonis Osa. *Wonderful Ways to Prepare Nigerian Dishes with American Ingredients.* Adamsville: Action Printing, n.d.

African Caribbean Institute of Jamaica. *A Panorama of African Recipes.* Kingston, Jamaica: N.p., 1980.

Aillaud, G. J., et al. *Herbes, Drogues et Épices en Méditerranée.* Paris: Éditions du Centre National de la Recherche Scientifique, 1988.

Allen, Charles, ed. *Tales from the Dark Continent: Images of British Colonial Africa in the Twentieth Century.* New York: St. Martin's Press, 1979.

Andoh, Anthony. *The Science and Romance of Selected Herbs Used in Medicine and Religious Ceremony.* San Francisco: The North Scale Institute, 1991.

Anonymous. *Eating in Africa.* Capetown: Howard Timmins, 1958.

Anthonio, H. O., and M. Isoun. *Nigerian Cookbook.* London: Macmillan, 1982.

Bailey, Adrian. *Cook's Ingredients.* New York: Bantam, 1980.

Barlow, Sean, and Banning Eyre. *Afropop! An Illustrated Guide to Contemporary African Music.* Edison: Chartwell, 1995.

Barth, Henry. *Travels and Discoveries in North and Central Africa: Being a Journal of an Expedition Undertaken Under the Auspices of H.B.M.'s Government in the Years 1849–1855.* 3 vols. New York: Harper & Brothers, 1857.

Bascom, William. "Yoruba Food" in *The Journal of American Folklore,* vol. 21, no. 1 (January 1951): 35–41.

———. "Yoruba Cooking" in *Africa* magazine, vol. 21 (April 1951), cited in Gary Edwards and John Mason, *Onje Fun Orisa (Food for the Gods).* New York: Yoruba Theological Archministry, 1981.

Battuta, Ibn. *The Travels of Ibn Battuta.* Trans. H.A.R. Gibb. 3 vols. 1958. Millwood: Kraus Reprint, 1986.

Bayley, Monica. *Black Africa Cook Book.* San Francisco: Determined Productions, 1977.

Becher, Daniel. *Fruits et Légumes Exotiques: Comment ça se mange?* Paris: La Compagnie du Livre, 1994.

Benkirane, Fettouma. *Moroccan Cooking: The Best Recipes.* Paris: Sochepress, 1983.

Beye, Abdoul Khadre. *Étude de l'Art Culinaire Sénégambien Traditionnel.* Dakar: Offset Imprimerie, 1957.

Bharadwaj, Monisha. *The Indian Spice Kitchen.* New York: Dutton, 1997.

Biarnes, Monique. *La Cuisine Sénégalaise.* Dakar: Société Africaine d'Édition, 1972.

Blakeney, E. H., ed. *The Histories of Herodotus.* Trans. George Rawlinson. 2 vols. 1910. London: Dent, 1964.

Bokomo Cook Book. No city; no publisher, 1935.

Bovill, E. W. *The Niger Explored.* London: Oxford University Press, 1968.

Burton, Richard, Sir. *A Mission to Gelele, King of Dahome.* Ed. C. W. Newbury. New York: Frederick A. Praeger, 1966.

Caillie, René. *Travels Through Central Africa to Timbuctoo: and Across the Great Desert, to Morocco, Performed in the Years 1824–1828.* 3d ed. 2 vols. 1830. London: Frank Cass, 1968.

Camara Cascudo, Luis da. *História da Alimentação no Brasil.* 2 vols. São Paulo: Editora Nacional, 1967–68.

The Cape Restaurant Guide. Greenpoint: Image Press, 1996.

Cartwright, D., and C. Robertson. *How to Cook for Your Family.* Nairobi: Longman, 1975.

Cavazzi de Montecuccolo, João Antonio. *Descrição Histórica dos Três Reinos do Congo, Matamba e Angola.* 2 vols. Lisboa: Junta de Investigacoes do Ultramar, 1965.

Clapperton, Hugh. *Journal of a Second Expedition into the Interior of Africa from the Bight of Benin to Soccatoo.* 1829. London: Frank Cass, 1966.

Clergeaud, Lionel. *Fruits et Légumes Exotiques: Recettes à Découvrir.* Lucerne: Dormonval, 1996.

Clevely, Andi, et al. *The Encyclopedia of Herbs and Spices.* New York: Hermes House, 1997.

Coffe, Jean-Pierre. *Le Marché.* Paris: TFI Editions, 1996.

Conneau, Captain Theophilus. *A Slaver's Log Book of 20 Years' Residence in Africa.* Englewood Cliffs, N.J.: Prentice-Hall, 1976.

Coughlan, Robert. *Tropical Africa.* New York: Time Incorporated, 1966.

Coyle, L. Patrick. *The World Encyclopedia of Food.* New York: Facts on File, 1982.

Curpenen, Ludmilla. *La Cuisine de l'Île Maurice.* Paris: Éditions Publisud, 1994.

Danan, Simy, and Jacques Denarnaud. *La Nouvelle Cuisine Judéo-Marocaine.* Paris: ACR Édition PocheCouleur, 1994.

Day, Irene F. *The Moroccan Cookbook.* New York: Quick Fox, 1975.

de Lourdes Chantre, Maria. *111 Receitas de Cozinha Africana.* Mem Martins: Publicações Europa-America, 1981.

Dede, Alice. *Ghanaian Favourite Dishes.* Accra: Anowuo Educational Publications,1969.

Diop, Saurele. *Cuisine Sénégalaise: D'hier et d'aujourd'hui.* St. Louis (Senegal): n.p., n.d.

Duckitt, Hildagonda J. *Hilda's "Where is it?" of Recipes.* 1891. London: Chapman & Hall Ltd., 1914.

———. *Traditional South African Cookery.* New York: Hippocrene Books, 1996.

Duncan, John. *Travels in Western Africa, in 1845 & 1846: Comprising a Journey from Whydah, Through the Kingdom of Dahomey, to Adofoodia, in the Interior.* 2 vols. 1847. New York: Johnson Reprint Corp., 1967.

Edet, Laura. *Classic Nigerian Cookbook.* London: Divine Grace Publishers, 1996.

Eldon, Kathy, and Eamon Mullan. *Tastes of Kenya.* Nairobi: Kenway, 1981.

Erasmus, Yvonne. *The Trilingual Cookery Book: Simple Recipes in English, South Sotho & Zulu.* Trans. (Zulu) Constance Motsumi and (South Sotho) Eddie Malukwa. Capetown: Howard Timmins, 1972.

Felix, Guy. *Genuine Cuisine of Mauritius.* Singapore: Singapore National Printers, 1988.

Fortin, François. *The Visual Food Encyclopedia.* New York: Macmillan, 1996.

Gerber, Hilda. *Cape Cookery.* Capetown: Howard Timmins, 1950.

Ghana Medical and Education Departments. *Ghana Nutrition and Cookery.* Edinburgh: Thomas Nelson and Sons, 1960.

Gorer, Geoffrey. *Africa Dances: A Book About West African Negroes.* New York: W. W. Norton, 1962.

Guggisberg, Rosanne. *Cooking with an African Flavour.* Nairobi: Sapra Studio, 1973.

Hachten, Harva. *Kitchen Safari.* New York: Atheneum, 1970.

Hafner, Dorinda. *A Taste of Africa.* Berkeley: Ten Speed Press, 1994.

Hal, Fatema. *Les Saveurs et les Gestes.* Paris: Stock, 1996.

Hall, Mary. *A Woman's Trek from the Cape to Cairo.* London: Methuen & Co., 1907.

Hamdun, Said, and Noel King, eds. *Ibn Battuta in Black Africa.* Princeton: Markus Wiener Publishers, 1994.

Hammann, Marlene. *Potjiekos from Huisgenoot.* Capetown: Human & Rousseau, 1987.

Hammoutene, Cherifa. *La Cuisine de Nos Grand-mères Algériennes.* Monaco: Éditions du Rocher, 1983.

Harris, Colin. *A Taste of West Africa.* New York: Thomson Learning, 1994.

Harris, Jessica B. *Iron Pots and Wooden Spoons: Africa's Gifts to New World Cooking.* New York: Atheneum, 1989.

———. *Sky Juice and Flying Fish: Traditional Caribbean Cooking.* New York: Fireside, 1991.

————. *Tasting Brazil: Regional Recipes and Reminiscences.* New York: Macmillan, 1993.

————. *The Welcome Table: African American Heritage Cooking.* New York: Simon & Schuster, 1995.

Hayward, Yvonne., ed. *A Zimbabwean Cookery Book.* Gweru: Mambo Press, 1990.

Herbst, Sharon Tyler. *The New Food Lover's Companion.* 2d ed. Hauppauge: Barron's, 1995.

Hess, Karen. *The Carolina Rice Kitchen: The African Connection.* Columbia, S.C.: University of South Carolina Press, 1992.

Higham, Mary. *Household Cookery for South Africa.* Johannesburg: RL Esson & Co., 1936.

Holloway, Joseph E., ed. *Africanisms in American Culture.* Bloomington, IN: University of Indiana Press, 1990.

Hultman, Tami. *The Africa News Cookbook: African Cooking for Western Kitchens.* New York: Penguin Books, 1985.

Iliffe, John. *Africans: The History of a Continent.* Cambridge: Cambridge University Press, 1995.

Inquai, Tebereh. *A Taste of Africa.* Cambridge: The National Extension College, 1992.

Jackson, James Grey. *An Account of the Empire of Morocco.* 3d ed. 1809. London: Frank Cass, 1968.

Jaffin, Leone. *150 Recettes: Et mille et un souvenirs d'une juive d'Algérie.* Paris: Encre Éditions, 1980.

Jardim, Mimi. *Cooking the Portuguese Way.* London: Viking, 1991.

Jobson, Richard. *The Golden Trade, or A Discovery of the River Gambia and the Golden Trade of the Aethiopians.* 3d ed. 1623. London: Dawsons of Pall Mall, 1968.

Johnston, Rhoda Omosunlola. *Never a Dull Moment: Memoirs of a Nigerian Educator.* Lagos: Fadec, 1995.

Jones, Neville. *The Stone Age in Rhodesia.* New York: Negro Universities Press, 1969.

Jones, Paul, and Barry Andrews. *A Taste of Mauritius.* London: Macmillan Education, 1982.

Kanie, Maurice Anoma. *La Côte d'Ivoire et Sa Cuisine.* No city; no publisher, 1975.

Karsenty, Irène, and Lucienne Karsenty. *Cuisine Pied-Noir.* Paris: Éditions Denoël, 1974.

Kouki, Mohamed. *La Cuisine Tunisienne.* Tunis: Naffati, 1989.

Kraus, Barbara, ed. *The Cookbook of the United Nations.* New York: Simon & Schuster, 1970.

Laasri, Ahmed. *260 Recettes de Cuisine Marocaine.* Paris: Jacques Grancher, 1996.

Laleye, Barnabe. *La Cuisine Africaine et Antillaise.* Paris: Éditions Publisud, 1985.

————. *La Cuisine Ivoirienne.* Dakar: Société Africaine d'Edition, 1974.

Le Petit Livre d'Or de la Cuisine Réunionnaise. N.p.: Orphie, 1996.

Le Système francophone d'information agricole (SYFIA). *L'Afrique, Côte Cuisines: Regards Africains sur l'Alimentation.* Montpellier: Syros, 1994.

Leo, Johannes. *A Geographical Historie of Africa.* 1600. Amsterdam: Theatrum Orbis Terrarum Ltd., 1969.

Lewicki, Thadeuz. *West African Food in the Middle Ages: According to Arabic Sources.* Cambridge: Cambridge University Press, 1974.

Margen, Sheldon, et al. *The Wellness Encyclopedia of Food and Nutrition.* New York: Rebus, 1992.

Marks, Copeland. *Sephardic Cooking.* New York: Donald I. Fine, 1992.

————. *The Great Book of Couscous.* New York: Donald I. Fine, 1994.

Mars, J. A., and E. M. Tooleyo. *The Kudeti Book of Yoruba Cookery.* 3d ed. 1934. Lagos: C.S.S. Bookshop, 1979.

Meredith, Henry. *An Account of the Gold Coast of Africa: With a Brief History of the African Company.* 2d ed. 1812. London: Frank Cass, 1967.

Mesfin, Daniel J. *Exotic Ethiopian Cooking.* Falls Church: Ethiopian Cookbook Enterprises, 1993.

Nabwire, Constance, and Bertha Vining Montgomery. *Cooking the African Way.* Minneapolis: Lerner Publications, 1988.

Newman, James L. *The Peopling of Africa: A Geographic Interpretation.* New Haven: Yale University Press, 1995.

Newton, Alex. *West Africa: A Travel Survival Kit.* Victoria: Lonely Planet Publications, 1988.

Norman, Jill. *The Complete Book of Spices: A Practical Guide to Spices & Aromatic Seeds.* London: Dorling Kindersley, 1990.

Odarty, Bill. *A Safari of African Cooking.* New York: Visa Choice, 1992.

Ortiz, Elisabeth Lambert. *The Encyclopedia of Herbs, Spices & Flavorings: The Complete Practical Guide for Cooks.* London: Dorling Kindersley, 1992.

Osseo-Asare, Fran. *A Good Soup Attracts Chairs.* Gretna: Pelican, 1993.

Peachey, Stuart. *Early 17th Century Imported Foods.* Bristol: Stuart Press, 1993.

Percival, Robert. *An Account of the Cape of Good Hope.* 1804. New York: Negro Universities Press, 1969.

Phillipson, David A. *African Archeology.* 2d ed. Cambridge: Cambridge University Press, 1995.

Redgrove, Stanley H. *Spices and Condiments.* London: Sir Isaac Pitman & Sons, 1933.

Ritzberg, Charles. *Classical Afrikan Cuisines.* New York: Afrikan World Infosystems, 1993.

Robins, Myrna. *The Cape Cookbook.* Diep River: Chameleon Press, 1994.

Sandler, Bea. *The African Cookbook.* New York: Citadel Press, 1993.

Schwartz, Oded. *Preserving.* London: Dorling Kindersley, 1996.

Simson, Sally. *The Cape of Good Cooks.* Rivonia: William Waterman Publications, 1994.

Sokolov, Raymond. *Why We Eat What We Eat.* New York: Summit, 1991.

Stagg, Camille. *The Best of the Cook's Advisor.* Chicago: Camille Stagg & Associates, 1991.

Strandes, Justus. *The Portuguese Period in East Africa.* Trans. Jean F. Wallwork. 4th ed. 1899. Nairobi: East African Literature Bureau, 1968.

Susser, Allen. *The Great Citrus Book.* Berkeley: Ten Speed Press, 1997.

Tannehill, Reay. *Food in History.* New York: Crown, 1988.

Toussaint-Samat, Maguelonne. *Couscous.* Tournai: Casterman, 1994.

van der Post, Laurens. *First Catch Your Eland.* New York: William Morrow and Co., 1978.

Villers, Anne, and Marie Françoise Delarozière. *Cuisines d'Afrique.* Provence: Edisud, 1995.

Weaver, William Woys. *Heirloom Vegetable Gardening.* New York: Henry Holt, 1997.

Williams, R. O. *Miss Williams' Cookery Book.* London: Longmans, Green and Co., 1957.

Wolfert, Paula. *Couscous and Other Good Food from Morocco.* New York: Harper & Row, 1973.

Yahmed, Danielle Ben. *Les Merveilles de la Cuisine Africaine.* Paris: Éditions J.A., 1979.

Zeitoun, Edmond. *250 Recettes de Cuisine Tunisienne.* Paris: Jacques Grancher, 1977.

INDEX

(Page numbers in *italic* refer to illustrations.)

METRIC EQUIVALENCIES

Liquid and Dry Measure Equivalencies

Customary	Metric
¼ teaspoon	1.25 milliliters
½ teaspoon	2.5 milliliters
1 teaspoon	5 milliliters
1 tablespoon	15 milliliters
1 fluid ounce	30 milliliters
¼ cup	60 milliliters
⅓ cup	80 milliliters
½ cup	120 milliliters
1 cup	240 millilliters
1 pint (2 cups)	480 millilliters
1 quart (4 cups)	960 millilliters (.96 liter)
1 gallon (4 quarts)	3.84 liters
1 ounce (by weight)	28 grams
¼ pound (4 ounces)	114 grams
1 pound (16 ounces)	454 grams
2.2 pounds	1 kilogram (1000 grams)

Oven-Temperature Equivalencies

Description	°Fahrenheit	°Celsius
Cool	200	90
Very slow	250	120
Slow	300–325	150–160
Moderately slow	325–350	160–180
Moderate	350–375	180–190
Moderately hot	375–400	190–200
Hot	400–450	200–230
Very hot	450–500	230–260